RUSSIAN ACADEMY OF SCIENCES

INSTITUTE FOR AFRICAN STUDIES

AFRICAN STUDIES IN RUSSIA

Works of the Institute for African Studies of the Russian Academy of Sciences

Yearbook 2010–2013

MEABOOKS Inc.
Lac-Beauport, Quebec
2015

REPRINT

Originally published by Institute for African Studies of the Russian Academy of Sciences in 2014.

This reprint edition by Meabooks Inc., Africana publishers and booksellers.

www.meabooks.com

ISBN: 978-0-9939969-4-8

African Studies in Russia. Works of the Institute for African Studies of the Russian Academy of Sciences. Yearbook 2010–2013. – Moscow, 2014, 188 p.

The publication is the latest in the *African Studies in Russia* series of compilations and contains full articles and annotations of the most important – from the point of view of editors – works of Russian Africanists over a certain period. The authors work at the Institute for African Studies of the Russian Academy of Sciences (RAS).

The present issue covers the years 2010 to 2013 and consists of two sections. The first section presents conceptual articles on Africa published in authoritative journals. The second section offers synopses of books by Russian authors on economics, cultural anthropology, social and political development, gender studies, and international relations of African countries.

The main objective of the triennial series of compilations is to introduce new findings of Russian Africanists to interested foreign scholars who do not speak Russian.

CONTENTS

ARTICLES

SYNOPSIS

ARTICLES

Leonid Fituni
Irina Abramova

PATTERNS OF FORMATION AND TRANSITION OF MODELS OF GLOBAL ECONOMIC DEVELOPMENT[*]

At the beginning of the 21st century world economic development was marked by a number of processes and shocks indicating the fundamental change taking place in the global economy. The development paradigms and paradigms of relations between economic entities, which have existed for decades, are now undergoing profound changes. Where the removal of accumulated imbalances and contradictions is unreasonably delayed, or the path of peaceful evolutionary transformation becomes impossible, there the contradiction between the obsolete "old" and the emerging "new" pushes for a solution through a crisis.

Modern economics assumes that the defining features of the global economy in the late 20th – early 21st centuries were system processes: internationalization, globalization and integration. They are transforming the global economy towards overcoming internal barriers of state borders, ideally turning it (which in the real world is still, in the authors' opinion, unattainable) into an integrated whole – a huge economic macrocell with a powerful center core surrounded by the protoplasm of the global periphery. According to the 20th century models of global economic development, the role of the latter is to protect the core, ensure its continued growth and development, protect it against adverse external impacts and facilitate the healing of internal pathologies.

However, in recent decades, the apparent center-periphery dichotomy has undergone substantial corrosion. The process of redistribution of global power and influence and of strengthening of new poles of the emerging polycentric international system has become pronounced. There have been tectonic shifts in the balance of power between leading economic centers of power. Some countries, such as China, India, Brazil and others, previously attributed to the global periphery, began to achieve an unprecedented (for them) economic power and geopolitical importance. At the same time, the traditional center of the globalized economy slowly began to lose at least some of the levers of control over the world economy, which had been fully at its command until then. According to the Russian Ministry of Foreign Af-

---

[*] First published in *World Economy and International Relations*. Issue 7, 2012.

fairs, "Against this background, there is a relative decline in the influence and capabilities of the countries which are attributed to the historical West, weakening their role as the "engine" of global development"[1].

A great many researchers who focus on studying global processes and who belong to different scientific schools and profess different methodological cal approaches almost unconditionally agree that the ongoing processes signify a change of epoch. The authors of this paper put forward the hypothesis that such a "change of epoch" is associated with a qualitative transformation of the models of global economic development (MGED).

MGED as an economic category

MGED transition can be interpreted as a natural, conscious adaptation of the leading global economies to the changing technological, environmental and *"populational"* (implying a broader than purely demographic range of issues) shifts in the development of the mankind. However, we also cannot but consider these ongoing processes to be objective natural "leaps", which are revolutionary in the philosophical sense, and that means, in comparison with the first case, a higher probability of unforeseen developments, dramatic effects and bitter conflicts and, most importantly, unpredictable outcomes.

Either way, these processes lie in the context of the general trend toward globalization that has been dominating and determining the development of the global economy in recent decades.

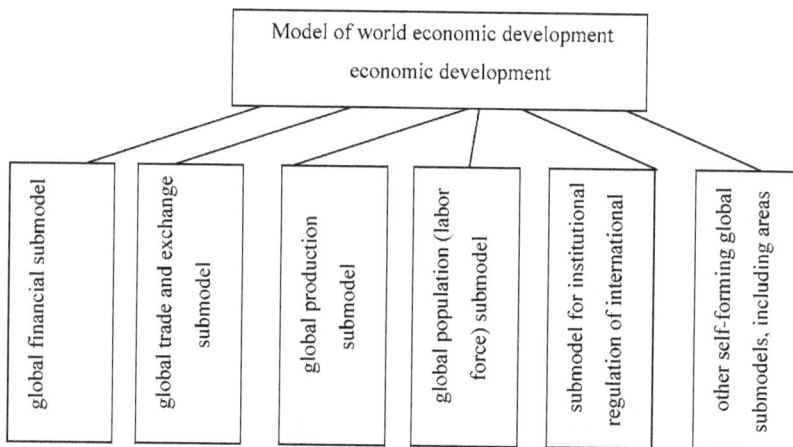

Figure 1. Submodel structure of MGED

When we talk about MGED, we mean first of all stable and repeating paradigms of the formation of international public relations associated with

6

production, distribution, exchange and consumption in the world economy, developed at a certain historical stage of human development, and generally reflecting the current balance of power in the world economy given the level and nature of technological and economic development.

At any given historical period, the active MGED reflects the level of the contemporary world economy and the balance of power in it. If there is a fundamental shift in the balance of these components, there follows a complete or partial change of MGED. Typically, these changes are evolutionary, not revolutionary. They mature for decades due to the long-term accumulation of qualitative characteristics of the future model of relations – a more appropriate one in the face of new global circumstances and, therefore, more efficient.

In terms of system analysis, a model of the world (global) economic development can be seen as a complex system that incorporates a number of relatively independent subsystems (submodels). The latter in turn also have a complex structure that can be divided into smaller elements. The most important of these include: the global financial submodel (often referred to as the global financial system), global trade and exchange submodel, global production submodel, global population (labor force) submodel, submodel for institutional regulation of international economic relations, etc. (Fig. 1)^2

The aforementioned subsystems (submodels) are not isolated from each other. Moreover, they are not simply linked, but partially overlap each other, creating a sort of "areas of mutual contact and overlap." These mutually overlapping areas in some cases obtain new quality characteristics and, consequently, may be regarded as new subsystems.

The most important characteristic of any of the models (including the submodels) is that they include objective material components, which exist in a specific state and at a specific level of development and form the model (e.g. financial, production and human resources, technological, etc.), as well as subjective institutional components (regulatory institutions, "rules of the game" in the industry, etc.). Therefore, the emergence, development and transition of models are subject to the general laws of the dialectic of the objective and the subjective.

With regard to the internal dynamics of the general models of global economic development, it should be noted that a change of the global model of economic development does not imply synchronous and simultaneous replacement of all its submodels. Moreover, some of them persist in the old form for a long time not only after the maturity of other elements of a new model, but even after the latter has acquired a dominant position in the world.

Because of the internal features or specific external circumstances some submodels are more conservative than others. The global currency and trade submodel is very mobile, even volatile. The global financial submodel, as the experience of the 20th century shows, is also quite mobile and changes faster and more often than, for example, the global production submodel. It was noticed that during the 19th–20th centuries a change of the financial submodel (the gold standard, the gold exchange standard, the classic Bretton Woods system, the Jamaican system, etc.) acted as the harbinger of the imminent change of the global economic model (less often) and/or of the onset of a global crisis (more often).

In this sense, it could probably be argued that a change of the global financial submodel is an integral part and one of the earlier indicators of the onset of the final phase of the change of active models of global economic development.

The global reproduction and population mobility (labor force) submodel is one of the most conservative. This is due to the fact that its system elements depend strongly on the "generational" stereotypes of behavior, and the transformation of such submodels is a direct function of generational change. During the 20th century they changed very slowly and rarely, and when changing retained most of the key features of the previous submodel. For the purity of the description of the behavior of these submodels, it is necessary, however, to state that by the end of the 20th – beginning of the 21st century an apparent trend to accelerate their transformation was in place. It seems that this was due to spreading and deepening processes of globalization, integration and internationalization, which lead to major changes in the demographic behavior of population and to the gradual elimination of barriers to cross-border movement of human resources.

MGED's place in economic and political transitology

Why, from the point of view of the authors, is it necessary to regard MGED as an independent scientific category and to study the process of MGED transition separately as an objectively existing reality of the modern global economy?

In our opinion, the isolation and separation of MGED as an economic category makes up an important missing link in contemporary scientific knowledge. It allows us to understand the essential characteristics, driving mechanisms and possible outcomes of complex social and economic changes of specific depth and importance which are taking place in the world economy, including the ones which pertain to the ongoing global crisis processes and transitions.

In fact, when we speak about MGED transition, we focus on a qualitatively separate "mesoprocess", which, given its depth and implications, occupies its own specific median level between the transitions of formational and cyclical nature.

The objective reality of the world economy confirms the validity and usefulness of such a structural classification of the processes of economic transition. Indeed, on the one hand, the ongoing global cataclysms do not mark a change of economic formations. They are developing within the same global economy characterized by the dominance of capitalist (modern market) relations. The fact that it contains significant socialist "inclusions" (China, Vietnam, Cuba) in general does not change its essence, as these countries largely depend on market relations for access to the global market and, increasingly, for the functioning of domestic economy.

MGED transition is not accompanied by a fundamental change in property relations or in the distribution of newly created value. The transition is about overcoming the backlog of very serious problems, inconsistencies and imbalances in the world economy and, what is very important, about altering the balance of power between active players (usually, between those who have already managed to capture key positions in a particular area and the newcomers who are gaining power). During this process, changes of an institutional nature take place, rules of the game are adjusted, but the fundamentals of the relations are not reshaped cardinally. They are only corrected to a greater or lesser extent in order to remove accumulated obstacles to further growth and development. In technical terms, the system gets cleaned and modernized.

At the same time, the depth and systemic nature of the current crisis is clearly beyond the scope of short-term cyclical fluctuations. In order to survive and overcome the accumulated imbalances, to get rid of the dead weight impeding development, the global economic system and its relations model objectively demand renovation. This happens regardless of the will of individuals, groups or states.

Moreover, for some actors (mainly, for "traditional key players") it is important to preserve the established framework of relations, rules of the game, and global hierarchical and subordination systems to the greatest extent possible, whilst for others (especially for new "rising" members) it is essential to adapt those to their own needs, to legitimize and institutionalize their own conquests, thus surpassing the "old-timers". As the essential characteristic of the described process of MGED transition, changes in the balance of power are just as important as any aspect of the removal of the accumulated imbalances and contradictions.

In fact, both of these aspects are in a dialectical unity because at least some of the contradictions within the existing model at any given moment arise from shifts in the balance of power within it. Each new "contraposition of partners" in the framework of MGED in turn exacerbates purely "technological" imbalances (financial, trade, and between the spheres of production and circulation, etc.) in the world economy.

What are the stages of MGED transition in modern times? While not considering the following periodization of the evolution of MGED to be the only one possible, the authors suggest that over the last century the world economy experienced transitions between three of them[3]. The economic essence of the first one was bitter inter-imperialist rivalry during the transition from industrial capitalism to its monopolistic phase[4]. The United States and Germany (but not only) were the primary new "rising" actors. This phase ended with the global economic crisis of the 1930s, "voluntary" (the Anschluss, Munich Agreement, Memel ultimatum) or forceful (occupation) incorporations of some European states in the Third Reich, and the World War II, the end of which paved the way for the establishment of a new MGED.

Its main feature was the co-existence of the global systems of capitalism and socialism (which included both elements of competition and cooperation) and the collapse of the colonial system in the 1960s. The competition of these systems, including the economic "war of annihilation" between them, was the main characteristic of this MGED.

Old actors were hard-pressed by new ones, primarily the Soviet Union and the socialist camp. The latter category, however, may also include Japan and newly industrialized countries at the later stages. Within the framework of this model, there began a process of transferring production capacity from industrial to developing countries, which changed their position in the world economy, transformed the structure of international trade and the nature of inter-country cooperation ties. In addition, there emerged an influential but disunited new power in the world economy – oil-producing countries, which strongly affected the character of resource exchange between the center and the periphery. This MGED lasted until the fall of the Soviet Union, collapse of the world socialist system and incorporation of its part into the EU. It coincided with hitherto unprecedented progress in internationalization of the world economy, which entered the era of globalization, and with the transition of some of the countries of the center to post-industrial development.

The third MGED of the century began to establish itself from the moment when a transient intermediate stage of unipolarity in world politics gave way to an evident tendency towards the formation of a polycentric world. There has been a rise of heavily populated developing countries, in particular China, India and Brazil. Russia has begun to resurge in a new capacity. The key economic characteristic of the emerging MGED, apparently, is the new paradigm of global wealth distribution and dominance of global development issues (in particular, connected with demographics and natural resources) over purely national ones.

The boundary periods of MGED transitions are always accompanied by the most profound geopolitical cataclysms, which for some global players turn out as greatest catastrophes, while for others – as historic victories.

10

Needless to say, in real life both outcomes affect the well-being and sometimes even physical existence of large numbers of people. This means that the study of the formation, development and transition of MGED as a separate category has not only theoretical but also practical significance in terms of developing applied strategies of country development and political decision-making.

New MGED, the middle class and the limits of growth

What changes are coming or have already materialized due to the advent of a new world economic model at the beginning of the 21st century?

For about four decades, until the beginning of this century, the seven leading Western economies (U.S., Japan, Germany, France, Britain, Italy and Canada) accounted for an average of about 65% of the gross world product (GWP) (based on the current exchange rate). Despite the evolution of the MGED, crises and economic problems of various kinds, the deviation from this value did not exceed 3%. Since the beginning of this century and the formation of a new MGED, this situation slowly began to change in favor of countries just recently considered to be the world periphery. By 2010, according to the IMF, the total share of the "magnificent seven" fell down to 48% of the GWP[5]. At the same time, the resource problems of the world economy intensified. The developed countries faced the current financial and economic crisis, most severe since the Great Depression.

In the first decade of the 21st century, the rise of large developing countries (DC) finally became one of the factors forming the backbone of the new MGED[6]. Between 1990 and 2010, the GDP growth in the DCs exceeded, on average, 5-6%, i.e. they were twice as high as in developed countries. In 2010, the DCs produced more than 45% of the GWP at purchasing power parity. The share of the DCs in the world imports had risen to 38% by 2010; in the exports it had exceeded 40%. All the while, the trade among the developing countries was growing both in absolute and relative terms (43% of foreign trade turnover in 2010). The share of the DCs in the manufactured exports rose from 12% in 1960 to 70% in 2010, while the share of foreign direct investment (FDI) in the DCs increased from 26.8% in 2007 to 45% in 2010. DCs are becoming increasingly important exporters of capital. In 1985, the share of FDI originating in the DCs did not exceed 6% of the total, whilst in 2009 this indicator reached 21%. In 1995, the DCs accounted for only 1.1% of foreign assets of the largest 2500 TNCs, but in 2010 this figure reached 9%.

In 1995, only 1.1% of foreign assets of 2500 largest TNCs were located in the DCs, but in 2010 this figure reached 9%. Even in terms of labor productivity, the gap between the developed and many developing countries has a tendency to decrease, although it remains significant[7].

At the beginning of the 21st century, the region of East and South Asia became a new growth pole of the world economy due to the contribution of the dynamically developing China and India. According to a convincing forecast of the IMEMO's researchers, these countries will become new leaders of globalization, making the main contribution to the global growth, which will call into question the absolute dominance of the former leader[8].

The rise of a number of developing countries leads to the establishment of new rules of the game in the global economic space as it has the following consequences: 1) gradual change in the geographical distribution of world production; 2) changes in its structure; 3) transformation of global trade; 4) evolution of the global financial flows in terms of their focus, volume and nature; 5) change of the global consumption model; 6) changes in the quality and structure of the global labor market.

However, even within the currently emerging MGED there already are visible embryos of new contradictions and imbalances.

When China's GDP exceeds U.S. GDP, per capita income in China will still be 3-4 times lower than the U.S. figure. And here comes the most important qualitative change in the economic model of the world. It may happen in the next 30 years that for the first time in the modern history the world's largest economies will not at the same time be the richest (in terms of per capita figures), and hence the two key imperatives of the near future.

Firstly, the international business will have to change the prevailing business strategies and adapt to the needs of the less well-off but more numerous consumers. Secondly, social and political instability in the world will continue to grow because, on the one hand, the lack of social-oriented policies in the developing countries increases protest potential, and, on the other hand, in an attempt to artificially maintain their leading position, developed countries will not apply their disappearing economic influence but rather non-economic methods, including the use of institutional, military and political leverage still at their command. Recent events in the Middle East and North Africa (and elsewhere) are a vivid example of this[9].

The outgoing MGED was based on middle class consumer demand in developed countries. The transition to a postindustrial society washes away the material production of the advanced Western economies, encouraging transnational corporations (TNCs) to transfer resource-intensive, labor-intensive and polluting industries to developing countries, where the costs are lower. Solvent demand in the most developed economies is increasingly met by innovative financial products and the growth in consumer and mortgage lending. The illusion of a "permanent boom" allowed the middle class in the West to minimize their savings and direct them on current consumption, creating a false impression of stable and solvent demand in these economies. However, in fact a large part of the latter was provided by the deferred income, loans or real assets (collaterals such as house, car, etc.).

The current financial crisis has forced consumers to save a larger portion of income than before. The middle class of developed countries , which, according to the neo-classical political economy, is the primary source of entrepreneurship and innovation and, therefore, the basis for economic growth (through new ideas, physical capital investment and human capital accumulation), suddenly ceased to generate effective demand required to maintain economic growth in accordance with the established growth model. In particular, the demand for financial instruments fell significantly, which primarily affected the foreign exchange and financial markets.

The crisis has led to a review of the views on the ratio of the real and financial sectors in the framework of the outgoing MGED. At the beginning of 2012, in the face of the second wave of the crisis, leaders of some Western countries, as if recollecting themselves, one by one issued statements about the need to return physical production to the U.S. and the EU[10]. France is beginning the process of introducing a tax on financial transactions. The central point of President Barack Obama's 2012 address to the nation was a tax reform aimed at returning manufacturing jobs to the U.S. The proposed policy should (at least) equalize the conditions for companies for creating jobs in the United States and abroad, or (better yet) create advantages for the Americans. In fact, Obama declared a war on outsourcing and advocated for measures of investment and trade protectionism, but worded it relatively mildly[11].

It is still unclear whether the "repatriation" of physical production becomes one of the trends of the new MGED. However, it is clear that by the beginning of the 21st century much of the physical production had found itself in the developing world, and the slogan "new industrialization", which is supposed to generate (or regenerate) domestic demand, had become a kind of mantra for politicians in both the West and the East. In can also be heard in Russia (if you listen hard), though as usual it comes late and muffled.

At the same time, it is also becoming apparent that a large proportion of solvent demand has permanently escaped the "old" center. Moreover, the new MGED provides for global economic growth based largely on domestic demand generated in young "rising" economic powers.

The establishment of the new MGED, in which most of the accelerated growth takes places in the "rising" economies, especially China and India, will lead to fundamental shifts in the social structure of the population of the planet. According to OECD data, the size of the global middle class will increase by 3 billion people in demographically dominant developing countries over just the next 20 years[12]. The growth of the middle class is now taking place almost exclusively in countries of Asia and Latin America, while in the 2030s it is expected to shift to Africa. This will inevitably affect the global balance of resource consumption necessary for development, as well as the structure of the global production and consumption.

It is expected that if the demand of the new middle class is met, the global car fleet will reach 1.7 billion units in 2030. The demand for food production will increase drastically not only because of the absolute population growth in developing countries, but, according to experts, also due to a 20% increase in the number of calories consumed per capita in these countries by 2030. For example, meat consumption of an average Chinese will go up by 40% (up to 75 kg per year), although it will still remain much lower than in the U.S. The quantitative and qualitative growth of consumption will require a comparable increase in spending on infrastructure, housing, etc.[13]

Lastly, it is easy to deduce that such a sharp increase in the consumption of world resources by "new consumers" in the framework of the nascent MGED will wittingly or unwittingly impose restrictions on the paradigm of consumption of the same resources by the "old" centers of economic power. With the expected drop in resource sufficiency of the West, its middle class, at least in theory, could face the prospect of an imposed decline in consumption standards. Where is the way out of the situation given that the expansion of consumer demand lies at the heart of economic growth in the West?

For western democracies this will be the most complicated economic and political challenge. History teaches us that "underfeeding burghers" generates fascism and external aggression. In view of the limited and non-renewable nature of a number of natural resources, the new and old global actors will be involved in a "zero-sum game" for resources, in which the gains of one side are exactly balanced by the losses of the other. Behind these "games" we can quite clearly see the prospect of "resource wars"[14].

Resource aspect of the balance of power

Within the new MGED researchers expect a significant change in the influence of the resource factor. The growing shortage of resources is one of the root causes of the growing and latently ripening local, regional and global crises of the new millennium. As the beginning of this century clearly showed, the reason for the West's action is largely the pursuit of control over increasingly scarce supplies of natural resources despite all attempts to cover up the true motives of its behavior on the world stage with higher goals and ideals – the protection of peace, freedom, democracy, fight against the proliferation of weapons of mass destruction[15].

The relative increase in importance of the resource factor for global economic development and, consequently, global politics can be clearly illustrated by comparing the figures of population growth and production of key mineral commodities. For example, between 1950 and 2011 the world's population grew from 2.5 to 7 billion people, or 2.8 times, while oil production increased

14

8.4 times over the same period (from 522 to about 4,400 million tons), natural gas production – 21 times (from 190 to nearly 4,000 billion cubic meters), and the same is true for almost all types of mineral resources[16].

The upward trend in per capita consumption of most types of natural resources will probably continue in the new MGED. It also should not be forgotten that mineral resources are distributed unevenly across the planet. Typically, the largest consumers of these resources are by no means their leading producers but, on the contrary, countries with limited or no natural reserves on their sovereign territory.

For the first time in decades (in fact, since the 1970s and the first report by the Club of Rome titled "Limits to growth") reputable researchers once again began to speak seriously about the potential for triggering the Malthusian trap, but in contrast to the predictive model developed by the graduate of Jesus College, Cambridge, in 1791, not only with regard to food but to all resources[17]. However, based on the historical experience of development, they stipulate that the "trap" might be avoided provided adequate productivity growth in the extractive industries is ensured. However, the estimated parameters of the required growth seem to be extremely high, at least for now.

According to research by McKinsey Global Institute, world prices on natural resources (energy, food, water and industrial raw materials, as well as the key intermediate for the global production of industrial products – steel) were decreasing in the first third of the 20th century and then for the most of it (except for relatively short fluctuations) stayed at a relatively low level[18].

Based on the data of McKinsey researchers (Fig. 2), we believe it is possible to conclude that the past and existing MGED supported primarily economic growth in the world's economic centers that existed at a particular point in history. The graph shows that during the 20th century the MGI Commodity Index fell by almost a half in real terms. This in itself is a clear confirmation of the viability and effectiveness of the MGED of the respective periods, taking into account that the population of the planet increased by four times during the period. The world production increased by approximately 20 times over the same time, resulting in a growth in demand for various resources of somewhere between 600 and 2000%.[19]

In accordance with the aforementioned periodization, there were three MGEDs during the considered period of time (112 years) (upper part of the graph in Fig. 2). In the course of the first MGED the commodity prices declined sharply; during the second – the index remained relatively stable, with some fluctuations and at the level lower than that at the beginning of the century. Near the end of the second MGED prices on some raw materials skyrocketed (oil crisis, etc.). The establishment of a new (the third in our classification) MGED was accompanied by a new rise in prices on raw materials, and the commodity index returned to the levels from which the graph started.

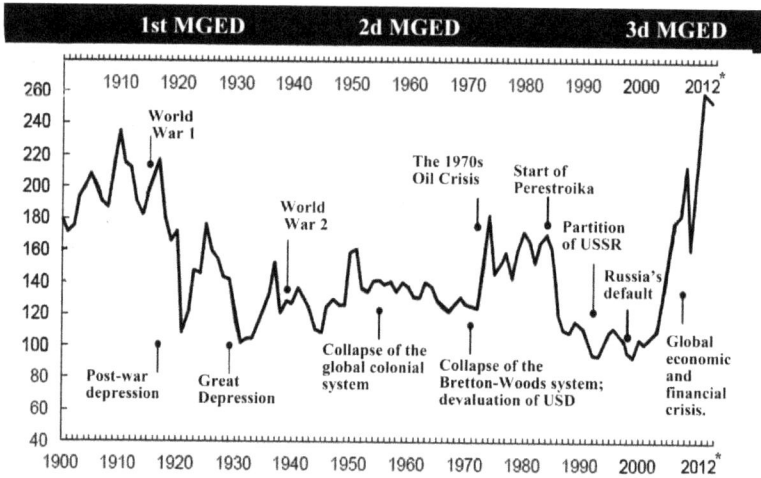

1st MGED	2d MGED	3d MGED

Fig. 2. Changes in the MGI Commodity Index as MGED transitions occur (at constant prices, 1999–2001=100)

Source: created and adapted based on the graph and data from: *Dobbs R. et al.* Op. cit. P. 22 and *UN Monthly Bulletin of Statistics Online*, 1st quarter 2012 (http://unstats.un.org/unsd/mbs/app/data search table.aspx)

During the 20th century in the course of MGED transitions the commodity index decreased from the levels seen at the beginning of the century, but that did not mean a reduction in the intensity of the global consumption of resources. One of the decisive factors for decreasing the intensity of the consumption of raw materials in the world in the last quarter of the 20th century was the collapse of the Soviet Union, which was the world's second largest consumer of industrial raw materials for most of that century. According to the report by the McKinsey Institute, the disappearance of the Soviet Union "improved the situation with regard to the intensity of the global consumption of resources."[20]

The rapid growth of demand in emerging markets, which has taken place in the last 10-15 years, particularly in Asia, has essentially turned the situation around and reverted the downward price trend of the previous 100 years despite the fact that Russia still has not returned to the previous levels of resource consumption. In the framework of the emerging MGED it will not be easy to solve the problem of meeting the resource needs of development and ensuring productivity growth in the extractive and resource-intensive industries. In general, readily available resources will account for only 20% of the total consumption, while scarce resources will account for more than 40%. In addition, the main deposits of fossil fuels and minerals are located in coun-

16

tries significantly inferior to advanced economies in terms of labor productivity. For example, according to the ILO, labor productivity in Russia was 4 times lower than in the G-7 countries. The figure is 3 times for the Middle East and Latin America, and 12 – for sub-Saharan Africa[21]. In order to raise productivity to acceptable levels more than $1 trillion will be required annually, which is hardly feasible in a global recession[22].

Thus, the next MGED carries the risk of a protracted period of at least two decades of high and volatile prices on resources. Under these circumstances, there is a gradual transformation of the world market of minerals from the "buyer's market" to the "seller's market". Given that resources are limited and new strong competitors for access to these resources have emerged, sellers may to some extent dictate the terms and derive additional benefits from the situation.

Developing economies, which are rich in natural resources, can and, quite logically, should take advantage of a very favorable situation on the world market of fossil fuels and minerals in order to accelerate their own economic and social development and improve their standing in the world economy. In our opinion, the reasonable use of the "resource leverage" in view of modern historical conditions, shifts in the global balance of power, as well as mineral and energy depletion, can contribute to promoting a number of yesterday's outsiders in terms of economic development to subjects of the global economy of the 21st century. The above process is one of the features of the emerging MGED.

Subjective aspect of MGED transition

MGED transition is an objective process which develops regardless of the will of individuals. At the same time, its objectively self-organizing features can be used in subjective group (country, ideological, clan) interests. In this sense, the links between the discussed MGED transition, current global economic crisis and emerging realities of global governance are very interesting but so far very poorly researched.

MGED transition under the current circumstances is experiencing the growing impact of desovereignization and other processes related to the category of global governance. Such governance involves (at least declaratively) the establishment of organizational forms that most closely meet the corresponding global public demands. The study of global governance goes beyond the scope of this article, but our study would not only be incomplete but also distorted if we did not take into account the relation between the two phenomena and did not try to determine the nature of the interaction.

Because such global governance levers as the expansion of regulatory mechanisms, globalization of institutions, determination of development goals and objectives, reform of international institutions are not but elements and directions of the reform of the existing MGED, formal, semi-formal and informal international institutions of global governance (so different in status, nature and importance like the UN, IMF , G-8 , G-20 , OECD , Davos Forum , Bilderberg Club, etc., and, more recently, BRICS) are involved in determining the nature of the transformation of the model of world economic development.

As an outcome and a natural extension of the process of globalization the emerging MGED increasingly includes non-state, supranational actors, their associations and institutions, which is due to the increasing trans-nationalization of production processes and of the global economy in general. It is not just about the increasing role and number of multinationals of different sizes, profiles and characteristics, but also of many NGOs, lobby groups and trade associations, informal groups and networks.

Whether the range of actors who have an impact on the formation of the new model is narrow or wide will determine its level of democracy, functionality and viability. It is no secret that even participation of relatively large "new economies" in international negotiations on key topical issues of global development does not guarantee the replacement of old and obsolete elements of MGED. In this respect, illustrative is very modest progress in the redistribution of quotas and places in the management of the IMF or in solving disputes at the WTO concerning the EU's agricultural subsidies.

Judging by the themes of the majority of national scientific publications, global governance is one of the central problems in global studies. Therefore, the question of whether the process of forming a new MGED can be controlled (and, if so, how) is not idle.

Without denying the objective nature of the processes taking place in the global economy, the authors feel the need to focus on the increasingly growing "virtualization" of its important components during the transition to the emerging MGED. This phenomenon is largely associated with the entry of the centre, which still remains its main engine, into the post-industrial age and the formation of an information society on a global scale.

Due to globalization and trans-nationalization of the production processes, they are becoming increasingly public. An information society operates in a way that constantly forces private owners to obey its decisions, which are broadcasted via external information channels. Under globalization, regardless of the will of a capitalist, he is socialized due to the pressure of growing volumes of network information available to him – both reliable and purely manipulative (market quotes, decisions of associations of producers and consumers, findings of rating agencies, news about emerging country and industry risks, etc.). Because of the growing informatization, the actions of entrepreneurs become more predictable and preplanned, are coordinated with or adapted to the actions of colleagues and competitors, they apply ready solutions, etc. During crises the same factor leads to similar decision-making by millions of independent entrepreneurs, who panic in the same way, which makes their decisions especially devastating.

In other words, the new MGED provides the conditions for the growth of the importance of subjective factors in global economic development, which in certain circumstances may prevail over its objective factors. Increasingly often there are situations when actions of market subjects are not based on real market signals but on subjective information, often of suggestive and manipulative nature (ratings, unfounded forecasts, lobbying, ideological labels and stereotypes, economic boycotts, sanctions, misinterpreted public good, etc.), which is spread by interested parties. The increasing "virtualization" of the new MGED, which is primarily a consequence of the disconnection from the real economy, is a serious threat. It can drastically distort market signals, directing governments, institutions and market actors themselves down the wrong track.

The participants of the process of MGED transition are trying to influence the transformation to their advantage, which is quite natural. For Russia, for example, fundamentally important is the question of under what conditions its integration into the world economy takes place or, in other words, what will be Russia's position in the new MGED. Will Russia be only satisfying various demands under the new model, or will its partners not only in words but in deeds implicitly conform to Russia's own wishes?

We should not forget that the power of global economic actors is measured not only and not so much by their territory, population and fast GDP growth. Despite the significance of the aforementioned factors with regard to the increasing importance of the resource component in international development in the coming decades, other kinds of resources – human, financial, intellectual, technological, informational, military, etc. – will play no lesser and often much greater role than energy resources and raw materials.

The ongoing gradual erosion of national sovereignty has bred many concepts of common human resource heritage which are far-reaching in their effects. For example, the internationally recognized principle of permanent sovereignty over national natural resources is put into question in different forms increasingly often[23]. At the same time, the principle of sovereign ownership of other types of development resources – financial, technological, etc. – is not questioned. Since the first types of resources are controlled mainly by developing countries, while the second – by developed ones, the desire of "old centers of power" to employ institutional levers to use the global resource base to their advantage becomes obvious.

These changes do not signify the democratization of relations within the new MGED. Modern liberal approaches put power relations (and, by default, global governance relations) mainly in the categories of International Public

Law and Public Policy. Non-political influence on the formation of a new economic model of global development is mostly non-transparent and, with few exceptions, lies outside the framework of open public discourse.

One of the historical problems in controllability and viability of any MGED is the increasing concentration of capital on a global scale. In the new MGED this process will go hand in hand with the trans-nationalization of capital. At the same time, in our opinion, it would be wrong to characterize the current or future MGED exclusively as "the world of TNCs". TNC is just a modern form of capitalist (market) organization whose main interest is maximizing profits. Moreover, these TNCs are controlled by certain interest groups and owned and operated by narrow groups of people united by common economic (especially financial) and, which is not often mentioned, ideological principles and objectives. The number of such financial and ideological groups (FIG) in the world is by more than an order of magnitude smaller than that of TNCs[24].

In 2011 the British magazine *New Scientist* published a research study by a team of scientists who were specialists in complex systems at the Swiss Federal Institute of Technology in Zurich and who empirically proved over-concentration of global wealth and power in the hands of less than 150 market actors. The researchers used a technique previously applied in the modeling of nature systems for the processing of the most complete (at that time) database on the corporate structure of the world economy and created a global model of asset ownership by TNCs.

Of the 37 million companies and investors worldwide, they identified 43,060 TNCs, and then tried to identify the shareholders of these companies and their interrelationships. It revealed a core of 1,318 holders (corporations, organizations and individuals) closely related to each other. Each of these companies has a relationship with at least two other firms, and the average number of connections between them is 20. Although they account for 20% of the global operating profit, they control 60% of the global income through ownership stakes in industrial companies and "blue chips". Further investigation revealed an even more closely interwoven group of so-called superobjects, which included 147 companies that control 40% of the world's wealth. Most of them are major financial institutions such as Barclays Bank, JP Morgan Chase, Deutsche Bank, Credit Suisse and Goldman Sachs[25].

It should be noted that the results of this study are important not only from the point of view of identifying the real mechanisms of wealth distribution and management within the MGED. It also provides strong evidence of the limits of stability of the system. In fact, the current crisis has confirmed that these networks can be highly volatile. External shocks or loss of key links may lead to very serious consequences if not a collapse of the entire system. Such levels of dependence are essential to understanding both the nature and development vectors of MGED.

An analysis of the architecture of global economic power can somewhat contribute to strengthening the stability of MGED, which, naturally, involves an analysis of the system and identification of its vulnerabilities. In theory (in practice, unfortunately, there is no such certainty) in such situation economists could make recommendations on how to avoid critical disasters in the world economic system or at least to minimize the associated risks and possible damage.

* * *

Despite the importance of the aforementioned issues, the discussion of MGED transition should not be limited to such aspects as the development of global production capacities and global struggle between the world's centers of economic power. The transition of models typically proceeds evolutionarily through the accumulation of new qualitative features that replace the old ones. But in some cases an escalation of contradictions is possible, and that requires revolutionary solutions, which can be implemented in the global economy – in contrast to the political sphere – only through the concerted action of all actors.

Thus, model transition is a deeper and less dynamic process than a simple cyclical change in the situation on the global market even if the latter takes place over long periods of time. Here we deal with certain irreversible changes, new global economic realities, which get fixed in a new context of the relation between the participants of the international division of labor.

Because submodels develop asynchronously (as discussed above), it is difficult to speak about specific time limits for MGED transitions. Nevertheless, the graph above clearly shows that each "death" of a preceding MGED and "birth" of a succeeding one was accompanied by geopolitical catastrophe of global proportions – the Second World War, the collapse of the Soviet Union, etc. MGED transition was accompanied by a change in the "resource balance of power" in the world. In addition, to a certain extent the MGED theory explains or, at least, allows to take a fresh look at the causes of pendulum-like gains and reductions in the state's role in the world economy as a whole. The last 150-200 years show that this role grows at the junctions of MGED and gradually decreases as the latter establish themselves, just to begin to grow once again as imbalances accumulate, i.e. the eventual crisis of any "aging" MGED takes off.

Since the systematic study of the phenomenon of MGED has just started, the authors of the article do not claim to provide an exhaustive and/or the only possible definition. This is a long-term task for large research groups. In addition, the object of our research is continually evolving, and so inevitably there will be new issues and events waiting to be discovered and analyzed. At this stage, we considered our most important task to develop the very formulation of the problem and, if possible, an accurate description of the phenomenon at the scientific level available today. The problem, of course, remains open to scientific discussion and reformulation in line with new knowledge and evidence.

---

[1] http://www.mid.ru/brp_4.nsf/0/45D5CC6F7FlEACF0442579 9A005B12EC

[2] In practice, when there is no need to specifically emphasize the aspect of hierarchy and complexity, the term "model" (e.g. "population reproduction model") is sometimes used with respect to each of the submodels, which creates some inconvenience, but rarely leads to serious confusion. A typical example is the so-called model of the development of newly industrialized countries (NICs) – a product of the interaction of specific regional, financial, demographic, and production and exchange submodels, which have generated a new relatively self-dependent quality. Other examples of such synthetic systems, which we call "models", include the global and regional integration models, global model of transnational management of economic processes, global labor mobility model, etc. Thus, from the point of view of the hierarchical organization of the system, we are talking about a variety of submodels of the single global economic model – MGED.

[3] The authors consider it necessary to emphasize that a model transition is not an instantaneous process. Moreover, since any model consists of a set of asynchronously developing submodels, there are no clear boundaries between successive MGEDs. A transition period usually drags on for decades. Rudiments of the previous model can exist for a very long time even after the establishment of a new MWED.

[4] If you study the period of 150–200 years (starting around the first third of the 19th century and till now), it is relatively easy to distinguish qualitatively specific periods of global development, which gave rise to the corresponding independent MGEDs: 1) the period of the mature industrial capitalism and the formation of colonial empires (roughly until the end of the 19th century), 2) during the bitter inter-imperialist rivalry (from the beginning of 20th century, or a little earlier, and until the World War II), and 3) the period of "inter-imperialist cooperation", the Cold War and the confrontation between the two systems (the final milestone is the decade during which the Soviet Union collapsed, conventionally – until the majority of Eastern European countries was incorporated in the EU), and 4) the current stage of the emergence and formation of a polycentric world.

[5] According to the IMF's World Economic Outlook Database. September 2011. Report for Selected Countries and Subjects (http://www.imf.org/external/pubs/ft/weo/2011/02/weodata/weorept.aspx?pr.x=45&pr.y=3&sy=2010).

[6] The limits of the meaning of DC are somewhat blurred. Many scientists question the classification of China, Turkey, Mexico and some other countries as "developing countries", while supporters of traditional approaches, including most of the leading international organizations, continue to consider them as such. Recognizing the importance of the classification of the world in terms of socio-economic development from a methodological point of view, the authors could not fit a detailed discussion of

the issue within the limited space of this article. The authors' views on the issue, including the economic and mathematical justification of their position, can be found in the monograph *"Возникающие" и "насостоявшиеся" государства в мировой экономике и политике* [*Emerging and "failed" states in the world economy and politics*] by Abramova I.O., Fituni L.L., SapuntsovA.L. (M., 2007).

[7] UNCTAD. Handbook of Statistics 2010. N.Y. and Geneva, 2010. P. 16-23.

[8] *The World Economy: Forecast till 2020.* Ed. A.A. Dynkin. M., 2007. P. 64-65.

[9] For more detail, see *Fituni L.L.* "Арабская весна": трансформация политических парадигм в контексте международных отношений ["The Arab Spring": transformation of political paradigms in the context of international relations"]. *Мировая экономика и международные отношения* [*World Economy and International Relations*], 2012. Issue 1, P. 3.

[10] For example, see *Discours du President de la Republique a Toulon*, ler decembre 2011 (http://www.elysee.fr/president/les-actualites/discours/2011/discours-du-presi-dent-de-la-repu-bli-que-a-toulon.l2553.html); Intervention de M. le President de la Republique. Sommet sur la Crise Palais de l'Elysee. 18 Janvier 2012 (http://www.elysee.fr/president/les-actualites/ declarations/2012/intervention-du-pre-sident-de-la-republi-que-a.12814.html); Remarks by the President in State of the Union Address. January 24, 2012 (http://www.whitehouse.gov/the-press-office/2012/ 01/24/remarks-president-state-union-address).

[11] Remarks by the President in State of the Union Address. January 24. 2012 (http://www.whitehouse.gov/the-press-office/2012/01/24/remarks-president-state-union-address).

[12] Hereinafter statistical data and digital projections on the status and role of the middle class in MWED transformation according to: Kharas H. *The Emerging Middle Class in Developing Countries* / / OECD Development Centre Working Paper № 285. January 2010. According to OECD, an individual is considered part of the middle class if he spends $10 to $100 per day at purchasing power parity (PPP).

[13] Ibid.

[14] An example that already can be observed is the furious reaction of the West towards the so-called "expansion of China in Africa" and its attempts to hinder it. Although Beijing does not proclaim the Dark Continent to be its "zone of vital interests", China imports from Africa significant amounts of raw materials necessary for the sustained growth of its economy. In principle, the PRC has the exact same rights in this regard as the West. As a reminder, China still has only a fraction of the economic influence that former colonial powers and currently the United States have exerted in Africa for centuries.

[15] *Abramova I., Fituni L.* Competing for Africa's Natural Resources. International Affairs: A Russian Journal of World Politics, Diplomacy and International Relations. 2009. v 55. № 3. C. 47-58.

[16] Key World Energy Statistics, 2011. International Energy Agency. Paris, 2011. P. 10, 12.

[17] *Dobbs R., Oppenheim J., Thompson K, Brinkman M., Zornes M.* Resource Revolution: Meeting the World's Energy, Materials, Food, and Water Needs. McKinsey Global Institute. November 2011.

[18] McKinsey analysts adapted the research methodology of the World Bank known as the commodity price index, which was introduced by Grilli and Jan (See: Grilli E., Maw Cheng Yang. "Primary Commodity Prices, Manufactured Goods Prices, and the Terms of Trade of Developing Countries: What the Long Run Shows." The World Bank Economic Review. Vol. 2, № 1 (1988): pp. 1-47), creating their own index of commodity prices (MGI Commodity Index) based on databases of 28 key commodities divided into four subgroups : energy , food, agricultural raw materials and metals. The indices of Grilli and Jan were adjusted taking into account long time-series of prices on energy resources (oil, natural gas and coal) and steel. The latter was chosen as a separate single category because of its special importance to the economy and growth in general. The results were adjusted to remove the effects of inflation and currency fluctuations. Individual products within each of the subgroups were assigned appropriate weight based on the share of these products in world trade (by value).

[19] *Dobbs R.* et al. Op. cit. P. 2.

[20] Ibid. P. 23

[21] http://www.ilo.org/global/about-the-ilo/press-and-media-centre/news/WCMS_083976/ lang-en/index.htm

[22] *Dobbs R.* et al. Op. cit. P. 73.

[23] Resolution 1803 (XVII) of the UN General Assembly, December 14, 1962.

[24] *Fituni L.L.* Новый порядок на века? Политическая структура современного мира: состояние, проблемы, перспективы. [*Russia in the world of FIGs: the limits of growth and the illusions of revival / New world order for the ages? Political structure of the modern world: situation, problems and prospects*]. Moscow, 2000.

[25] New Scientist. 19.10.2011.

Irina Abramova

URBANIZATION IN AFRICA
DRIVER OR IMPEDIMENT TO ECONOMIC GROWTH?[*]

The African continent occupies a special place in the global economic and social order. The same can be said about the process of urbanization in Africa: while replicating with varying degrees of accuracy many tendencies inherent to other countries, this process, however, reveals a number of specific features that are peculiar to the African context.

African cities in the global urbanization space

The rate of urbanization in Africa is 3-4 times higher than the corresponding figures for Europe at the time of the Industrial Revolution and has not decreased for four decades already. Despite the fact that in 2012 the level of urbanization in Sub-Saharan Africa amounted to only 38.6% (for comparison: the figure for developing countries is 45.9%, for North African countries – 54.6%), the growth rate of the urban population in Sub-Saharan Africa was the highest (4-5% in the 1980s–1990s and over 3% in the 2000s). The most rapidly growing urban population was in Burundi, Reunion, Uganda, Angola, Botswana, Mozambique, Burkina Faso, Cape Verde, and Guinea-Bissau (an average of 4-6% annually)[1].

Currently, the African continent is experiencing a phase of quantitative and qualitative demographic changes, one of which is the process of accelerated urbanization. Back in 1990 two-thirds of the African population lived in rural areas, but by 2030 760 million Africans, or more than 50% of Africa's population, will live in cities. By 2050, the urban population of the continent will exceed 1.2 billion people, which will be greater than combined urban and rural population of the West[2].

Since population density of the African continent is quite differentiated, the level of urbanization in Africa also varies from country to country and from region to region.

As seen from Table 1, the least urbanized sub-region of Africa is East Africa, where less than a quarter of the total population lives in cities, although the rate of urban population growth there is higher than in Africa as a whole. Only in North Africa and Southern African countries most of the population lives in cities, while the rates of urban population growth and total population growth here are the lowest. However, in all parts of the continent the rate of urban population growth is higher than the rate of total population

---

[*] First published in *Azia i Afrika segodnya*. Issue 8, 2013.

growth. This means that in the coming years the level of urbanization in Africa will be growing quite rapidly.

Table 1
Key indicators of urbanization in Africa's sub-regions

Sub-region	Level of urbaniza- tion in 2012 (%)	Rate of urban population growth 2005–2012	Population in 2012 (million)		Rate of population growth in 2005–2012
			Urban population	Total population	
North Africa	54.61	2.45	116.258	212.927	2.2
West Africa	44.85	4.05	137.271	306.067	3.5
East Africa	23.6	3.86	77.194	327.093	3.4
Central Africa	43.1	5.9	55.592	128.909	3.8
Southern Africa	58.7	2.1	34.021	57.957	1.47
All Africa	40.6	3.71	420.336	1033.034	2.6

Calculated by the author based on: State of World Cities 2012/2013. Prosperity of Cities. UN-HABITAT. Nairobi, Kenya. 2012; The State of African Cities 2010: Governance, Inequality and Urban Land Markets. UN-HABITAT. Nairobi, Kenya. 2010.

Nearly two-thirds of Africa's urban population (61.7%) live in cities with the population of less than 750 thousand inhabitants (for the world, the figure is 52%), i.e. in cities rather small by global standards (see Table 2). For Africa, these "small towns" are quite large. It is these very towns which in the coming years will make the key contribution to the growth of Africa's urban population. This means that it is important to strengthen governance in these cities in order to effectively address the problems of rapid urban growth, urban planning, housing, infrastructure and living standards of the residents.

This certainly does not mean that Africa's largest city should be given less attention. They will also continue to grow quite rapidly, although not as fast as small and medium-sized cities. In absolute terms, the population of major cities will increase most significantly in the coming years. They will account for over one third of the total increase in Africa's urban population.

In 1950, Africa had only two cities with more than 1 million people – Cairo and Alexandria. In 2010, there were 50 such cities. The average size of African city-millionaire was 2.8 million and the entire population of these cities exceeded 144 million people. By 2015, there will be already 59 "millionaire cities" on the continent, with an average of 3.1 million residents, and the entire population of Africa's megacities will exceed 170 million[3].

Table 2

Distribution of African cities by their size in 2010 and 2025

Size	> 10 million	5–10 million	1–5 million	0.75–1 million	< 0.75
Number of cities in 2010	2	3	45	20	No data
Population (million)	21.579	24.504	97.917	17.053	259.271
Share in the total urban population	5.13	5.83	23.30	4.05	61.68
Number of cities in 2025	3	8	73	34	No data

Calculated by the author based on: The State of African Cities 2010: Governance, Inequality and Urban Land Markets. UN-HABITAT, Nairobi, Kenya. 2010, p. 244–247.

Currently Africa's biggest agglomerations are Cairo (Egypt), Lagos (Nigeria) and Kinshasa (DRC). The growth rates of these megacities are among the highest in the corresponding global category of cities. Today, Cairo (without Giza and other suburbs) has 12 million people, Lagos – 10 million, and Kinshasa – 8 million. In 2015, Cairo will have 13.5 million residents, Lagos – 12.5 million, Kinshasa – 11.3 million, and they will occupy the 11th, 17th and 19th places, respectively, among the 20 largest urban agglomerations in the world.

Table 3

Ten fastest growing African cities

City	Absolute growth in 2010–2020 (thousands)	City	Relative growth in 2010–2020 (%)
Kinshasa	4034	Ouagadougou	81.0
Lagos	3584	Niamey	56.7
Luanda	2308	Kampala	56.6
Dar es Salaam	1754	Dar es Salaam	52.3
Nairobi	1669	Mbuji-Mayi	50.0
Ouagadougou	1548	Lubumbashi	49.3
Cairo	1539	Abuja	49.2
Abidjan	1375	Luanda	48.3

City	Absolute growth in 2010–2020 (thousands)	City	Relative growth in 2010–2020 (%)
Kano	1100	Bamako	47.9
Addis Ababa	1051	Nairobi	47.3

Source: The State of African Cities 2010, p. 54–55.

As seen from Table 3, the largest absolute contributions to the growth of the urban population in the coming years will be made by Kinshasa, the capital of the DRC, (more than 4 million people), Lagos, the largest city in Nigeria, (3.6 million) and Luanda, the capital of Angola, (2.3 million), while Cairo's population – the largest in Africa to date – will grow by only 1.5 million[4]. In relative terms, the rates of urban growth will be highest in Ouagadougou, the capital of Burkina Faso, Niamey, the capital of Niger, and Kampala, the capital of Uganda.

By 2025, Kinshasa will become the largest African city with the population of 16.7 million people (11th in the world), followed by Lagos (15.8 million, the 12th place) and Cairo without suburbs (15.5 million, 13th place).

In addition to the accelerated growth of African megacities, there is a tendency of forming large urbanization systems that concentrate around one, two or three major cities, and gradually lure surrounding towns and countryside into their orbit of influence. This process has a strong synergic effect when adding up numerical values – in this case populations of towns and cities – leads to important qualitative changes in their development, which manifests itself in an accelerated socio-economic growth of urban areas and their simultaneous isolation from the rest of the country or group of countries.

The examples of such urbanization systems include the following: the Nile Delta area in Egypt with a population of 67 million people, which includes the Greater Cairo (more than 20 million inhabitants), Alexandria, Port Said and Suez and many medium and small cities; Gauteng area in South Africa with the population of 10.5 million inhabitants, which incorporates Johannesburg, Pretoria/Tshwane and Emfule/Vereeniging, and finally, an area in the Gulf of Guinea with 25 million people, which incorporates Ibadan, Lagos, Cotonou, Lome and Accra. These urban areas accumulate enormous human, natural, financial and other resources, which enable them to grow rapidly in comparison with other areas of the African continent. In the coming decades, the importance of these systems in the development of Africa will only increase.

How does the life of an African change with the move to a city?

Of course, the process of urbanization in Africa cannot be reduced solely to the accelerated growth of urban population and its concentration mostly in metropolitan areas. It is a complex structural phenomenon that affects qualitative aspects of functioning of both urban areas and country as a whole.

The urbanization process is usually accompanied by an increase in per capita income. This trend has manifested itself in Europe, North and Latin America and in much of Asia. However, Africa, unlike other regions of the world, has not demonstrated this trend in any country at any time. Particularly negative in this regard was the period between 1970 and 1995. During this period Africa's urban population grew on average 4.7% annually, while per capita GDP declined by 0.7% per annum. This inverse relationship between indicators of urbanization and per capita income is a unique phenomenon even among the world's poorest countries.

At the same time, the accelerated growth of African cities is not accompanied by an increase in industrial production, as it was the case in the developed countries of Europe and America. Slightly more than 9% of the African workforce was employed in industry compared to 18% in Asia, where there was a comparable rate of urbanization[5]. Not being a result of industrialization, Africa's explosive urban growth of recent decades, with few exceptions, was not associated with any significant increase in labor productivity in the agricultural sector.

Until the early 2000s, a peculiarity of the African urbanization was that the continent's urban population continued to grow rapidly despite low and (in some cases) negative growth of public production. Stagnation in the African economy did not restrain urbanization, whilst the latter, in turn, did not stimulate economic growth.

In this regard, in the 1980s–1990s, there was a fairly widespread concept of the so-called "false urbanization" or "hyper urbanization", according to which African cities were not considered as engines of economic growth and structural change. Instead, according to supporters of this concept, they were part of the reason and one of the main manifestations of the economic and social crisis that engulfed the continent[6].

The author of this study is not a supporter of the concept of "false urbanization". Despite all its inconsistency, the process of urban growth in Africa stimulates socio-economic development, albeit in distorted and non-traditional forms, and cities themselves, amid limited material, financial and other resources, are becoming a sort of "outposts of growth", providing simultaneously a bridge between African countries and the world market.

At the same time, the author agrees with the statement that the trend we see in Africa towards urbanization in the absence of economic growth can be partly explained by distorted incentives that encourage workers to move to the city in order to receive subsidies and other social benefits rather than to have an opportunity to find a better paying job. African cities benefit from

29

trade and food pricing policies, which favored urban consumers over rural producers.

National governments of most African states have often tried to influence the pace of urbanization and where and how it takes place. Often, however, these efforts were limited to the transfer of resources from agriculture to finance the development of "modern" economic sectors concentrated in cities. In fact, much of the money was invested in the creation of the public sector, which was characterized by low efficiency but created a significant number of jobs. Urban formal sector workers and government employees had access to subsidized food and housing as well as to pension programs and employment funds, while rural population was forced to sell their products at low prices and had limited access to government support. Subsidizing basic goods in cities was done for political reasons: it ensured relative social stability in large cities, where conflicts could start for smaller reason due to high density of population.

Main incentives for rural-urban migration

Although governments of a number of African states have tried to reduce the gap between urban and rural areas, the process of deepening the gap has gone too far and has led to an excessive rate of migration from rural to urban areas. In other words, what lay at the heart of rural-urban migration in Africa was not just economic attractiveness of cities, but also, to a large extent, factors pushing people out from the countryside, including widespread farm bankruptcies, land scarcity, and the relative and absolute overpopulation in agrarian communities.

Furthermore, wars and civil unrest on the African continent for decades have been forcing millions of people to flee to cities. Migration flows were also influenced by weather conditions, particularly drought. In Mauritania, the population of Nouakchott doubled in just one year during the drought of mid-1985.

Capitals and major cities – trade, financial, administrative and cultural centers – received main flows of migrants from the African village. In the 1980s, the contribution of migration to urban population growth in Africa reached 50%[7]. Since the beginning of the 1990s, the proportion of migrants in the total urban population growth has begun to decline, and now it does not exceed 40%[8]. African cities are increasingly relying on own resources for growth, i.e. natural growth of the urban population.

Nevertheless, we should not expect the outflow of residents from the African village to weaken in the near future. The tendency of reverse migration from cities to the countryside in Zambia, Tanzania, Uganda and some other countries because of the high cost of living in cities, which was incipient in the early 1990s, proved to be unstable.

Migration flows do not decrease during structural economic adjustment or social and economic upheavals. Conversely, the scale of migration, both legal and illegal, increases significantly. Another thing is that these flows in the context of globalization are increasingly beginning to rely on foreign labor markets, overcoming not only national but also continental boundaries. The bulk of these flows will be absorbed by the global city. Migration from the crisis-stricken rural areas of Africa will continue to "feed" both African and global urbanization, exacerbating problems of urban development and exporting these difficulties to the developed world.

Administrative efforts to stop migration to cities hinder African poor to improve their economic situation and can create other problems for migrants. For example, the introduction of restrictions on migration in Dar es Salaam (Tanzania) increased the vulnerability of the poor to corrupt officials demanding bribes for issuing permits to enter the city (the situation is very similar to the issuance of registration permits for migrants in Russia in exchange for bribes)[9].

Economic and social contrasts

Urbanization processes in Africa under the conditions of weak economy, high rates of population growth and high population mobility increasingly acquire crisis outlines.

The crisis has affected almost all aspects of life in African cities – employment, education and health, food and welfare benefits, environmental situation and access to urban social services, and much more.

The problem of widespread urban poverty has come to the forefront in all its complexity and severity. According to the World Bank (WB), in the 1980s urban residents accounted for 29% of Africans living in poverty; in the 1990s, the figure reached 40%[10]. The gap between the African continent and the developed world remains and even tends to increase. In 2010, the GDP of the Western countries with the population of 890 million people (of which 700 million are urban residents) exceeded 16 times Africa's GDP, while the population of the latter was greater than that in the West (1,033 billion people, of whom 420 million were urban residents). By the end of the 2000s, more than 15% of the urban population of Africa continued to live on $1 a day; as a result of the global financial and economic crisis the number has undoubtedly increased[11].

It should be noted, however, that the average income of residents of African cities is higher than that of villagers. The data on migrants we collected during our field study in 2005–2012 provides irrefutable evidence that by the means of migration poor Africans respond to economic incentives, especially higher wages, better than the locals, and tend to be in a better position after the move. According to our estimates, the income of migrants after migration increases 1.5 times[12]. In other words, the process of urbanization objectively facilitates an increase in African living standards, providing the best opportunity to increase earnings. However, costs in African cities are also substantially higher and more diverse than in the countryside.

Absolute poverty is the inability to satisfy basic needs. The growth in relative and absolute poverty in African cities continues against the backdrop of the widening gap between the richest and the poorest segments of the population. Wealth and earnings are increasingly concentrated in the hands of the small urban elite – bureaucratic elite, bourgeoisie, highly qualified specialists, who gained new opportunities for enrichment during economic restructuring. In view of the inconsistency of the available statistics on income distribution, incompleteness of initial materials of the research, as well as the use of different methods of calculation, one can only try to identify the most common trends.

According to calculations by V.A. Melyantsev, the average unweighted quintile coefficient of income differentiation increased in Tropical Africa from 9–11 in the 1980s–1990s to 14.9 in the 2000s[13]. According to our estimates, in Africa in general, the Gini index of income distribution increased from 43% to 51% between 2000 and 2010. In some countries it was higher. For example, in the Comoros in 2010 it was 64.3%, in Botswana – 61%, in Angola – 58.6%, in South Africa – 57.8%, in Lesotho – 52.5%, in Swaziland – 51%.[14] It is noteworthy that the coefficient of income inequality is higher in countries with high rates of urbanization. According to our calculations for ARE, the Gini index for the Egyptian cities was 46%, while the figure for the villages was 39%[15]. Consequently, it is in the cities where the gap between the rich and the poor is most pronounced.

The gap between the living standards of urban elites and the poor primarily affects consumption – both quantitatively and qualitatively. In addition, the contradiction between the emerging needs of the population and the actual level of consumption in cities is even greater because city life, in comparison to rural, provides for the emergence of a greater number of needs, and low living standards of the majority of citizens objectively limits the ability to meet these needs. At one extreme of African society there is rampant unproductive consumption, at the other – the poorest strata create demand below the outermost limits of their physical needs.

During the years of structural economic adjustment, as well as in times of financial and economic crises, the urban poor are the first to feel the marked decline in living standards. In 2008–2010, indicators of real income and consumption in low-income families in urban Ghana, Nigeria, Kenya and South Africa fell to the level of mere biological existence, and the life of the marginalized became the daily struggle for survival[16].

"Urbanization of poverty"

Another clear demonstration of the scale of urban poverty is growth of slums and squatter settlements on the outskirts of African cities. In two-thirds of African countries more than half of the urban population lives in slums. In Sudan, the Central African Republic (CAR), Chad, Angola, and Guinea-Bissau their share exceeds 80%. Even in relatively prosperous countries – Egypt, Morocco, and Algeria – a significant part of the urban population continues to live on the outskirts of the city life and does not have adequate housing (see Table 4).

Table 4

Slums in African cities

Country	Urban population in 2010 (million)	Share of slums in urban areas (%)	Number of slum dwellers (million)
5 least prosperous countries			
Sudan	14.771	94.2	13.914
CAR	1.536	94.1	1.446
Chad	2.463	91.3	2.247
Angola	8.501	86.5	7.352
Guinea-Bissau	0.407	83.1	0.390
5 most prosperous countries			
South Africa	28.119	28.7	8.077
Zimbabwe	4.667	18.0	0.239
Egypt	31.662	17.0	5.405
Morocco	18.469	13.0	2.422
Algeria	20.804	12.0	2.455

Source: The State of African Cities 2010, p. 29–30.

Inability to pay for increasingly expensive housing with very little or no income or its absence increases the risk of losing the roof over one's head. For example, in Luanda, the Angolan capital, the cost of a studio apartment not in the best district and without electricity but with utilities included is $5,000 per month; a decent apartment in a prestigious area costs $15,000 per month. Such money can only be paid by foreigners or local elites. Most of the population lives right in the streets in structures built from any available material.

Unimaginable filth and unsanitary conditions reign in African slums; electricity, water supply, sewerage, and garbage disposal are completely absent. Population density here is uncontrollable, and thousands of homeless sleep in the streets.

33

Problems of urban development, landscaping, transportation, healthcare, etc. are intensifying. Especially dangerous is the deepening environmental and social crisis. Environmental factor worsens the already low social indicators. Only in North African countries and South Africa most of the population of major cities has access to clean drinking water and sanitation.

In Tropical Africa we are seeing a very different picture. Currently only 63% of the population of Luanda, 60% of the Chadian capital N'Djamena, and 30% of the residents of Ibadan (Nigeria) have water supply and sewerage[17]. Despite the fact that in the 2000s due to the efforts of African governments and international aid access to clean water and sanitation on the continent was increased on average by 20–30%, a significant proportion of Africans are still deprived of these essential services[18].

Environmental degradation (accumulation of sewage and waste, water and air pollution, etc.) especially affects slum dwellers. It is very likely that the expansion of areas of environmental degradation at the expense of urban areas and its negative consequences for African cities will have long-term nature, especially given the global financial and economic crisis.

Many African countries are characterized by a phenomenon that can be called "urbanization of poverty". Rural poor migrate to cities and join the urban poor. Sprawling poverty in African cities is accompanied by a peculiar "restructuring" through changes in employment.

Urban labor market: limits to growth

The rapid growth of urban population means an increase in the proportion of people of working age in cities, i.e. of potential workforce. The army of urban workers is growing rapidly in Africa. In the 1990s, its rate of growth was 3%; in the 2000s, it went up to 4-5%. At the same time, there was unfavorable situation in urban labor markets in most African countries and new manpower remained unemployed. According to some reports, in a number of countries of Sub-Saharan Africa 70% of the urban economically active population have no permanent job and, therefore, no stable income needed to lead a full life[19].

Rapid urbanization in African cities has led to a redistribution of the labor force in urban sectors of the economy; in particular, there was rapid growth of the service sector and the informal sector (IFS). Employment in this sector is complex and controversial. It is dominated by unstable forms of employment, underemployment, low productivity and income, and orientation on specific demand. In some African countries, especially the poorest, the informal sector absorbs up to 60% of urban employment[20].

As a rule, income levels of most of the people employed in the IFS do not exceed the survival threshold. The most common activities in the IFS are primitive outdoor trade and traditional services. In is a common practice to combine different jobs (carter and watchman, temporary worker and shopkeeper, etc.). Migrants who fill the ranks of the ISF retain not only their traditional norms of life, but also the usual compulsion to engage in rural labor. In a difficult economic situation, not only migrants, but also all urban poor, including civil servants and intellectuals, engage in agriculture or urban gardening (in gardens, on vacant lots, on the outskirts). It is a typical marginal activity at the crossroads of economic sectors, structures, urban and rural lifestyles.

This kind of economic activity, which provides only unstable income, often coexists with beggary, theft, and vagrancy. In the context of large-scale urban unemployment, the prospect of becoming a lumpen is very real, but that of becoming a modern worker is extremely low. Visible growth of employment in the ISF does not eliminate the problems of urban poverty and pauperization. The city becomes the base of a broad marginal social category, which is characterized by deprivation, absolute poverty, stagnation on the sidelines of economic life and social existence. The ISF in the urban context cultivates social categories characterized by unstable and inefficient employment with incomes no higher that the survival threshold.

Of course, there exist upper layers of the ISF linked to the modern sector of the economy (small business, etc.), which form social groups that are transitional to modern social groups. Yet growing population pressure on urban labor market in the context of job deficit increases unemployment, hidden unemployment, and underemployment in the informal sector. Pauperism and poverty in such setting reproduce constantly; the number of people in a state of extreme social deprivation is only growing. Thus, Africa at the turn of the century is characterized by the type of urbanization associated with the marginalization of a significant part of the urban population.

Urban marginal mass not involved in modern economic relations swells faster than new social structures are formed. Nevertheless, the African city plays an important and even decisive role in the social transformation of society, forming those strata that represent the modern sector of the economy. In the process of urbanization, employment in the national economy increases and human resources are used more efficiently through reallocation of labor between urban and rural areas, agriculture and urban sectors of the economy. According to the World Bank, over the last 40 years the share of agricultural employment in African countries fell from 77% to 60%: from 85% to 75% for Sub-Saharan Africa and from 51% to 32% for North Africa[21].

Cities also contribute to improving the quality of labor by educating and training it. Urbanization significantly expands the scope of hired labor in the economy and thereby makes a substantial contribution to the modern structure of employment. In African cities female employment also increases: cities provide women with more opportunities to work and study.

Thus, the formation of modern economic sectors and types of employment in African cities is continuous, but its rate is not high enough and lags behind the rate at which the number of people not involved in new economic relations increases. As a result, the share of modern economic sectors in urban employment in African countries is usually below 50%.

The structural macroeconomic restructuring initiated by international financial institutions has not created the foundations for the growth of social strata, including the stratum of employees working for modern economic structures. In the first years after independence, the main driver of growth in the number of hired workers, primarily in cities, was the formation of the public sector. The size of the army of hired labor doubled in Africa during the period.

Due to the measures taken by most of the African states to reduce direct government participation in the manufacturing sector, the number of employees in the modern sector of the economy decreased significantly. This affected all spheres of public production – industry, energy, infrastructure, state apparatus, health and education services. As a result, the share of hired labor in the modern urban employment began to decline. According to the ECA, by the end of the 2000s, the modern sector of the economy of most African countries employed only 8% of the workforce[22].

The last global financial crisis has made a huge impact on urban employment in African countries. The loss of jobs in the modern sector of the urban economy, including the public sector, destabilization of employment, and sharp deterioration in the living conditions of workers have accelerated pauperization of the modern sector. Many middle class groups, including social workers – teachers, doctors, etc., as well as part of the national bourgeoisie, are increasingly marginalized.

Youth is in a particularly difficult situation. Most of the urban unemployed (50–75%) are people under 25 years of age. Young intellectuals – recent graduates – who have difficulties finding suitable jobs after the abolition of the system of work assignment that existed in several countries in the 1980s–1990s are also lumpenized. Under these conditions, "brain drain" is increasing significantly. Those who are not able to go abroad continue to be dependent on relatives or friends, join the ranks of the ISF, or become unemployed. Thus, the army of the "new marginals" is replenished with the strata of the intelligentsia that have received education and training.

Women and children are the worst off. According to the UN, by 2025 more than 50% of the Africa children will be urban residents, and more than 60% of them will live in poverty[23].

The increasing number of angry and desperate people in African cities and swelling to a critical mass lumpenized population complicate the general socio-political situation in many African countries. Squatter slums and villages, which accumulate socially disordered and unprotected underclass, mostly young people, represent a kind of "risk zone", being a source of constant economic and social tensions. A crime wave swept African cities where prostitution, theft, and robbery thrive, especially among young people. Destructive processes in cognition and disposition of marginalized masses have consequences for any society, threatening if not a complete rupture of the social fabric than its significant weakening and dilution.

Marginal masses of urban residents are involved in riots and unrest of the general urban population, which have become ubiquitous on the continent. Suffice it to recall the events of the winter and spring of 2011 in North Africa. African conflicts increasingly often cross national boundaries, and African refugees and illegal migrants have become one of the world's major problems.

Is it possible to regulate urban growth in Africa?

Negative consequences of violent urbanization processes on the continent have confronted African governments with the need to find effective ways to solve this problem. Governments in most African countries are trying to purposefully influence the processes of urbanization.

However, as practice shows, the policy is not always successful. Trying to regulate urban growth in Africa, governments of African countries often distort the objective processes of urbanization, choosing locations for the construction of public enterprises and creating special economic zones for political rather than economic reasons. For instance, the largest state-owned enterprise in Egypt – the metallurgical complex in Helwan – was placed near the capital but not near the source of raw materials. As a result of the decision, the polluting steel plant operates almost in the center of the largest urban area in the country (Greater Cairo), which not only increases the cost of transportation of raw materials, but also creates huge environmental problems for the local population.

The African countries that have established or are establishing special economic zones by offering preferential tax system, in fact, encourage economic activity in a particular privileged area at the expense of others. After all, when, for example, trade liberalization was carried out in coastal areas, which was typical, for example, for a number of West African States, their inland regions found themselves at a considerable disadvantage. In fact, the policy of preferential development of certain regions or cities perpetuates the dual economy – with modern cities on the coast and the rest of a country at a disadvantage. The coastal cities of Egypt, which were the first to gain from the open door policy, as well as such cities as Port Sudan, Lagos, Accra and several others still retain their benefits, despite the fact that their special status was revoked.

But the most significant hidden form of distortion brought by governments in the process of geographical distribution of production facilities and urban growth is bureaucratic centralization of decision-making and large-scale corruption. They are inherent in most African states. Bureaucrats in central governments want to tightly control the process of issuing various licenses, permits, loans and grants. In these circumstances, manufacturers tend to stay in capitals or other bureaucratic centers in order to be able to effectively solve such problems. In the 1990s, Morocco, Egypt and Tunisia liberalized capital markets and export-import operations, creating new opportunities for small and medium-sized companies. However, the issuance of permits for commercial activities remained centralized, and the concentration of small and medium-sized companies in major cities of these countries only increased.

The disappointing results of previous attempts by African governments to prevent migration from rural to urban areas or to accelerate growth of specific cities lead to an unambiguous conclusion: by far the majority of the African governments are not able to make decisions about where people should live or production facilities should be constructed.

An ideal government policy would be to ensure a level playing field so that large, medium and small cities and rural areas are on an equal footing to compete with each other. However, such policies require not just the removal of subsidies and tax incentives. As a country is urbanized, investment in public infrastructure should be increased. Industrial production in remote cities and regions requires modern communications, roads and electricity to make the production of competitive products, their transportation to the market and communication with buyers and sellers possible. It is the central governments that play a key role in making decisions about whether to make such investments, and if yes, where and when. To resist pressure to concentrate investments in capitals or one or two large cities, institutional mechanisms to allow other regions to participate in decision-making about fund allocation are necessary. The task of creating such mechanisms should also be attributed to the state authority.

As practice has shown, other repressive measures of African governments to manage urbanization processes – such as demolition of slums, destruction of urban gardens, and banning street trade, vagrancy and beggary, etc. – do not produce the desired effect. Therefore, African governments need to focus on the development of a comprehensive policy in the field of demography and human resources to mitigate the consequences of unemployment and poverty. This includes legislative regulation of migration flows, promotion of small business and entrepreneurship, stimulation of labor-intensive industries, organization of public works, development of small and medium-sized cities, training labor force, and so on.

* * *

Governments of African countries with the aid of the international community are trying to compensate for the social costs of economic restructur-

38

ing and the impact of the financial crisis by adopting special programs to combat poverty and ensure social protection of the most vulnerable urban residents. Such efforts on the part of African governments will be still needed in the future, although they have not yet had any substantial impact on the state of things.

Obviously, it will take joint efforts of the entire world community to solve the problems of African cities, which are increasingly becoming international in character.

[1] State of World Cities 2012/2013. Prosperity of Cities. UN-HABITAT. Nairobi, Kenya. 2012, p. 29-30.

[2] The State of African Cities 2010: Governance, Inequality and Urban Land Markets. UN-HABITAT, Nairobi, Kenya. 2010, p. 19.

[3] Calculated by the author based on: The State of African Cities 2010.., p. 244-247.

[4] It should be reiterated that this the figure is for Cairo but not for the Greater Cairo, which includes Giza, Helwan and a number of suburbs and whose population exceeds 20 million people.

[5] World Urbanisation Prospects. The 2000 Revision. DESA, United Nations, N.Y. 2001, p. 6-7.

[6] See, for example: World Bank. World Development Report 1999/2000. Wash., 2000; Tarver J.D. Urbanization in Africa: A Handbook. L., 1995.

[7] *Todaro M.* Economic Development in the Third World. N.Y., 1989, p. 286.

[8] The State of African Cities 2010.., p. 23-24.

[9] The data was obtained by the author from interviews of Tanzanian migrants in 2009–2011.

[10] Urbanization in the Developing World: Current Trends and Need Responses. Wash., 1992, p. 1.

[11] The State of African Cities 2010.., p. 29.

[12] *Абрамова И.О.* Африканская миграция: опыт системного анализа [*Abramova I.O.* African Migration: The Experience of Systems Analysis]. М., 2009. P. 67.

[13] *Melyantsev V.A.* Developing Countries in the Age of Transformations. M., 2009, p. 163.

[14] Human Development Report 2011. UNDP., Vienna, 2011, p. 95-97.

[15] Calculated based on: *Abramova I.O.* Arab City on the Eve of the New Millennium. Moscow, 2005. M., 2005, P. 169. The State of African Cities 2010...

[16] African Economic Outlook 2010. OECD/ADB. Addis Ababa, 2010, p. 35.

[17] The State of African Cities 2010.., p. 180-183.

[18] Human Development Report 2011, UNDP, p. 176.

[19] The Journal of Development Studies. L., 2006. Vol. 42, No 5, p. 675.

[20] Africa Development. Dakar. 2005. Vol. XXX, No 2, p. 87.

[21] Africa Development Indicators 2012. The World Bank. Washington, 2012, p. 309.

[22] Human Development Report 2011.., p. 97.

[23] Economic Report on Africa, 2010. U.N. ECA. N.Y., 2010, p. 58.

Irina Matsenko

SUB-SAHARAN AFRICA: IMPLEMENTATION OF THE MILLENNIUM DEVELOPMENT GOALS[*]

It has been over ten years since the adoption of the UN Millennium Declaration (2000), which nominated eight Millennium Development Goals (MDGs) for the period until 2015. These goals include eradicating extreme poverty and hunger, achieving universal primary education, promoting gender equality and empowering women, reducing child mortality rates, improving maternal health, combating HIV/AIDS, malaria, and other diseases, ensuring environmental sustainability and developing a global partnership for development.

From the outset Sub-Saharan Africa (SSA) has seriously lagged behind other developing regions in the implementation of the MDGs. Suffice it to say that in 1990 (the base year for monitoring MDGs) the poverty rate in the region was estimated at 58% of the population (the highest in the world)[1]; in absolute terms, it was about 300 million people living in extreme poverty, i.e. on less than $1.25 a day. In other words, every second African lived (and still lives) below the poverty line (one in four in the world).

The global financial and economic crisis has further aggravated the situation with the implementation of the MDGs, slowing progress in this direction. It is necessary to note that the crisis of 2008 was preceded by a period of significant improvement in human development indicators in many African countries due to the unprecedented economic growth in 2000–2007[2]. Particularly noticeable overall progress was achieved in expanding primary school enrollment, combating AIDS and reducing child mortality rates. For instance, the world's greatest expansion of primary school enrollment (by 36%) of the last decade was observed in SSA countries, although the region still lags behind other developing regions in absolute terms. Owing to the intensification of combating AIDS and other infectious diseases, the annual number of new HIV-infected people in SSA countries has fallen by more than 25% since the mid-1990s, while the mortality rate of children under five years of age has decreased by 22% over the same period.

With regard to all other MDGs (eradicating extreme poverty and hunger, reducing unemployment, promoting gender equality, reducing maternal mortality, etc.), most SSA countries are still very far from achieving the Declaration's goals. Moreover, in absolute terms poverty, hunger and unemployment are growing (although they are decreasing in relative terms), gender inequal-

---

[*] First published in *Azia i Afrika segodnya*. Issue 8, 2012.

ity remains high, particularly in the field of education and labor, and maternal mortality is not reducing.

Poverty. The poverty dynamics for SSA countries: 57% (1990), 58% (1999) and 51% (2005) (in developing countries – 42, 31 and 25 % respectively)[3]. In quantitative terms, the total number of people living below the poverty line has decreased in all regions of the world except SSA, where as a result of rapid population growth it increased in 1990-2005 by 100 million people, reaching 390 million. The global crisis added approximately 50-60 million people to the figure. Thus, despite the sharp downward trend in the proportion of people living in extreme poverty in SSA countries which has been in place since the late 1990s, the region remains the only one on the planet where poverty continues to grow. This means that the first and main MDG of halving extreme poverty (the target of 29%) will not be achieved here, in contrast to all other developing regions.

However, a statement of this fact does not fully reflect the real picture, because this region has actually made progress in recent years. For more than ten years SSA countries have been exerting significant effort to implement virtually all of the MDGs, including poverty reduction, but their path to these goals has been much more difficult in comparison with other regions due to their lower initial level. It is extremely difficult for African states to overcome the distance separating them from the poverty target in such a short historical period because in 1990 large parts of Africa were far below the poverty line. In addition, African countries began their reforms later than other regions and therefore later benefited from accelerating revenue growth.

The obvious fact that Sub-Saharan Africa as a whole will not be able to reach the target of halving poverty by 2015 does not mean that individual states will not be able to do this. The continent is very heterogeneous, so one should not consider just averages. According to the monitoring of the MDGs, Gambia and Mauritania have already cut poverty in half compared to 1990 and thus have achieved the 2015 target; several other countries – Botswana , Ghana, Senegal, Cameroon, Cape Verde, Kenya and Ethiopia – are getting close to achieving the target[4]. High rates of poverty reduction have recently been observed in several other countries (Mali, Guinea, Central African Republic).

Thus, we can assume that despite the substantial lag of the Sub-Saharan region as a whole in terms of halving extreme poverty by 2015, a number of countries, which are successfully progressing in this direction, will be able to achieve the first MDG if not by the deadline then shortly thereafter.

Hunger. Since 1990, the percentage of hungry people in SSA countries has decreased from 31 to 26%, but this change is not sufficient to compensate for population growth and put the region on track to meet the MDG of halving the proportion of people who suffer from hunger by 2015. The recent global food and financial crisis has sharply aggravated the food situation in Africa, which could not but affect the solution of problems of malnutrition and hunger[5]. To date, 265 million Africans living in Sub-Saharan Africa suffer from hunger[6].

Employment. This problem has always been huge in Africa[7]. According to recent estimates, SSA countries are still experiencing very high overall unemployment (according to official figures – 8%, but unofficial estimates are several times higher). The share of informal employment as well as the so-called vulnerable employment (self-employed and unpaid household workers who typically work in unstable and insecure jobs) varies from 70 to 80% of the workforce in the countries of Sub-Saharan Africa, which is the highest such figure in the world. Moreover, this region has the world's highest proportion of the "working poor ", who represent about 60% of the employed population (the working poor are those who have income below $1.25 a day)[8].

The recent global crisis has resulted in a marked decrease in employment and productivity in Africa. Due to the loss of jobs, increasingly more Africans have been forced to accept unsafe and unstable positions. According to the International Labour Organization (ILO), in 2009-2011 this kind of employment accounted for about 77% of all jobs in the SSA countries, and the proportion of the working poor grew by 6% (from 58 to 64%), which is a worrisome indicator and practically nullifies the gradual improvement observed in the pre-crisis period[9].

Universal primary education. In the pre-crisis period the resumption of economic growth on the continent led to some progress in the development of the education sector. The most notable achievement was an almost 40% increase in primary school enrollment in Sub-Saharan Africa, which came as the result of government policies coupled with international support. The level of primary school enrollment in SSA reached 76% in 2010 compared with 58% in 1999, although the region as a whole still lags behind other developing regions in this regard (e.g. North Africa – 96%)[10]. In 11 countries (Benin, Burundi, Ethiopia, Kenya, Lesotho, Madagascar, Malawi, Mali, Mozambique, Tanzania and Uganda) primary education fees have been abolished, which has allowed children from low-income families to go to school.

However, in Sub-Saharan Africa 32 million children of primary school age do not go to school (this number constitutes almost half of all such children in the world), while 30% of those who enter the first grade do not graduate[11]. Most of these children come from poor families where the dilemma "school or work" is decided in favor of the latter.

It is quite obvious that despite the significant progress made in the 2000s the MGD of achieving universal primary education will not be implemented in Africa by 2015. Nevertheless, according to recent UN data, some of the poorest countries of SSA, in particular Burundi, Madagascar, Tanzania, Rwanda, Sao Tome and Principe and Togo have already achieved or are close to achieving universal primary education (net enrollment ratio of over 95%)[12]. Similar progress has been made in wealthy nations of southern and northern sub-regions such as Botswana, South Africa, Seychelles, Mauritius, Algeria and Tunisia.

Gender equality. Growing enrollment leads to a reduction in the gender gap in this area. Many countries of Sub-Saharan Africa have adopted measures to eliminate the barriers to girls' education, which resulted in decreasing gender inequality in primary schools of the region in general. For example, in 2010 in primary school there were 92 girls for every 100 boys (in 1999 – 85), while in middle and high school the situation became even worse than in 1999 (79 and 63 girls for every 100 boys in 2010, but 82 and 67 in 1999), in contrast to all other regions where gender inequality has decreased at all school levels[13]. Consequently, SSA countries, despite all efforts to improve the situation in the field of gender equality in education, are still far from achieving the MDG of eliminating gender inequality at all levels of education by 2015.

Child mortality. Over the last two decades there has been made considerable progress in reducing child mortality in all countries of the world.

The mortality rate of children under five years of age fell by a third in developing countries: from 99 to 66 per 1,000 live births over the period from 1990 to 2010, which is a significant improvement, but not sufficient to achieve the MDG of reducing child mortality by two-thirds.

Child mortality is the highest in SSA countries, which are home to 20% of all children under five years of age. The mortality rate for this age (121 per 1,000 live births) is twice the figure throughout the developing world, and a significant number of countries of the region demonstrate no tendency to reduce it. The region still accounts for half of all child deaths in the world. The main causes are pneumonia, diarrhea, malaria and AIDS, as well as malnutrition[14].

Nonetheless, there are also positive examples. For example, since 1990 the child mortality rate has decreased in Malawi, Eritrea, Ethiopia, Equatorial Guinea, Zambia, Mozambique, Niger, Ghana and other countries. Overall, the child mortality rate in SSA has decreased by 22% since 1990, indicating a positive trend, but the rate of improvement is clearly insufficient to achieve the corresponding MDG.

Maternal mortality. Of all the MDGs the least feasible is improving maternal health as required by the goals, namely the reduction of maternal mortality by three-fourths in 1990–2015. Over half a million women worldwide die each year from treatable complications of pregnancy and childbirth, and 99% of such deaths take place in developing countries. The situation in SSA countries is the most depressing. There has been practically no reduction in their extremely high maternal mortality rate (640 per 100.000 live births), which is more than twice the figure for all developing countries (290). More than half of all maternal deaths occur in SSA, where the "leaders" in terms of this indicator (more than 1000 per 100.000 live births) are Somalia, Chad and Guinea-Bissau[15]. The most common causes of maternal death are blood loss during delivery, high blood pressure, as well as malaria, HIV/AIDS and cardiovascular diseases.

Diseases. In Sub-Saharan Africa just HIV/AIDS, malaria and tuberculosis, which are known as the "big three" diseases, annually kill an estimated three million people[16]. The AIDS pandemic has become a disaster for Africa. In 2010, there were about 33 million people living with HIV, of which more than two-thirds lived in SSA. Nearly three-fourths of deaths related to AIDS took place the region. Although in recent years the high rates of the spread of HIV/AIDS and related mortality have begun to decline, the magnitude of this problem is still the greatest in Sub-Saharan Africa, where 70% of new HIV infections worldwide were recorded in 2010[17]. Characteristically, in the region almost 60% of HIV-infected adults are women, indicating the feminization of the disease.

Despite these staggering numbers, in recent years some progress has been made in the fight against AIDS owing to medical developments and their implementation. These include prevention programs and antiretroviral therapy, which have led to a decrease in the number of people newly infected with HIV or dying from AIDS. However, still today two-thirds of Africans who are infected with HIV and are in urgent need of treatment do not have access to appropriate therapy. Africa lacks medical personnel, financial resources, equipment and drugs necessary for the prevention and treatment of this terrible disease. It is necessary to pool efforts at the international and national levels, intensify cooperation between the international community and African governments, and engage Africa's private sector and civil society.

Among traditional tropical diseases that are widespread in Africa malaria is the greatest threat. The disease kills a human every minute. 90% of global deaths from this disease take place in the SSA countries; the majority of deaths (80%) occur among children under five years of age: it is exactly malaria which is considered the main cause of children mortality in the region. Half the world's population carries the risk of contracting the disease. At the same time, according to the World Health Organization (WHO), in 2010 the SSA countries accounted for 80% of the cases of malaria. Among these countries the most affected were Nigeria, DRC and Burkina Faso[18].

The number of cases of tuberculosis as well as deaths from it has been declining in all regions except Sub-Saharan Africa. Over the last 20 years the incidence of tuberculosis in SSA has increased from 300 to 490 per 100.000

people, while the corresponding death rate has grown from 33 to 53 per 100.000 people[19]. In conjunction with AIDS tuberculosis causes enormous physical and material losses, leading to a reduction in income and poverty of the ill and their families, which in turn increases poverty and slows economic growth, particularly in South Africa, which has become the epicenter of the dual epidemic.

In general, despite the increased efforts of the international community and the African countries themselves to combat infectious diseases in the last decade, the current trends in Sub-Saharan Africa indicate that the region will not achieve the MDG of "having halted by 2015 and begun to reverse the incidence of malaria, HIV/AIDS and other major diseases".

Access to drinking water and basic sanitation. Today, about 1.1 billion people in developing countries do not have adequate access to water, while 2.6 billion lack basic sanitation, and the reason for this, according to experts of the UN Development Programme (UNDP), lies not in the physical absence of water but government authority, poverty and inequality. The worst situation with access to water and sanitation is in Sub-Saharan Africa. For instance, according to the UN, more than 40% of the population of the region lack access to clean drinking water, and about 70% have no access to basic sanitation facilities[20].

Despite the global nature of the problem of water supply and sanitation, it does not occupy a prominent place on the international agenda, in contrast, for example, to the attention paid by the international community to the HIV/AIDS pandemic and the problem of universal education. Nevertheless, it is a MDG which provides for halving by 2015 the proportion of people without sustainable access to safe drinking water and basic sanitation. It is projected that at the current rate of development Sub-Saharan Africa will be able to reach the target for water only in 2040 and for sanitation – in 2076.

A global partnership for development. Although the brunt of the responsibility for achieving the MDGs lies with developing countries, international support and assistance from developed countries are essential, especially for the poorest countries[21]. The specific tasks within the goal of establishing a global partnership include an increase in official development assistance (ODA), ensuring access to the markets of developed countries and debt relief.

With regard to ODA, the promises given by G8 leaders in Gleneagles (Scotland, 2005) to double the annual aid to Africa by 2010 were not fulfilled. It is estimated that Africa has received $18 billion less than planned, and the region as a whole will receive no more than $11 billion instead of the $25 billion promised in Gleneagles. The prospects of ODA are also alarming. For example, due to the fact that a number of donor countries has put in place budget constraints because of the global crisis, in 2011–2013 the annual growth of ODA to developing countries, including African ones, is expected to fall to 1% from 13% in the previous three years[22].

In order to implement the MGD of ensuring access to developed markets and the successful completion of the Doha Round of the World Trade Organization (WTO), it is necessary to eliminate all barriers to exports from developing countries, including the reduction of customs duties and the reduction of farm subsidies in developed countries, which, above all, requires political will.

Despite the progress in the realization of programs for debt relief, the implementation of major existing initiatives for debt relief is coming to an end, while a number of low- and lower-middle-income economies are still in debt crisis or face the risk of it. According to the latest estimates by the International Monetary Fund (IMF), such African countries are Burkina Faso, Burundi, DRC, Djibouti, Gambia, Guinea, Comoros, Côte d'Ivoire, Sudan and Zimbabwe[23].

Overall, the achievement of the MDGs by 2015 requires the immediate implementation of donor commitments in terms of ODA, market access and debt relief for developing countries. The 2010 United Nations Summit on the MDGs voiced serious concern that Sub-Saharan Africa is substantially lagging behind in the implementation of the set objectives and recognized the urgent need for additional effort in providing aid, expansion of trade and debt relief.

---

[1] The Millennium Development Goals Report, 2011. UN., N.Y., 2011. P. 6.

[2] *Фитуни Л.Л.* Экономика Африки: вызовы посткризисного развития // Африка и Азия сегодня. 2010, № 8. [*Fituni L.L.* Экономика Африки: вызовы посткризисного развития Economy of Africa: Challenges of Post-Crisis Development// Azia i Africa segodnya. Issue 8, 2010.]

[3] The Millennium Development Goals Report, 2009. UN., N.Y., 2009. P. 6.

[4] Assessing Progress in Africa toward the Millennium Development Goals, 2011. UNECA. N.Y., 2011. P. 4; Rethinking Poverty. Report on the World Social Situation 2010. UN., N.Y., 2009. P. 23.

[5] *Фитуни Л.Л.* Место Африки в посткризисной мировой экономике. Статья 3 (заключительная) // Азия и Африка сегодня. 2011, № 2. [*Fituni L.L.* Место Африки в посткризисной мировой экономике. Статья 3 (заключительная) Africa's Place in the Post-Crisis World Economy. Article 3, concluding // Azia i Africa segodnya. Issue 2, 2011.]

[6] Finance & Development. IMF. Washington, March 2010. P. 40.

[7] *Абрамова И.О.* Рынок труда в странах Африки: количественные и качественные характеристики // Проблемы современной экономики. 2013, № 4. [*Abramova I.O.* Labor Market in African Countries: Quantity and Quality Features // Problemy sovremennoy ekonomiki. Issue 4, 2013.]

[8] Changing patterns in the world of work. ILO. Geneva, 2006. P. 37; Decent Work for Africa's Development. ILO. Geneva, 2003. P. 8-9, 11.

[9] The Millennium Development Goals Report, 2010. UN., N.Y., 2010. P. 9-10.

[10] The Millennium Development Goals Report, 2012. UN., N.Y., 2012. P. 16.

[11] Ibid, P. 17.

[12] The Millennium Development Goals Report, 2011. P. 17.

[13] Ibid. P. 20.

[14] The State of the World's Children 2012. UNICEF. N.Y., 2012. P. 91.

[15] Ibid. P. 116-118.

[16] The Health of the People: the African Regional Health Report. WHO. Geneva, 2006. P. 37.

[17] The Millennium Development Goals Report, 2011. P. 36-37.

[18] World Malaria Report 2011. WHO. Geneva, 2011. P. viii.

[19] The Millennium Development Goals Report, 2011. P. 46; The Millennium Development Goals Report, 2010. P. 51.

[20] *Абрамова И.О., Фитуни Л.Л.* Цена «голубого золота»: проблема водных ресурсов в современном социально-экономическом развитии Африки // Азия и Африка сегодня. 2008, № 12 [*Abramova I.O., Fituni L.L.* Price of "Blue Gold": the Problem of Water Resources in Contemporary Social-Economic Development of Africa // Azia i Africa segodnya. Issue 12, 2008]; The Millennium Development Goals Report, 2010. P. 58, 61.

[21] *Рощин Г.Е.* Африка и международная помощь // Азия и Африка сегодня. 2012, № 7. [*Roshchin G.E.* Африка и международная помощь Africa and International Aid // Azia i Africa segodnya. Issue 7, 2012.]

[22] The Millennium Development Goals Report, 2011. P. 59, 60.

[23] The Global Partnership for. Development: Time to Deliver. UN., N.Y., 2011. P. 57.

Georgiy Roshchin

INTERNATIONAL CORPORATIONS IN AFRICA: HOW THEY COOPERATE WITH THE NATIONAL BUSINESS AND WHAT CHANGES BRING TO THE ECONOMY OF THE BLACK CONTINENT[*]

Attracting foreign capital is one of the main priorities of the investment policies of most African states. Foreign direct investment (FDI) is considered here, as elsewhere in the world, as an important channel of access to the resources of transnational corporations (TNCs), which are necessary for the development and modernization of their economy.

According to UNCTAD, in 2009 the total FDI inflow to Africa amounted to $52.6 billion, in 2010 – $43.1 billion, and in 2011 – $42.7 billion[1]. The decline was caused primarily by the social upheavals taking place in the Arab North Africa. Unrest and instability in Egypt and Libya have caused many potential investors to refrain from investing their capital to these countries. As a result, Africa's share in global investment flows slightly declined from 3.3% in 2010 to 2.8% in 2011[2].

Meanwhile, in Sub-Saharan Africa (SSA), the FDI inflow increased in 2011 by almost a quarter over the previous year and amounted to $34.9 billion, which exceeded the record of the past few years – $34.7 billion (2008)[3].

Oil-producing countries of SSA and South Africa are the leaders in attracting FDI. In 2011, foreign investors considered Nigeria to be the best destination for investment. The country managed to raise $8.9 billion, i.e. every fifth dollar that came to Africa in the form of FDI. Nigeria was followed by South Africa – $5.8 billion, Ghana – $3.2 billion, Mozambique – $2.1 billion, Zambia – $2 billion, Chad – $1.9 billion, the DRC – $1.7 billion[4]. Uganda, Tanzania, Lesotho, Senegal, Botswana, and Namibia were also successful in attracting FDI. These countries are characterized by political and economic stability, high annual GDP growth, active realization of privatization programs, and successful implementation of measures to encourage FDI inflows.

Determinants of FDI inflows

Assessing the prospects for the development of the African economy, UNCTAD experts pay special attention to changes in world commodity

---

[*] First published in *Azia i Afrika segodnya*. Issue 12, 2013.

prices. A scenario set out in UNCTAD World Investment Report 2012 provides for an increase in FDI inflows to Africa in 2013 to $70–85 billion, in 2014 – to $75–100 billion. This forecast seems probable if high prices on raw materials and the current rates of economic growth are maintained[5]. Naturally, in the event of a decline in these indicators, one should expect a reduction in budget revenues in several African countries and in FDI inflows to their extracting industries. A slowdown in export revenues will hit countries with less diversified economies, especially where oil and other minerals and metals are main export products, the hardest.

The UN World Economic Situation and Prospects 2013 report projected Africa's GDP to grow 4.8%. The high rate will be supported by the commission of new facilities in the oil and mining sectors in several countries (Guinea, Ghana, DRC, Lesotho, Liberia, Madagascar, Mauritania, Mozambique, Niger, Sierra Leone), growing investment in infrastructure projects, and expanding co-operation with Asian countries. At the same time, the continent's largest economy – South Africa's – will grow almost twice slower than in 2012 due to a wave of strikes in its mining industry and the negative impact of economic crisis in the eurozone, which became one of the main markets for South Africa's high added value products[6].

Today Africa's contribution to the global GDP is 2.5%, but excluding the largest African economies – South Africa and Nigeria – 1.3%[7].

High GDP growth rates in Africa may facilitate FDI inflows to African countries. However, there is a risk that the FDI inflow from the developed countries will be less than expected. The reason for this is that there are structural problems in economies of these countries and in the global financial system.

Post-crisis development of the global business environment, including the situation in countries with highly developed economies, generally involves many uncertainties. These risk factors include the unpredictability of global economic governance, as well as budget and financial imbalances. The economy of the eurozone is still in recession, which has been exacerbated by a tightening of monetary and fiscal policy and financial sector instability. According to UN forecasts, the economy will grow only 0.3% in 2013 and 1.4% in 2014. The rate of unemployment in the euro area has reached a record level of 12%. The U.S. economy remained tepid in 2013, with GDP growing at a modest at 1.7 %, which is much lower than in 2012[8].

The continuation of the crisis in the eurozone and the difficulties in its banking sector could result in additional problems for multinationals, which will find it harder to raise capital for international projects, including in African countries. The ongoing restructuring of TNCs, particularly in the financial sector, may be accompanied by sale rather than usual acquisition of foreign assets. The impact of factors that increase uncertainty in politics in the fiscal field and in the sphere of investment activity cannot be ruled out. If such risks become dominant, it would be premature to expect an increase in FDI globally.

However, it should be taken into account that although the main FDI flow to Africa comes from the U.S. and Europe, investment from other developing countries, where the projections for the sector are more optimistic, is playing an increasingly significant role in a number of African states.

At the time, the Chinese were actively involved in the construction of large projects in Africa, particularly the important *Tanzam* railway, which connected Tanzania and Zambia. Now the key interest for the Chinese is oil. The PRC is expressing huge interest in significant oil deposits discovered in Uganda and Kenya. Nearby, in South Sudan, there are also rich oil fields. However, because of the conflict between the two Sudans – North and South – the development of these hydrocarbon resources by China seems problematic. China has intended to build and subsequently develop an oil pipeline system linked to the Kenyan seaport of Mombasa, which will open the shortest and safest way to China for tankers carrying Kenyan and South Sudanese oil[9].

Chinese companies are implementing numerous projects throughout Africa, including ports, railways and stadiums[10]. Particularly impressive are the construction works in the campus of the University of Nairobi, which are carried out by the Chinese company *Wu Yi*. The project includes not only the construction of a 21-story building of unique architecture, but also of a helicopter landing pad. *Wu Yi* has recently completed the construction of a 50-kilometer eight-lane stretch of the *Thika Superhighway*, which is rightly considered the pride of Kenya. *Wu Yi* is preparing to implement 18 more projects in the country[11].

India is slightly inferior to China in the scale of its cooperation with Africa: India's 2012 trade turnover with African countries was about $65 billion, compared with China's $200 billion. Indian companies – mostly small private firms – cooperate with African companies mainly in such areas as IT-technology, car-making and vehicle maintenance, agriculture and education[12]. Recently the Indians (just like the Chinese) have started to eye African natural gas resources[13]. According to some experts, Indian business is inferior to Chinese in terms of the agility and speed of the implementation of projects; in addition, the Chinese are ready to take more entrepreneurial risks.

"The African slice of the pie" is increasingly attracting the attention of entrepreneurs from other countries, particularly from Brazil[14] and the Republic of Korea[15].

In recent years, an important factor in FDI inflows to Sub-Saharan countries has become the development of the service sector. In addition to the traditional investment in capital-intensive extractive industries (ore mining and oil and gas sectors), the inflow of foreign capital in the banking, retail and telecommunications sectors is gaining importance. Information infrastructure (cell phones, pagers, the Internet) in Africa is becoming one of the most attractive objects for foreign private investors. For example, in 2006 the companies *MTN* (South Africa) and *Econet* (Kuwait) invested $285 million each in the development of mobile networks in Nigeria[16]. This is facilitated by the rapid pace of urbanization, as well as by the formation of an own middle class in Africa, which has considerable disposable income.

Middle-income consumers usually use a higher level of services, including financial (particularly, mortgages), telecommunications (especially in the field of mobile telephony), educational and healthcare; they also purchase relatively expensive durable consumer products. For example, in 2011 the passenger vehicle imports to the SSA countries increased significantly[17]. There is no doubt that the same trend continued in 2013.

Changes in the forms and modes of doing business

The TNCs interact with the developing countries using a wide range of models of production and investment besides FDI and classic trade. A typical type of such interaction is a joint venture (JV). For many TNCs international cooperation has become one of the leading strategies to enter new markets and build long-term investment activity.

There is a number of circumstances that make joint ventures attractive to multinationals. In particular, they receive certain guarantees against nationalization, enjoy – just like national companies – economic benefits, have greater access to local raw materials and markets, and build relationships with government and administrative apparatus.

While yielding some of the control over the joint ventures to host countries, multinational corporations compensate for this concession by spreading the investment risk associated with fluctuations in world prices, exchange rates and banking interest rates. Even with a majority stake in the hands of a local business, it often cannot effectively control the joint venture because what is most important is the monopoly of TNCs on modern technology, their organizational and managerial experience, brand ownership and marketing skills. This allows corporations whose representatives are a minority on the boards of directors to have the power of veto in such key management areas as borrowing and spending funds to expand production and management operations, equity issue, asset sales, pricing and product distribution, appointments of senior management, etc.

In addition, the control over joint ventures is achieved by incorporating them into in-house systems of specialization and cooperation on the basis of full technological cycle and corporate distribution networks. In every such system, a separate company functions as a part of a corporate production line and is deprived of any opportunity to pursue an independent policy.

The contribution of African countries to the establishment and ongoing activities of joint ventures in the extractive industry may initially be carried out only upon receipts of profit. The capital for the development of a joint venture is provided by a foreign company in exchange for the ownership of a stake in the company. The host government may not invest any funds; its investment may consist of provided infrastructure, ancillary services, the so-called "fee for access to resources", which all foreign investors are obliged to pay, etc.

One of the most important motives for a developing country to enter into a partnership with a foreign firm is the ability to ensure the participation of foreign specialists in the modernization of management and organization of the processes of production and marketing. The cooperation with representatives of leading corporations from developed countries is the main source of modern managerial and technical expertise for national staff in African countries.

In many cases the acquired skills allow local professionals to practically take over the management of production and commercial activities of a JV. Such companies, which cause a chain reaction of growing activity of foreign and local investors, are becoming a tool to strengthen the competitive environment and encourage the most economically capable national enterprises.

A significant role in the investment policy of TNCs is played by non-equity modes (NEMs) of international operations. NEMs are very diverse and include contract industrial and agricultural production, outsourcing[18], franchising[19], licensing, management contracts, renting[20], engineering[21], consulting and other types of contractual relationships, through which TNCs coordinate activities within their global value chains (GVCs).

Incidentally, some of these forms of investment cooperation between companies of developed and developing countries have long been used and can only conditionally be called new given their growing importance in international economic practice.

According to UNCTAD estimates, in 2010 the volume of sales through the NEMs in Africa exceeded $2 trillion. Of this amount, contract manufacturing and services outsourcing accounted for $1.1–1.3 trillion, franchising – $330–350 billion, licensing – $340–360 billion, and management contracts – about $100 billion[22]. These estimates cover only the most important sectors, where different NEMs are applied, and, therefore, are incomplete. The figure does not include, for example, the sales data for such a NEM as contract farming, which is common in 110 developing and transitional countries. In Mozambique this NEM employs about 400 thousand small farmers[23].

In developing countries NEMs provide a significant number of jobs. In many industries, primarily in contract manufacturing and services outsourcing, the developing countries account for almost the entire contingent of employees and almost all exports of these NEMs. Growing financial resources of the continent's most developed countries allow them instead of granting concessions to conclude contracts for the exploration and extraction of minerals, construction of industrial facilities, and, in some cases, for subsequent production management and distribution. Large African national companies can now just buy technologies and technical services without giving a stake in a local business to foreign providers. The import of licenses and know-how gives a considerable gain in time and considerable cost savings in research and development (R&D).

For their part, managers of many international corporations find a business based on the sale of technology and know-how and the use of highly-qualified employees no less profitable and, actually, safer (especially in developing countries) than the exploitation of local resources on the basis of asset ownership.

NEMs are inextricably linked to international trade and determine its structure in many industries. In industries such as electronics, garments, footwear and toys, contract manufacturing represents more than 50% of global exports[24]. Thus, for the countries seeking to rely on export-led growth model, NEMs can be an important "highway to the market".

The implementation of NEM projects promotes technological potential of the host countries. Among other things, Western entrepreneurs and businessmen from China and India usually offer their local partners extensive quality training of domestic personnel and support in the promotion and implementation of new technologies. For example, in South Africa quick-service restaurants and retail account for almost 50 per cent of international franchised systems. African partners had been offered a business model and assistance in the establishment of a new franchise and training its personnel[25].

* * *

FDI remains a key driver of global and, hence, African economic performance. However, this performance is still subject to numerous risks. The post-crisis recovery in FDI is slow and unevenly distributed. The development of investment policies for states and transnational corporations is becoming increasingly challenging due to the evolution of the world economy and the blurring of boundaries between FDI, non-equity modes of international operations and trade.

---

[1] UNCTAD. World Investment Report 2012. Towards a New Generation of Investment Policies. N.Y., 2012. P. 38.

[2] Ibidem.
[3] Ibid. P. 169.
[4] UNCTAD. World Investment Report 2012. Towards a New Generation of Investment Policies. N.Y., 2012. P. 169–170.
[5] Ibid. Table 2. P. 6.
[6] BIKI. M., 19 February 2013. P. 1, 4.
[7] Africa South of the Sahara 2013. Routledge. London and New York, 2012. P. 3.
[8] BIKI. M., 19 February 2013. P. 1, 4.
[9] *Drabkin A.* In Africa – in Chinese // Pravda, Vol. 110, 8-9 October 2013.
[10] For details, see: *Deitch T.L., Usacheva V.V.* International Conference In Mumbai: New Players And African Diaspora // Asia and Africa Today. 2013, Vol. 4; *Boguslavsky A.R.* Current Trends of China Policy in Africa // Asia and Africa Today. 2013, Vol. 4; *Kovalchuk A.P.* How The World Helps Africa To Overcome Crisis And To Increase The Rates Of Economic Development // Asia and Africa Today. 2013, Vol. 5.
[11] www.escortservicemoscow.ru/2013/08 (15.08.2013) China and India: The Struggle for Business in Africa.
[12] For details, see: Индия стремится не отстать» ["India is trying to keep up"] – a section in the article *Дейч Т.Л., Усов В.А.* «Восходящие» державы на Африканском континенте: пример Анголы [*Deitch T.L., Usov V.A.* "Emerging Powers" on the African Continent: Angola Case] // Azia i Africa segodnya. Issue 7, 2013. P. 36-41.
[13] www.escortservicemoscow.ru/2013/08 (27.08.2013) The Struggle for Africa's resources.
[14] See: *Borzova A.Yu.*, Brazil – Africa: an Example of a Highly Effective Cooperation // Asia and Africa Today. 2013, Vol. 9.
[15] See: *Morekhodov M.A.* South Korea and African Countries: Economic Cooperation Today and Tomorrow // Asia and Africa Today. 2013, Vol. 7; and *Morehodov M.A.* South Korean Trillion. Some Sources and Causes of Impressive Economic Success of the Republic of Korea // Asia and Africa Today. 2013, Vol. 3.
[16] Экономическая инфраструктура стран Африки [Economic Infrastructure of African Countries]. M., Institute for African Studies, 2012. P. 225-226; TAD. Investment Policy Review. Nigeria/ New York and Geneva, 2009. P. 18.
[17] UN. Africa Renewal. N.Y., April 2011. Vol. 25. N 1. P. 13–15; BIKI. M., 17 July 2012. P. 4.
[18] Outsourcing is the contracting out of a business process or production function to a third-party specialized in the corresponding area. A contract usually is concluded for a relatively long period – at least one year. The functions which are typically outsourced include accounting, office maintenance, translation, logistics, advertising and security.
[19] Franchising is the practice of using another firm's trademark and business model. Franchise agreement regulates the terms of the contract between the franchisor and the franchisee. The key point in the contract is the regulation of the amount of royalty paid for the use of the franchise.
[20] Renting is an agreement where a payment is made for the temporary use of a good, service or property owned by another.

[21] Engineering is a type of a commercial operation when one party provides another (the customer) with a set of services or a specific service related to the design, construction and commissioning of the object, development of new technological processes, etc.

[22] UNCTAD. World Investment Report 2011/ Non-equity Modes of International Production and Development. N.Y. 2011. P. 123.

[23] Ibid. P. 140.

[24] Ibid. P. 155.

[25] Ibid. P. 138.

Igor Sledzevskiy

AFRICA'S CHALLENGE: THE CIVILIZATIONAL CRISIS OF CATCHING-UP DEVELOPMENT*

The disappointing results of the development of most of the African states in the post-colonial period and, above all, their growing dependency on external aid have exposed the failure of the ideology of catching-up modernization, which in the 20th century was the foundation of all attempts to incorporate African societies into the global development agenda. In terms of social and political integration, stability and progress in human development, Africa employs inadequate strategies and tools to transform archaic and post-archaic African societies into modern ones. The post-colonial period, which was marked by the slogan of accelerated modernization, not only did not promote Africa in this regard but also outlined a developmental crisis, which manifested itself in the collapse of traditional environmental and social systems and the transformation of a large part of the continent into a disadvantaged region of the world in terms of food self-sufficiency.

In the wake of the decline of national economies, domestic unrest and humanitarian disasters, attention turned to the civilizational dimension of Africa's development. The civilizational dimension clearly plays a role when the least developed countries of the Sub-Saharan region are considered the Fourth World, which is "unable to adopt the modern type of progress", rating agencies categorize African countries as insolvent, and Sub-Saharan Africa is viewed as a seat of instability and chaos, "a sea of primitiveness", etc. There is also growing civilizational (ethical) criticism of the results of the post-colonial development as not conforming to the moral norms of the unity of humanity. Today the criticism finds public support in Africa: in its philosophy, political science, and theology. The blame for "Africa's crisis" is put not solely on "unfair globalization", but also on the behavior of corrupt ruling elites, which failed to avoid a "slavish imitation of the West", as well as on the behavior of the common man who puts up with poverty and social disorder.

In the post-colonial criticism of Africa's civilizational development one should not see only the manifestation of the sentiments of Afro-pessimism and clichés of dependent civilizational consciousness. This criticism has deeper roots. It is directly linked to a social and moral crisis of the model of catching-up modernization in its post-colonial (essentially, neo-colonial)

---

* First published in the collection *Africa: new globalization portal: Yearbook – 2012*. Moscow: Peoples' Friendship University of Russia, 2012, p. 29–35.

form. In some respects, while being natural and necessary, in the former African colonies catching-up modernization acquired a sense of a compulsory and universal ticket "to the modernity", a kind of a normative and almost mandatory project. Both philosophy and pragmatics of this project are still connected with the ideals and myths of the colonial era, especially with the ideas of the civilizing process, which was aimed at changing traditions and customs of people by the colonial powers and always in their favor.

However, with the collapse of the colonial empires, the main condition for the viability of the project – the presence of a separate political center independent of local communities and capable of drawing them into the state and society in the European sense – disappeared or weakened significantly. Even during the colonial period this condition was maintained with enormous effort and constant deviations from civilized standards of living in metropolitan countries. When the ownership of the government passed to African ruling groups, it retained little more than a symbolic value. Reduction in the inflow of external resources and sharp decline in interest in Africa after the end of the Cold War also undermined the external (symbolic) civilizational status of many African states as members of the international system. From this point of view, Africa's crisis of catching-up development can be defined as a civilizational crisis. In the context of civilizational ideas, it is driving weak African states into a "shadow zone" of the global unrest.

The important manifestations of catching-up development in former African colonies include the practice of adopting institutions of the modern state as the cornerstone of their political system, which fulfils a number of duties to the country and society. However, even at the level of the minimum standards of carrying out social functions – ensuring public safety and order – the state remains ineffective or ephemeral in many of the newly independent states of Africa. There could be noted numerous deviant patterns and trends of the functioning of the supreme power which are, in fact, incompatible with the functions of the enforcement of public order and stability. The ability to use hypertrophied violence, establishment of "naked power" regimes in some African countries in the 1980s and 1990s, corrupt looting of entire countries, destruction of formal political systems, and the wave of civil wars and conflicts that swept across the continent at that time have clearly demonstrated the degeneration of the adopted forms of statehood, the weakening or collapse of its formal institutions, and the increasing political disintegration of African societies. A systemic expression of a large-scale destruction in the political sphere was the formation and rapid strengthening of African kleptocracy as a type of government founded on the extreme commercialization and privatization of public institutions on the basis of organized corruption. The supremacy of kleptocracy is something completely opposite of the social role of the state and the official catching-up modernization goals. Some Russian political analysts (L.V. Geveling, A.I. Neklessa) noted the trend of formation of "political anti-systems" on the continent and warned about the threat of the emergence of African "anti-states" as one of the signs of growing global unrest and social "underground".

However, in my view, it would be a mistake to reduce the results of the development of African countries after their independence almost exclusively to images of degrading sociality, decaying society, social chaos, etc. African popular culture has never had the atomized individual – the person not included in social and communication networks, mutual aid associations, cultural associations, etc. on ethnic, regional, or kinship principle – as the dominant social type. Apparently, we can talk about the trend of own (endogenous) African social development, which to some extent is associated with catching-up modernization but, at the same time, cannot be reduced to the vector of assimilation of foreign, adopted samples and development incentives. To a certain degree, these trends are linked to the archaic substrate of African traditions, but reflect it on a new stage of development and in a much more complicated socio-economic structure of society (even in comparison with the level of organizational complexity of these societies 25–30 years ago). One could note rather dynamic processes of evolution of post-traditional African societies, which are manifested in the growth of the size of social systems, their growing differentiation, and development and complexification of social communications.

The "informal sector" ("informal structures") of employment and social organization of the population is the nexus of these processes. The development and public role of the sector cannot be fully defined and measured in terms of either traditional (archaic) African institutions or in terms of the modernized (industrial) society. The sector is composed of representatives of different social groups and to some extent performs the function of social integration. The key for those who are included in this sector is to perform a certain informal role of connecting legal and illegal or deviant social activities. Informal relations within the sector are based on a combination of prescribed and achieved social positions: kinship and clannishness, on the one hand, and impersonal, formal positions in the modernized sector of economic and social activity.

Organizationally, the informal sector is a social network, more or less adapted to urban life, modern economy and the structure of the government. The core of the sector is formed on the basis of modernized patron-client relations, while its top consists of power structures that incorporate representatives of the political and business elite. At the same time, activity and self-organization of these informal power structures to some extent reproduces the archetypal patterns of African chiefdoms and early states. One can find here the obligatory exchange of favors, tributary relations between subordinate and superior leaders, and formation of single social networks by these leaders.

The informal structures are, in essence, a special type of sociality that can transform formal structures of the government, business, or social and political organizations and movements in accordance with its own principles and rules. "Informal sociality" can implicitly or explicitly adjust the allocation of economic resources and financial flows, influence the development and size of the shadow economy and crime sector: cut budget revenues, reduce the incomes of specific groups of the population, and increase or control the earnings of others. The term "informal sociality" includes the rapid development of ethnic social networks, which expand and seriously modernize the importance of social kinship, patron-client relations, and, with regard to the political sphere – the development of a neo-patrimonial type of power based on personal relations of domination/subordination. "Informal sociality" provides for the conversion of old cultural meanings in the direction of greater rationalization and universalization of their values, bringing them closer to new social practices.

Indeed, the growth and complexification of the "informal sociality" and the increasing diversity of its structures and manifestations can hardly be equated with the development in its normative value, which considers it exclusively in terms of progress towards something higher and better. To a certain extent (but only in a focused, differentiated analysis), in "informal sociality" one can see manifestations of dynamic development, structural complexification of social archaism, its conversion into a neo-archaic one, which is adapted to the conditions of the complex and stratified society, centralized state structures and modern communications. For instance, the deviant forms of archaic traditions, which previously were limited to the sacred power of the rulers (absolute, uncontrolled authority of the leaders, anti-corporate behavior, etc), are becoming stronger. At the same time, as a form of endogenous (African) development, the structures of the network type do not preclude modernizing shifts associated with the development of formal public institutions, differentiation of their areas of responsibility and the emergence of universal impersonal roles. This not only increases the level of self-organization of African societies but also creates the preconditions for the development on the basis of their own internal resources.

Yevgeniy Korendyasov
Andrey Urnov
Vladimir Shubin

AFRICA, RUSSIA AND THE 50TH ANNIVERSARY OF THE OAU/AU[*]

In December 2010, the world celebrated the 50th Anniversary of the Year of Africa, while on 25 May, 2013 another golden jubilee was celebrated – the 50th Anniversary of the founding of the Organization of African Unity (OAU) and its successor – the African Union (AU). The event that took place in Addis Ababa in 1963 became known as the Africa Day and certainly deserves to be called historic.

On the occasion of the anniversary, Russian President Vladimir Putin sent a congratulatory message to the heads of states and governments of Africa, which said: "The founding of this unique structure half a century ago was a milestone on the path of the peoples of Africa towards peace, security, stability, good-neighborliness and mutual understanding on the continent. The African Union is an effective mechanism for multilateral political, economic and humanitarian cooperation and coordination of the activities of its members in the global arena"[1].

From the OAU to the AU

The OAU has become a comprehensive organization in the full sense of the word. All states of the continent that have acquired independence since the founding of the OAU have joined it. Is it not an eloquent testimony to the desire for unity and to strength of Pan-African ideas!

At that time the process of decolonization was still far from complete, and it came natural that the elimination of all forms of colonialism and racism was proclaimed the most important task of the OAU[2]. But not the only one.

Among the objectives of the OAU is the protection and strengthening of the "hard-won" independence, sovereignty and territorial integrity of the African countries, which was included in the Preamble to the OAU Charter and directly tied to the struggle against neo-colonialism in all its forms[3].

We should give African leaders their due. Despite all the differences – sometimes quite profound – in their perception of the world and their political leanings, they were able to agree that the common enemy of Africa is neocolonialism.

---

[*] First published in *Azia i Afrika segodnya*. Issue 9, 2013.

According to the Charter, the way to win against neocolonialism is through constructive endeavor – "harnessing the natural and human resources of the continent for the total advancement of its peoples in all spheres of human endeavor"[4].

The organization was given the purpose of promoting the unity and solidarity of the African States, coordinating and intensifying their cooperation in various fields: from politics and economics to defense and security[5].

The OAU existed for almost 40 years. In July 2002, it was replaced by the African Union.

In the late 1990s – early 2000s much was being said and written about the weaknesses and shortcomings of the OAU and that it exhausted its potential. The need for a new organization was, indeed, overdue. The initiative to create it came from the late Libyan leader Muammar Gaddafi. African leaders came to the conclusion that to reach its objectives the continent needed a more powerful and effective mechanism and a higher degree of cohesion and coordination. Besides, the AU was created as a more democratic structure – along with the Pan-African Parliament and the Economic, Social and Cultural Council, which represent civil society and the African Diaspora.

The problem of development stands atop the agenda, especially against the backdrop of the economic difficulties faced by Africa in the late 20th century. It is no accident that the New Partnership for Africa's Development (NEPAD) was established at the same time as the AU. They are a kind of "twin brothers". The AU, of course, is the elder brother, although it was created after the adoption of this program.

Speaking of Africa's economic difficulties and troubles, it would be worthwhile to give an instructive example.

In 1988, Julius Nyerere (at the time he was no longer president of Tanzania) was visiting the World Bank when asked a question: "Why did you fail?"

The wise Mwalimu ("teacher", as he was called in Tanzania and beyond) answered as follows. As the legacy of the British Empire, Tanzania inherited the illiteracy rate of 85%, two engineers and 15 doctors. "When I left the office, we had the illiteracy rate of 9% and thousands of engineers and doctors. Today, there are one-third less students, our public health system and social services are in ruins." "Over the last 30 years," said Nyerere, "Tanzania has been doing what was demanded of it by the World Bank and the International Monetary Fund. So it is my question: "Why did you fail?"[6] This was how Nyerere evaluated the structural reforms of the World Bank and the IMF in Africa.

Considering the shortcomings of the OAU, we recognize that in general its role has been very positive and constructive, and its contribution to the history of Africa deserves the highest praise. Suffice it to recall how much did the OAU and its Liberation Committee do for the elimination of colonialism and racism.

In July 2013, the AU celebrated its 11th anniversary since the first AU summit in Durban. It has proved its viability, has given African unity a new quality, and has stimulated processes of integration. Indeed, the AU has weaknesses and shortcomings. It is now obvious, however, that those skeptics who at the founding of the AU claimed that it was "a new bottle for old wine" were deeply mistaken[7].

Africa is different today

The Commemoration of the 50th Anniversary of the OAU/AU and the 21st Ordinary Session of the Assembly of the Union took place on 25 and 26 May 2013 in Addis Ababa. The celebration was dedicated to the theme of the Pan-Africanism and African Renaissance.

The commemorative summit consisted of two sessions. The first was held at the AU convention center, which was built as a gift from China. Mr. Hailemariam Dessalegn, Chairperson of the African Union and Prime Minister of the Federal Democratic Republic of Ethiopia, gave an introductory speech, followed by Dr. Nkosazana Dlamini Zuma, Chairperson of the African Union Commission, who discussed various aspects of the main theme of the celebration. The keynote speakers included D. Kaberuka (Rwanda), President of the African Development Bank (AfDB), Amina Mama (Nigeria), specialist on gender issues, P.J. Patterson, former Prime Minister of Jamaica, and a representative of the Organization of African Youth (Zimbabwe).

Next there was a discussion with the participation of Heads of State and Government. An interesting fact: with the appointment of the new head of the AU Commission, the discipline at the meetings has increased dramatically – after three minutes set for each speech, the microphone is automatically muted.

The second meeting was of a different nature. The Millennium Hall welcomed not only official participants, but thousands of residents of Ethiopia's capital. The speeches by African leaders (made mainly on behalf of regional organizations) were punctuated by concert items and the screening of a film about the history of the OAU-AU. We should, perhaps, highlight the speech by President Yoweri Museveni, who was the only one to note the role of socialist countries (USSR, China and Cuba) in achieving African independence.

The main impression is that Afro-pessimism has been discarded, and the spirit of optimism has triumphed. Africa is confident of the future. Here is an excerpt from the official press release of the summit: "The 50th anniversary comes at a golden time for Africa as the continent, which was perceived a decade ago as a hopeless one, is now unequivocally on the rise"[8]. Participants cited specific figures confirming these successes: the average GDP growth in Africa was 5% and 6 out of 8 countries with the fastest growing economies were situated in Africa.

At the same time the summit manifested realism, including in the summit's slogan posted everywhere – in boardrooms and on posters in the streets of Addis Ababa – "Rise! Africa 2063: Prosperity and Peace". That refers to the implementation of the "African dream" (Africa Vision 2063), the dream of the founders of the OAU – to build, as Ethiopian Prime Minister Hailemariam Dessalegn, Chairperson of the AU, stated in the opening speech, "a peaceful, prosperous and united Africa"[9], the accomplishment of which is expected only in 50 years at the next anniversary of the AU.

Dr N. Dlamini Zuma, Chairperson of the AU Commission, rightly pointed out that Africa would have to answer to a lot of "tough questions"[10].

The attitude toward African integration is notably more sober. For instance, in his second speech, Hailemariam Dessalegn talked about Africa as only "economically integrated" in 50 years, while Y. Museveni explicitly stated his disagreement with the idea of political integration of the continent, which had been advanced by late Gaddafi. The Ugandan President called plans for regional integration more realistic and stressed that the East African Community aimed at becoming a political federation.

In general, there is still much to be done. The AU Commission's Strategic Plan 2014–2017 adopted during the 21st Ordinary Session of the AU outlines the overall priorities of the Commission for the four year period.

The eight priority areas of the Commission as stipulated in the Strategic Plan are:

1. Human capacity development focusing on health, education, science, research, technology and innovation;

2. Agriculture and agro processing;

3. Inclusive economic development through industrialization, infrastructure development, agriculture and trade and investment;

4. Peace, stability and good governance;

5. Mainstreaming women and youth into all our activities;

6. Resource mobilization;

7. Building a people-centered Union through active communication and branding; and

8. Strengthening the institutional capacity of the Union and all its organs[11].

Corresponding AU structures developed specific measures to promote and inform African citizens on the implementation of the Plan, in order to enable them to participate actively in this process.

The 50th Anniversary Solemn Declaration was another document adopted in Addis Ababa. With regard to the process of African integration, it placed the emphasis on the development and merger of the regional economic communities "as the building blocks of the Union", accelerating the attainment of the objectives of the African Economic community", and the implementation of "the Continental Free Trade Area"[12].

The Declaration promises "to rid the continent of wars, civil conflicts", ending "all wars in Africa" by 2020[13].

Africa does not isolate itself from the outside world, but is going to take "its rightful place in the political, security, economic, and social systems of global governance" towards "establishing Africa as a leading continent", "mobilizing our domestic resources", and "providing African solutions to African problems"[14].

At the summit much attention was paid to the African Diaspora, which was undoubtedly related to the theme of the Pan-Africanism, the authors of which were its representatives. For example, during the second plenary session Jamaican Prime Minister P.S. Miller highlighted the fact that the AU had recognized the Diaspora as its 6th region, along with the northern, western, central, eastern and southern parts of the African continent. However, it is unclear what such recognition could mean in practice.

Today the place and role of Africa in world affairs has increased significantly. Other regions are eager to interact with it and listen to its opinion.

This was also manifested in the high representation at the commemorative summit. The event was attended by UN Secretary General Ban Ki-moon, Brazilian President Dilma Rousseff and French President F. Hollande, Indian Vice-President Mohammad Hamid Ansari, India, PRC Vice-Premier Wang Yang, President of the National Assembly of Cuba E.L. Hernandez, and U.S. Secretary of State John Kerry. Russia was represented by Special Envoy of Russian President for Cooperation with African States M. Margelov.

With all the possible reservations (poverty, disease, etc.), Africa has made a major breakthrough in the field of economics. The eThekwini Declaration, which was adopted at the Fifth BRICS Summit held on 26-27 March 2013 in South Africa (eThekwini is the current name of Greater Durban), rightly speaks of "the steep growth trajectory of the African continent"[15].

In general, compared with the past, the situation in Africa is better in terms of security and crisis management, although the events in North Africa, Mali, Central African Republic, and Nigeria interrupted the seemingly stable tendency towards the stabilization of the continent.

The following is what representatives of the two states that maintain the most extensive and diverse relations with Africa say about the continent.

At the BRICS – Africa summit in Durban on March 27, 2013 Chinese President Xi Jinping said: "Our planet would not have achieved stability and prosperity without peace and development in Africa. Without the participation of African countries in international affairs there is no question of their appropriate resolution. Without Africa's voice the global governance system would be deprived of its vitality. The 21st century will be the century of Africa"[16].

U.S. President Barack Obama yet again visited Africa. "Africa we need to be deeply engaged in and intend to be. We have a lot to do," U.S. Secretary of State Kerry said during a House Foreign Affairs Committee hearing[17].

The Americans are concerned that China has overtaken them in investments in Africa. It is possible that the U.S. will invest more in the African economy.

Russia-Africa cooperation

The 50th Anniversary of the OAU/AU gives us an opportunity to reassess the history and current state of Russia-Africa relations.

If today's Africa is clearly superior to yesterday's Africa, the position of today's Russia in Africa is vastly inferior to the one achieved by the Soviet Union.

A lot has been written or said about Soviet policy in Africa during the Cold War – both good and critical. But few would deny that supporting the anti-colonial struggle of peoples and assisting liberated states in strengthening their independence was an important aspect of Soviet foreign policy. It was made in the framework of confrontation with the West, but this does not change the fact that in those years the Soviet Union stood on the side of Africa in the fight for the right cause. And this is important.

In the early post-Soviet years, Russia if not entirely left Africa then drastically reduced its presence there. The subject is debatable. Some believe that Russia has already come back to Africa. It seems, however, that a more correct thing to say would be: "Russia is coming back".

Russia is not the USSR. There is now more pragmatism, no ideological messianism, less ambition, and, alas, less power.

In February 2013 a new version of the Concept of the Foreign Policy of the Russian Federation was approved. "The main task of the international activity of Russia is to create favorable external conditions for the rise of its economy, its transfer to innovative rails, increasing living standards of people," – wrote Russian Foreign Minister Sergey Lavrov in his article "Russia's Foreign Policy Philosophy"[18].

National egoism? It is peculiar to all states. The question is how to achieve the set goals. It is important not to solve one's problems at the expense of others or imposing one's will, but through mutually beneficial cooperation on the basis of international law. Russia seeks to follow this course. Its policy is open and predictable.

Indeed, Russia has fewer ambitions today. But it has ambitions, and we do not keep it back. Russia has enough resources to play "the role of one of the key centers" internationally. According to S. Lavrov, it is about formation of a "polycentric system of international relations" "in the interests of ensuring collective leadership of the leading countries of the world that must be representative in terms of geography and civilizations"[19].

In the years following the Cold War Russia and Africa experienced detrimental effects of a unipolar model. On the issue of strengthening of multipolarity, Russia's and Africa's interests are the same, and this creates a good and healthy basis for their multilateral cooperation in the international arena.

The African Union is to become one of the centers of multipolarity, and Russia is ready to the extent possible to promote further growth of the AU's international influence and its contribution to the collective efforts aimed at providing answers to common challenges.

Let us be honest. Africa is not Russia's top priority. The Concept of the Foreign Policy of the Russian Federation puts the CIS region in the first place. This is unlikely to cause any questions.

However, Africa is mentioned in the concept. It states the following on the main directions of Russia's Africa policy: "Russia will enhance multifaceted interaction with African states on a bilateral and multilateral basis with a focus on improving political dialogue and promoting mutually beneficial trade and economic cooperation and contribute to settling and preventing regional conflicts and crises in Africa. Developing partnership with the African Union and other regional organizations is an important element of this policy"[20].

President Vladimir Putin in his message on the occasion of the 50th Anniversary of the OAU/AU indicated that the partnership with the African Union would be enhanced within the framework of the UN, G8, G20 and BRICS[21].

Briefly about how Russia is coming back to Africa

Political contacts. Over the last 13 years Russian Presidents Vladimir Putin and Dmitry Medvedev visited eight African states. Twelve African leaders visited Russia over the same period.

On March 26, 2013 Vladimir Putin made a short working visit to South Africa, where he took part in the BRICS summit. Within the scope of the bilateral Treaty of Friendship and Partnership (2006), V. Putin and South African President Jacob Zuma signed the Joint Declaration on the Establishment of a Comprehensive Strategic Partnership between the Russian Federation and the Republic of South Africa. The document demonstrates a commitment to multifaceted partnership. It addresses the need to give a strong impetus to the bilateral relations in all areas – political, economic, scientific, technological, cultural and other fields. The parties intend to cooperate in the fight against international terrorism, separatism, organized crime and drug trafficking.

The document also provides a new direction for bilateral cooperation – cooperation between integration organizations – by establishing regular contacts between Eurasian and African integration associations, i.e. between the Eurasian (Customs Union, Common Economic Space, – Eurasian Economic Union) and African regional organizations (African Union, Southern African Development Community (SADC), Southern African Customs Union(SACU)).

It was agreed that the President of the Russian Federation and the President of the Republic of South Africa will meet at least once every two years; the Ministers of Foreign Affairs of the two countries will meet at least once a year. In addition, regular inter-parliamentary exchanges, widening contacts at high level between relevant chambers and committees will take place[22].

The next meeting between V. Putin and J. Zuma took place in Sochi on May 26, 2013 – not in two years, but after just two months. The plan was outstripped.

Nevertheless, we must be realistic. During a visit to South Africa we emphasized a significant increase in trade between the two countries – from $580 million in 2011 to $964 million in 2012[23]. However, South Africa's minister responsible for the economy rightly reminded one of the authors of this article that this growth had started from a rather low level. South Africa welcomes Russian investment, but it is noted that they are, basically, traditional investments in the mining sector, while the country is interested in diversification.

Another important contact was the visit of Dr. N. Dlamini Zuma, Chairperson of the African Union Commission, to Moscow. Assessing the results of the talks held on April 29, 2013, Lavrov pointed out the closeness or conformity of the positions of Russia and the AU in connection with most international and regional issues[24].

Economic ties. Russia and Africa are brought together by the fact that nature has endowed both with huge mineral reserves. Not everybody likes it. Some call for "justice" and want to regard these resources as "common heritage." Russia and Africa have something to defend jointly.

Nonetheless, there is also its own dialectic. According to some experts, by 2018 the Russian Federation will have depleted profitable and currently exploited reserves of 13 types of minerals, including zinc, chromium, silica and even gold and oil[25]. The remaining reserves available in Russia are difficult to extract in terms of either geography or geology; their development requires huge investments and is very time-consuming, as a result of which their production in Africa, including transportation to Russia, is more cost-

68

effective. Consequently, Russia's interest in Africa's mineral resources is growing, and it creates another incentive for the development of economic cooperation with the continent.

Trade. From 2000 to 2012 the volume of trade between Russian and Africa grew 7.5 times. Absolute figures, however, are modest – an increase from $1.6 billion to $12.2 billion[26]. In doesn't compare to China's or American trade with Africa. In addition, more than half of Russia's turnover is with North Africa, where trade is dominated by mineral resources and food[27].

Yet growth is obvious. Russia has introduced zero tariffs for the least developed countries, most of which are African.

Russia traditionally supplies arms to Africa. In 2012 it sold arms for almost $1 billion. According to Rosoboronexport, it is about 25% of the African arms market[28].

Russian investments in Africa are also growing, although they are modest in absolute terms. According to Russian statistics, accumulated direct investment account for about $9 billion. Russian companies have stated their intention to invest $17 billion in 2013–2020[29]. However, at present the African Development Bank evaluates the amount of investments from the Russian Federation at $20 billion[30]. The discrepancy is large, but perhaps the AfDB provides more accurate information.

80–90% of investments account for exploration and extraction of mineral resources.

13 largest Russian companies work in 25 African countries. The leaders among them are Renova (manganese, ferroalloys), Rusal, Norilsk Nickel, Evraz (vanadium), and Lukoil. According to the signed contracts, the investment of each of these companies ranges from $1 billion to $2.5 billion. Lukoil has a plan to invest further $2–2.5 billion in addition to $1 billion. Gazprom is still far behind (about $500 million), but plans to invest an additional $3.5–4 billion. Severstal also has serious plans in Africa. The company wants to increase its current investment of $200 million to $2.5 billion in 2015 and to $6.5 billion in 2024[31].

Today, the majority of the projects take place in South Africa, Namibia, Angola, Nigeria, Equatorial Guinea, Gabon and Ghana.

Russia and aid programs for Africa. Russia has written off $20 billion in African debt to the USSR, which is a very significant move. In terms of this indicator, Russia occupies the 1st place among the members of the G8[32].

Russian official aid for development assistance (ODA) in 2011 increased by 8.8% compared with 2010. African countries situated south of the Sahara received 28% of this amount, or about $150 million[33].

Furthermore, Russia allocated $5 million for energy security, including for mitigating fluctuations in energy prices, in 2007-2010, $235 million to the Global Fund to Fight AIDS, Tuberculosis and Malaria, $244 million for food security in developing countries (2009–2011)[34]. In response to the droughts of 2007–2008 and 2011–2012, Russia helped Ethiopia, Kenya, Somalia, Mali, Guinea, DRC, and Côte d'Ivoire.

25,000 Africans received higher education in the USSR[35]. Over the past four years, Russia has allocated $43 million to the World Bank program aimed at improving education in developing countries, especially African countries. Today about 8,000 students from Africa are enrolled in Russian universities, about half of them receive state scholarships[36]. Previously African countries were granted 750 scholarships annually[37]. Since 2013 this figure will increase to one thousand. Certain difficulties with these scholarships are connected with the fact that they are provided without sufficient travel compensation and accommodation allowances.

Russia participates in <u>UN peacekeeping operations</u> in Africa. The contribution of Russian air groups in the implementation of these operations has been highly appreciated. Let's commemorate Russian pilots killed in South Sudan.

Russia prepares up to 400 African peacekeepers annually[38].

РФ признает право Африки на постоянное членство в СБ ООН.

Representatives of Russia and Africa productively cooperate in the UN. General approaches of the parties to the reform of the Security Council are close or identical. Both Russia and the African Union believe that the reform is overdue and that the Security Council should be expanded to make it more representative and effective. The Russian Federation recognizes the right of Africa to permanent membership in the UN Security Council.

It is more complicated when it gets to specifics. Africa demands two permanent and five non-permanent (up from the current three) seats on the UN Security Council[39].

According to Russia, expansion of the Security Council should not be excessive. It must remain compact and should not turn into a "mini-General Assembly." It is necessary to achieve the broadest possible support for the upcoming reform from UN member states. It is preferable to come to a consensus.

The situation is complicated by the fact that a permanent seat on the UN Security Council is claimed by three countries – Egypt, Nigeria and South Africa, and the AU member states have so far failed to agree on who should be delegated to the Council.

The Russian Federation and the PRC expressed their position on this issue in the eThekwini Declaration at the BRICS summit in March 2013. China and Russia reiterated the importance they attached to the status of Brazil, India and South Africa in international affairs and supported their aspiration to play a greater role in the UN[40]. However, what exactly is meant by "a greater role" is not explained.

Russia, Africa and BRICS

BRICS is a promising channel for Russia-Africa cooperation.

As noted in the Concept of participation of the Russian Federation in BRICS, its creation in 2006 "has been one of the most significant geopolitical events at the start of the new century"[41]. "The Russian Federation stands in favor of positioning BRICS in the world system as a new model of global relations, overarching the old dividing lines between East and West, and North and South"[42].

According to the eThekwini Declaration, the members "aim at progressively developing BRICS into a full-fledged mechanism of current and long-term coordination on a wide range of key issues of the world economy and politics"[43].

The fact that the 5th BRICS summit took place in South Africa certainly put the African vector of its policy in the spotlight. However, this is not a tribute to the conjuncture. Africa rightfully occupies an important place on the agenda of this forum. The discussion was conducted in the context of global issues, and the emphasis was placed on making long-term decisions.

The overarching theme was "BRICS and Africa: Partnership for Development, Integration and Industrialisation"[44]. After the summit BRICS held a retreat with African leaders under the theme "Unlocking Africa's potential: BRICS and Africa Cooperation on Infrastructure"[45]. Besides J. Zuma, Africa in this dialogue was represented by presidents of 11 countries, Ethiopian Prime Minister Hailemariam Dessalegn, Chairperson of the AU, and Dr. N. Dlamini Zuma, Chairperson of the African Union Commission[46].

The decisions made at the summit followed the policy framework of the AU. It can be said that BRICS and Africa spoke the same language in Durban.

The five members expressed concern "with the slow pace of the reform of the IMF", which "should strengthen the voice and representation of the poorest members of the IMF, including Sub-Saharan Africa"[47].

The participants of the summit expressed their intention to continue efforts for the "successful conclusion of the Doha Round" of the World Trade Organization (WTO), the results of which should address "key development concerns of the poorest and most vulnerable WTO members", and considered that the next Director-General of the WTO should be a representative of a developing country[48].

For their part, the leaders of the BRICS countries reaffirmed their "support for the Continent's integration processes" and recognized the strides made by the African Union and the New Partnership for Africa's Development (NEPAD) in this regard[49]. "We will seek to stimulate infrastructure investment on the basis of mutual benefit to support industrial development, job-creation, skills development, food and nutrition security and poverty eradication and sustainable development in Africa," says the Declaration[50].

The Declaration also indicates an important intention to develop multilateral agreements between banks of BRICS and Africa in the field of financing sustainable development projects and infrastructure[51].

In examining the situation on the continent, the summit participants expressed their "deep concern with instability stretching from North Africa, in particular the Sahel, and the Gulf of Guinea". Another point of concern is "reports of deterioration in humanitarian conditions in some countries"[52]. The Heads of the BRICS countries supported "the civilian efforts of the Malian Government and its international community partners in realizing the transitional program leading up to the presidential and legislative elections", expressed their readiness "to work with the international community to facilitate progress to a peaceful resolution of the conflict" in the Central African Republic (CAR), and welcomed "the signing in Addis Ababa on 24 February 2013 of the Peace, Security and Cooperation Framework for the Democratic Republic of the Congo and the Region"[53].

The Declaration acknowledges "the central role of the African Union (AU) and its Peace and Security Council (PSC) in conflict resolution in Africa" and calls upon the UNSC to enhance cooperation with the AU and the PSC[54].

At the retreat African leaders unanimously called for accelerated development of the partnership between Africa and BRICS.

A group of African ambassadors to the Russian Federation held a conference devoted to the 50th Anniversary of the OAU/AU in Moscow at the Peoples' Friendship University on May 23, 2013. The past and the present of the continent were discussed thoroughly, and predictions for the future were made. In his speech, Ambassador of Benin G. Kochofa rightly observed that BRICS represents polycentrism in practice, and African states benefit from it as their relations with the BRICS countries are more balanced than with the West. Moreover, the existence of BRICS gives them the freedom to choose partners.

We believe that the process of Russia-Africa cooperation will continue to expand and strengthen both at the continental and global levels.

---

[1] http://www.kremlin.ru/letters

[2] OAU Chapter and Rules of Procedure. Published by the Division of Press and Information of the OAU General Secretariat. May 1981. Addis Ababa, Ethiopia. Article II 1.d. P. 10.

[3] Ibid. Preamble. P. 9.

[4] Ibidem.

[5] Ibid.; Article II, 2.a-f. P. 10.

[6] A Dialogue of the Deaf // Essays on Africa and the United Nations. The Centre for Conflict Resolution. Cape Town. 2006. Fanele – an Imprint of Jacana Media (Pty) Ltd. P. 167.

[7] From the OAU to AU. The Challenge of African Unity and Development in the Twenty First Century. Nigerian Institute of International Affairs. Lagos. 2004. P. 16.

[8] May 25, 2013. Commemoration of the 50th Anniversary of the OAU/AU Opening and Debate on the Pan Africanism and African Renaissance. Press Release N29/21st AU Summit – http://summits.au.int/en/sites/defaults/files/PR%2029-21ST%20OA U%20SUMMIT%20-%20Africa%20AT%20FIFTY_f_0.pdf

[9] Ibidem.

[10] Ibid.

[11] African Union Commission's Strategic Plan 2014-2017 adopted by Assembly – http://summits.au.int/en/21stsummit/events/african-union-commission%E2%80%99s-stratrgic-plan-2014-2017-adopted-assembly

[12] African Union 50th Anniversary Solemn Declaration (C, Ci, Cii) – http://summits.au.int/en/sites/default/files/50%20DECLARATION%20EN.pdf

[13] Ibid. (E, Ei)

[14] Ibid. (G, Gi, H)

[15] The eThekwini Declaration and the eThekwini Action Plan. 27 March 2013. Article 12 -http://news.kremlin.ru/ref_notes/1430

[16] Xi Jinping. The dialogue of leaders of the BRICS countries and Africa – http://ru.china-embassy.org/rus/zgxw/t1027020.htm

[17] *Gerstein Josh.* Kerry floats Obama Africa trip. 4.17.13 – www.politico.com/politico44/2013/04/kelly-floats-obama-africa-trip-161926.html

[18] Mezhdunarodnaya Zhizn. 2013, Vol. 3. P. 2.

[19] Ibid. P.5.

[20] The Concept of the Foreign Policy of the Russian Federation. 12 February 2013. Regional priorities – http://www.mid.ru/brp_4.nsf/0/6D84DDEDEDBF7DA64457B 16 0051BF7F

[21] http://www.kremlin.ru/letters

[22] The Joint Declaration on the Establishment of a Comprehensive Strategic Partnership between the Russian Federation and the Republic of South Africa – http://news.kremlin.ru/ref_notes/1428

[23] The customs statistics on foreign trade of the Russian Federation 2011–2012.

[24] http://interaffairs.ru/read/php?item=9440

[25] Russia in the competition for Africa's mineral resources. M., 2011. P. 33, 38.

[26] *Ustinov I.N.* Foreign trade of Russia // Statistical handbook. M., 2001; The customs statistics on foreign trade of the Russian Federation 2011–2012.

[27] World Trade Atlas 2010; The customs statistics on foreign trade of the Russian Federation; UNECA; The African Development Bank Group. Chief Economist Complex. African Economic Brief: Russia's Economic Engagement with Africa. Vol. 2. Issue 7. 11 May, 2011.

[28] Modern Russia as an exporter of arms – www.memoid.ru/node/sovremennaya_Rossiya_kak_ehksportjor_oruzhiya; Rossiyskaya Gazeta. 17.12.2012.

[29] Sources: corporate annual reports; corporate press-releases; The African Development Bank Group. Chief Economist Complex...

[30] The African Development Bank Group. Chief Economist Complex... P. 3.

[31] Direct investments of major Russian companies in African countries. Sources: corporate annual reports; corporate press-releases; The African Development Bank Group. Chief Economist Complex...

[32] Speeches by Foreign Minister Sergey Lavrov at the reception for the heads of diplomatic missions of African countries on the occasion of Africa Day, May 27, 2009 and May 30, 2013 – http://www.mid.ru/bdomp/brp_4.nsf2fee282eb6df40e643256999005e6e8c/eb6c2edc14bfd3e7c32575c4003a751b!OpenDocument; http://www.mid.ru/brp_4.nsf/0/43A270363B8B27FE44257B7B004A56F4

[33] Report on Russia's participation in international development assistance in 2011. May 16, 2012 – http://www.hse.ru/org/hse/iori/news/52861851.html; Statements by the Ministry of Finance of Russia – http://www.minfin.ru/ru/press/speech/index.php?id4=16351

[34] Director of the department of international financial relations of the Ministry of Finance A. Bokarev on the contribution of the Russian Federation in international development. 2011 – http://www.minfin.ru/ru

[35] The African Countries 2002 г. M., the Institute for African Studies, 2002. P. 80.

[36] http://www.pravda.ru/restofworld/africa/18-10-2012/1131759-africa_debt-0

[37] http://www.mid.ru/bdomp/brp_4.nsf/2fee282eb6df40e643256999005e6e8c/eb6c2edc14bfd3e7c32575c4003a751b!OpenDocument

[38] Ibidem.

[39] The Common African Position on the Proposed Reform of the United Nations: "The Esulvini Consensus". African Executive Council. 7th Extraordinary Session. 7-8 March, 2005. Addis Ababa, Ethiopia. Ext/EX.CL/2(VII).

[40] The eThekwini Declaration. Article 20.

[41] The Concept of participation of the Russian Federation in BRICS. Article 3 – http://news.kremlin.ru/media/events/files/41d452a8a232b2f6f8a5.pdf

[42] Ibid. Article 10.

[43] The eThekwini Declaration. Article 2.

[44] Ibid. Article 1.

[45] Ibid. Article 3.

[46] http://ru.china-embassy.org/rus/zgxw/t1027020.htm

[47] Ibid. Article 13.

[48] Ibid. Articles 15, 16.

[49] Ibid. Articles 4, 5.

[50] Ibid. Article 5.

[51] Ibid. Article 12.

[52] Ibid. Article 24.

[53] Ibid. Articles 30, 31, 32.

[54] Ibid. Article 24.

Dmitri Bondarenko

"UNIVERSAL" CONCEPT OF HUMAN RIGHTS
AND "AFRICAN SPECIFICS"[*]

I consider it necessary to formulate the problems in a way that avoids ap-
plying a narrow political science approach, which comes down to calculating
the number of parties in a country, counting of votes in elections, and so on.
A different formulation of the same set of problems allows a much more serious context for analysis. I think that this analysis should start with the answer to the question of what actually a modern African state is, where human
rights are or aren't respected, the concept of human rights does or does not
exist, so on and so forth. Although since the end of the 1980s, when the Cold
War came to an end and a wave of democratization started in Africa, from a
formal point of view, the vast majority of the countries on the continent have
established themselves as multi-party democracies, including legal recognition of human rights in their Western interpretation, in many of these countries democracy is in varying degrees of ephemerality up to now. As before,
there are problems with human rights, in particular, with the ability to effectively defend them in court. Nevertheless, Africa's actual achievements in
this regard should not be underestimated: nowadays there are, in fact, fewer
and fewer odious regimes, which were so typical for the continent until the
end of the 1980s. Today, most of Africa's regimes can be described as more
or less "soft" authoritarian.

In this connection I would like to note that during my last trip to Africa
– Tanzania in April-May 2011 – I saw unmistakable signs of influence of
the so-called "Arab Spring" on this particular country in sub-Saharan Africa. I have been to Tanzania many times, and this time I witnessed phenomena that I certainly could not imagine as recently as a year ago. Just
two examples: I visited the School of Journalism in Dar-es-Salaam to read
a guest lecture. I was met by the rector who said, "Hello. Do you know
what is most lacking in Tanzania? Democracy". Another example: I came
to Morogoro town and saw a demonstration of students under the slogans
that demanded introduction of true freedom of speech in the country. The
demonstration was small – about sixty people. Of course, it could not be
compared with, for example, the events in Tahrir Square in Cairo. But one
should compare not with Tahrir but with Tanzania just a year earlier: once

[*] First published in *Cultural Aspects and Practice of Human Rights in Africa
(Roundtable Proceedings)*. Riabinin, A.L. (Ed.). Moscow: Higher School of Economics Publishing House, 2012, p. 26–32.

again, a year ago it was nearly impossible to see what I saw during this visit.

In my opinion, the key is the fact that the modern states of Tropical Africa (with a few exceptions; to a large extent one such exception is Ethiopia) are largely artificial entities in the sense that their borders and the very fact of their existence did not ensue from the logic of historical, socio-cultural and political development of Africa. The process proceeded in a more or less natural way only during Africa's pre-colonial period. The modern African states, in essence, are the legacy of colonialism in the sense that when the colonialists left, the world had already become "global". In fact, the world became "global" first and foremost owing to the accomplishments of the Europeans since the Age of Discovery. It is not by chance that the great historian Fernand Braudel has called the Discoveries "the heroic deed of the West". Today the modern state is the only form of political organization that allows a society to exist as a subject of international law and as a recognized socio-political wholeness. It should be understood that, to a certain extent, most of the modern African states are chimerical formations from the very beginning. They are gradually finding their way toward an inner organic structure, socio-cultural and national wholeness, but they are not there yet as they encompass different peoples with very different cultures and different pre-colonial histories; these peoples often have very little in common or even used to be enemies. On the other hand, the colonial boundaries, which these postcolonial states inherited, divided many kindred peoples, often even the same people, severed historical economic, social, political, and cultural ties and imposed new ones.

One may recall how the concept of human rights has developed in Europe – the Magna Carta in England, the States-General in France and so on. Thus, one should not understand the concept of human rights as an absolute and truly universal value at its start. Therefore I want to emphasize the historical and cultural conditionality and European civilizational essence of this concept. In the form in which it exists in the widespread theory and is rooted in historical, cultural, and political experience of the West, the concept of human rights is not something quite adequate for the basic principles of African societies. If we look at African communities, but not from the viewpoint of blatant Eurocentrism, we will see that they had their own historically evolving forms of hierarchy and interaction between individuals, society and authorities.

The real basis of the social and political life of the African peoples, the basic form of the existence of the African cultures is and has always been the community. This is a fundamental fact, which the colonizers did not succeed in changing despite all their effort and despite whatever system of

76

colonial control – "direct" or "indirect" – they implemented, and because of this Africa has maintained its civilizational identity despite all its distortions. Without understanding the fact that still today the community sets (either directly or – in the context of urbanization – indirectly) the *modus vivendi* of the overwhelming majority of Africans, we cannot comprehend the problem of human rights in Africa, as well as all the processes that take place there in general. The community is not the epitome of human rights in their contemporary European ("modern" and, supposedly, "universal") sense. But neither has it ever been the epitome of a totalitarian, anti-humanist principle.

The community has always ruled out autocracy, and there have always been institutions, if not elected in a literal sense, then where people are promoted on the basis of clear and understandable principles. The nature of the worldview defined by the community is not anthropocentric, but sociocentric, in which the society (the community itself) is at the forefront rather than the individual. Whereas the Modern European anthropocentrism welcomes self-determination of the individual through accentuating his/her unique individuality (personality), in an African community the individual is not "dissolved" in the collective, but feels indispensable and unique only as a part of it, and does not confront it but, on the contrary, is conscious of being its part and tries to liken to it internally, and via it – to the Cosmos. The "laws" of the Cosmos determine the laws of society, while the latter, in turn, define the place and role of an individual in it. Just what is good for the collective is also good for the individual. Of course, the collective is conceptualized in terms of the concepts and categories of community and kinship.

In connection with the above, it is worth mentioning various concepts of "African specificity", which in the 1960s-80s were established by many African leaders as their states' official ideology. These leaders appealed to traditional African culture in order to show that it was different from Western one, including the human rights aspects, and thus justify the need for society to follow the ideology designed to legitimize their hard-authoritarian or even openly dictatorial regimes. Probably the most famous of them is the concept of "Zaïrian exceptionalism", sometimes called "Mobutizm" after the name of its creator, Mobutu Sese Seko. While expanding his dictatorial powers in the country (in particular, through a direct violation of human rights and freedoms), Mobutu asserted that such a regime supposedly corresponded to the foundations of the Zaïrian culture and was ideally suited to traditional norms of the Zaïrian society. However, firstly, as noted above, Africa's indigenous social space does in no way encourage dictatorship, and, secondly, the very concepts of "the Zaïrian culture" and "Zaïrian exceptionalism" are absurd when used in connection with the foundations of African cultures and societies: Zaïre (now – the Democratic Republic of the Congo) is a product of colonialism, and the peoples of this modern state had never before been within a single socio-political organism and certainly had not possessed any common homogeneous "Zaïrian culture". In fact, Mobutizm was no reference to the real roots but was an invention by some pseudo-historians in a situation where the autochthonous communities of numerous Zaïrian peoples and their regulations, including those relevant to the issue of human rights, had largely been distorted (but not eradicated) during the colonial and early post-colonial periods. Only in such circumstances there became possible the emergence of Mobutizm and similar ideologies, which in reality were based not on the establishment of traditional social values in new historical conditions, but on the rejection of the values of Western civil society – the values that are inextricably linked to the concept of "human rights".

If we talk about contemporary Africa in connection with the concept of human rights developed in the West and imposed on the world as a supposedly universal concept, the following should be noted. The contemporary African society is divided. On the one hand, there are the educated youth and intellectuals. Indeed, these are primarily city residents who have access to modern media: the Internet, the press, and TV, including Western ones. For the most part, these are the people who recognize the concept of human rights in its Western form as an undoubted value even if they like to talk about the dominance of the West in their countries, negative aspects of globalization, etc. There is a large number of NGOs that operate in African countries, not only Western and international, but also indigenous African, including those fighting for human rights in general and for the establishment of civil society. At the same time, in any African country there are millions of people who are poor, uneducated and illiterate, not only in terms of the inability to read and write, but also in the sense of ignorance and misunderstanding of the norms of democracy.

Here is an example from my experience as an Africanist. The Republic of Benin. At one time, the higher percentage of students from Benin graduated with honors from Soviet universities than of any other nationality. This was because the French colonialists who once controlled Dahomey (present-day Benin) focused on developing a narrow layer of well-educated and highly skilled elite. Young representatives of this particular social group came to study to the Soviet Union. Since the late 1980s – early 1990s Benin has had a democratic political system with a genuine multi-party parliamentarism and where a president is not guaranteed re-election. The educated part of the Benin society is very proud of this and, in general, speaks ill of the period when their country tried to build socialism with the help of the Soviet Union. But at the same time Benin is a country where about 30% of the population are illiterate and another roughly 30% can be called semi-literate. These people have no idea about democracy or human rights. In my opinion, the problem with establishing any civil and democratic norms in Africa, including those related to human rights, arises largely from the lack of education. It is no accident that at the time when these concepts were being conceived in Europe eminent figures of the Enlightenment insisted that not only the rulers – "sages on the throne" – should be educated, but also the people, for the people should be able to enter into the "social contract" between them and the government consciously and abide by this contract. Democracy is a system designed for the educated middle class. This was well understood in antiquity: it is no accident, for example, that Solon took measures against both excessive enrichment and impoverishment of the Athenians. In case of Benin, on the one hand, there is a layer of people who understand the essence of democracy, including the concept of human rights, and who are committed to corresponding political ideals and social norms. But those 60% of Beninese – the poor and the uneducated (which is interrelated) – are also a part of the electorate, and these people are also involved in social and political life, for instance elections. Thus, two very different political cultures with different worldviews, lifestyles and social opportunities clash within the same national political process.

The path towards the establishment of human rights in Africa, both in theory and in practice, runs, most importantly, through education and enlightenment. First of all, because any system of education gives not only knowledge but, wittingly or unwittingly, a particular system of values; modern education – Western in essence, secular and anthropocentric in nature – is oriented towards the value system of civil society, in which human rights occupy the central role.

Only in a situation where the anthropocentric worldview and secular mindset dominate it is possible to implement the concept of human rights in its historically Western version. In contemporary Africa the level of secularity is quite low, and anthropocentrism is not a typical feature of the worldview of most of its inhabitants. This in no way makes Africans worse than Europeans. Europe has traveled a long historical path to its current spiritual and socio-political status. It is just necessary to note that the countries of sub-Saharan Africa at the moment lack preconditions of any kind – social, political, cultural, mental, etc. – to carry out a real (not formal) implementation of the Western concept of human rights. Perhaps, globalization may assist them in this regard, but, in my opinion, it remains an open question whether it makes sense to introduce in Africa the concept of human rights in its supposedly universal form, which, in fact, is Western. Apparently, the correct answer will depend on what globalization will bring: universal Westernization or the formation of a global civilization as a single socio-cultural foundation of a kind of federation of local civilizations. Personally I think the latter is more likely[1].

---

[1] See *Bondarenko D.M.* The Social World's Parts and Whole: Globalization and the Future of Some Non-Western Cultures in the Civilization and World-System Theories Perspectives. In J. Sheffield (ed.), *Systemic Development: Local Solutions in a Global Environment.* Litchfield Park, AZ: ISCE Publishing, 2009. P. 17–24.

Stanislav Mezentsev

USE OF FOREIGN MILITARY FORCE IN AFRICA (ON THE EXAMPLE OF THE HORN OF AFRICA)[*]

Recently there has been a further increase in the use of foreign military forces in Africa in general and in the Horn of Africa[1] in particular. Today the sub-region can be considered as a kind of reference for the analysis of various forms of the use of armed forces by the United States and other NATO countries in order to achieve their political, military-strategic and economic goals on the African continent.

The quantitative and qualitative increase in NATO's military presence in the Horn of Africa has a number of formal reasons. First, it is the extremely advantageous geostrategic position of the region, which is determined by its proximity to the main areas of oil production in the Arabian Peninsula, as well as to major sea lanes of global significance. Second, it is the relatively brief escalation of maritime piracy in the Gulf of Aden and off Somalia's shore. Finally, it is the high conflict potential of the Horn of Africa, where numerous intra- and inter-state armed conflicts and wars have not stopped for decades.

Peacekeeping in Africa and foreign military force
We can assume that the leading form of the use of foreign military forces in order to ensure regional security should be peacekeeping[2]. However, in fact, in recent years the reverse process has been taking place. There is a gradual reduction in direct involvement of foreign armed forces in peacekeeping activities under the auspices of the UN, which are increasingly being replaced by so-called "humanitarian interventions", of which more will be said below. At the same time, there is a steady increase in the use of foreign military force to conduct counter-terrorism activities and ensure forward presence in various countries on the African continent.

At the beginning of the 1990s, the participation of the U.S. military and other NATO armed forces in peacekeeping operations, including in Africa, was defined as one of the priorities. This provision was in particular embodied in the strategic military concept of the Bush Sr. administration, which officials dubbed *The Base Force*. Its direct developer – Colin Powell, at the time the Chairman of the Joint Chiefs of Staff – spoke in favor of increasing the level of American involvement in peacekeeping operations under the auspices of international organizations[3].

---

[*] First published in *Azia i Afrika segodnya*. Issue 11, 2013.

81

In 1992, the U.S. government initiated the involvement of the U.S. military in planning the humanitarian *Operation Restore Hope* in Somalia. The Unified Task Force (UNITAF), which had up to 37,000 troops, was deployed under the direct command of the U.S. It consisted of troops from 24 countries. The total expenditure on the two stages of the peacekeeping operation in Somalia was $1.687 billion[4]. However, the activities of foreign armed forces in Somalia proved to be ineffective. The UNOSOM II mission was one of the bloodiest in the history of UN peacekeeping operations. The casualties totaled 143 people[5].

According to American experts, *Operation Restore Hope* failed due to a phenomenon known in the American military theory as *mission creep*. U.S. Marines landed in Somalia to carry out primarily humanitarian tasks, but became involved in an internal conflict of low intensity. The objective was not met, the conflict became protracted, and the human and material losses led to discontent in the U.S.[6]

The fiasco of the peacekeeping operation in Somalia was one of the reasons that direct intervention in internal conflicts in "failed states", especially where there are no clearly defined U.S. interests, lost the support of the American public. Currently, the article on "the provision of support for multilateral peacekeeping operations" is only formally kept in the list of the strategic objectives of U.S. military policy[7].

Former colonial powers (Britain, France, Italy, Portugal), which traditionally demonstrate high political-military and economic activity in Africa, are also minimizing the direct involvement of their national armed forces in African peacekeeping operations. Such a policy is justifiable and understandable in terms of reducing the risk of incurring combat casualties, which is extremely unpopular in the West, especially in the context of resolving foreign and distant from their national interests African conflicts.

Since the 2000s Western countries have usually limited their involvement to sending their staff officers to crisis areas as military observers or administrative officers[8]. At the same time, the United States and other NATO countries have been strengthening their own control of political and economic aspects of development in Africa, especially in the post-crisis period. To do this, they retain and even increase their involvement in the creation of the Pan-African collective security system (PCSS) and its basic element – the African Standby Force (ASF). Today, virtually all activity in this direction is financed by Western donor countries, which also provide consulting support.

However, strict dependence of African countries on external financial assistance is in conflict with their own capability of independent decision-making during peacekeeping operations, not only at the strategic and operational but sometimes even at the tactical level. In this regard Cedric de Coning, a renowned expert in the field of African peacekeeping, quite rightly pointed out: "The success or failure of the further development of African peacekeeping capacity will be determined by whether the right balance will be found between the goals and objectives pursued in the political and military field by the Africans themselves and the interests of foreign donors and partners."[9]

It should be noted that recently the aspirations of the parties have not always coincided, especially with regard to shaping post-conflict future in many African countries.

Another important type of the use of foreign military force is the provision of military assistance to African countries in matters of national defense. U.S. military analysts directly point out that "the U.S. Army should form an advisory corps that will be sent to various regions of the world to serve allied armies as the basis of military and administrative training. However, the troops on the ground, including in Africa, should be provided by foreign allies."[10]

"Humanitarian intervention", "fight against international terrorism and piracy" – the reasons or excuses?

As already noted, in recent years the international relations concept of "humanitarian intervention" has come to the forefront of the theory and practice of the use of military force by the U.S. and its main NATO allies, primarily Britain and France. Typically, it is implemented in the form of armed intervention in an internal conflict under the banner of humanitarian activities (protection of safety zones, refugee security, food deliveries, restriction of activities or the ouster of "undemocratic" – from the Western point of view – regimes, etc.). This complex and fraught with dangerous political and military consequences trend in the use of military force by the US and NATO certainly deserves a separate detailed scientific analysis. Without going into a discussion of the concept of "humanitarian intervention" within the scope of this article, it should be emphasized, however, that it is always associated with the formulation and resolution of political, military, and, in many cases, economic problems.

Speaking about the development of U.S. military policy, it should be noted that as the country's leaderships change, it is subjected to certain evolutionary changes, including approaches to the scope and degree of American military involvement in conflicts abroad. With the accession of the Democratic administration of Barack Obama to the White House on January 20, 2009, the world became cautiously optimistic about possible structural changes in U.S. foreign policy, especially given the blunders and obvious failures in this area made by the former U.S. administration[11]. Of course if during the period from 1996 to 2005 Washington took on the role of the military leader and a direct participant of foreign military interventions by coalition forces (Yugoslavia, Afghanistan, Iraq), then the recent events in Tunisia, Egypt, Libya, Mali, and Syria demonstrate more secrecy, caution and flexibility in the actions of the United States. In recent conflicts and crises, U.S. forces are primarily engaged in providing logistical, intelligence and information, and consultative support to their NATO allies. The use of U.S. military personnel is limited to the deployment of special operations forces.

This does not mean that the United States will refuse to continue the offensive course of its foreign policy to achieve political, military-strategic and economic goals in various regions of the world. One can only speak about certain changes in tactics and strategy of the implementation of the set goals.

Under the new conditions of post-bipolar development and given the virtual absence of an external military threat, America has to be more careful when justifying its political and military actions abroad in order to gain support within the country and in the international arena. To achieve this, U.S. politicians carry on using traditional excuses – "the war on international terrorism", "protecting democracy internationally", "humanitarian responsibility", "improving the safety and security of U.S. citizens and facilities abroad," etc.

Noting the adjustment of U.S. military strategy in foreign countries, some observers express the hope that the political and military leadership of the country is beginning to learn from protracted and hopeless wars in Afghanistan and Iraq. Apparently, Washington is no longer willing or able to engage in endless wars with invisible enemies to help "ungrateful locals". Hence under the new circumstances U.S. leadership is considering more active involvement of other states and political forces in solving emerging issues, limiting the U.S. role to providing indirect support through the transfer of arms, money, military advisers and intelligence.

In the framework of the new policy on Africa, the United States is increasingly taking advantage of its allies – old colonial powers – with minimal risk to itself. In particular, in the latest internal crisis in Mali a French contingent was assigned the responsibility for implementing main military objectives. The U.S. coordinated and provided intelligence, transport and logistics support to the French *Operation Serval*. In addition, they provided financial and material assistance to ECOWAS[12] peacekeepers. In other regions, for example in Middle Eastern countries, the Americans actively involve local political and religious movements for the same purpose. The strategy, dubbed "leadership/game from behind", is becoming a common practice under the foreign policy of the Obama administration[13].

In recent years, the use of foreign military force has grown in connection with operations against international armed criminal groups, including sea pirates.

The problem of piracy off the coast of Somalia and in the Gulf of Aden and Northwestern Indian Ocean has long gained international importance. Pirate activities harm the development of the region and the world economy as a whole. According to various estimates, just the amount of ransom money paid to pirate gangs in 2010 was between \$4.9 and \$8.3 billion[14].

In the mid-2000s, the growing activity of pirates led to increased efforts of the international community to counter them, including with the use of foreign military forces. Since 2008, naval groups of the U.S. Navy, NATO and the European Union have participated in the multinational counter-piracy force in the waters of the Horn of Africa on a permanent basis. A number of major anti-piracy operations, such as *Operation Ocean Shield* and *Operation Atalanta*[15], which also involve U.S.-led Combined Task Force 151, are taking place in the region.

In late 2012 – early 2013 the number of pirate attacks in the Gulf of Aden and the Red Sea dropped significantly. A special report published in July 2013 by the International Chamber of Commerce and the International Maritime Bureau (IMB)[16] noted that in the first half of the year Somali piracy fell to its lowest levels since 2006: worldwide, the IMB recorded 138 piracy incidents in the first six months of 2013, compared with 177 incidents for the corresponding period in 2012. Seven hijackings were recorded during the period compared with 20 in the first half of 2012. In particular, nine piracy incidents including two hijackings were recorded in the first six months of 2013 off the coast of Somalia[17]. As of 30 June 2013, Somali pirates were holding 57 crew members for ransom on four vessels. They were also holding 11 crew members kidnapped in 2010 in unknown conditions and locations.

The report highlighted the trend of shifting the center of pirate activity from East Africa to the Gulf of Guinea, where in the first half of 2013 31 pirate attacks on merchant ships, including four hijackings, were recorded. Attacks off Nigeria accounted for 22 of the region's 31 incidents

IMB experts attribute this significant drop in the frequency and range of attacks by Somali pirates to the following:

– anti-piracy actions by international navies stationed in pirate prone areas;

– the deployment of privately contracted armed security personnel;

– wider use of special equipment installed on merchant ships;

– improving the level of special training of crews.

Most effective is when a group of several merchant ships is escorted by a warship through a pirate prone area. The naval convoys have not experienced a single pirate attack. The Russian Navy, which maintains a permanent presence in the Gulf of Aden, with warships operating on a rotation basis, also takes part in escort duty. However, the disadvantage of this anti-piracy method is its fairly high cost as ships need to wait at a collection point (7–12 vessels) to assemble a convoy, which leads to a significant increase in downtime and ship-owners' operating costs.

Another effective way to counter piracy is to have armed security personnel on board of a merchant vessel. This conclusion is supported by statistics showing that pirates have never managed to capture a ship protected this way, despite the fact that, for example, in 2011 45 such attempts were recorded. However, there is a problem with legislation concerning the storage and use of automatic firearms aboard civilian vessels. In 2012 the problem led to an incident in Nigeria where the Nigerian authorities arrested a ship, its crew and armed security guards on charges of illegal possession of automatic weapons. The court proceedings on the case are still in progress[18].

Regarding the effectiveness of anti-piracy measures off the coast of Somalia by naval group of the U.S., the EU and NATO, its results remain at a relatively low level. Navy representatives of participating countries informally recognize that the presence of naval groups in the Gulf of Aden does not fully meet the objectives of anti-piracy activities.

It should also be noted that some Somali politicians in recent years have increasingly doubted the genuineness of the interest of Western and Arab states in the practical resolution of the problem of piracy in the coastal waters. Independent military experts link this passivity to the fact that the status quo gives NATO countries a formal pretext to maintain a permanent naval presence in areas of strategically important sea lanes.

Foreign military force and private military and security companies

In the analysis of various forms of the use of foreign military force in the Horn of Africa, one should pay special attention to the growing involvement of private military and security companies (PMSCs) in combat activities, particularly in crisis areas.

As noted above, the international industry of private security services contractors which offer escort and armed defense at sea is actively developing. Currently the industry is represented by a significant number of foreign PMSCs. For example, these include *AdvanFort*, *G4S*, *IMSA*, MAST and others[19]. Typically, these structures are registered in the UK (which offers relatively simple – from a legal standpoint – registration procedure), in the U.S., or have offshore status. Most of the PMSCs employ retired professional military experts from the armed forces of the U.S., NATO countries, Israel, Russia, Ukraine, etc.

In addition, the practice of engaging PMSCs in peacekeeping and so-called "humanitarian" operations in a number of crisis areas of the world, including in Africa, is constantly expanding. The most famous PMSCs include such U.S. companies as *DynCorp International* and *XE Services*[20], which specialize in international military and police operations.

This kind of business formed in the days of national liberation wars during the decolonization of Africa in the 1960s and advanced the most in South

Africa. Currently there are more than 10,000 large security PMSCs employing 1.5 million professionals, who in terms of their special training and weaponry match regular army units. The U.S. alone has about 100 companies cooperating on a regular basis with the State Department, the Department of Defense and intelligence agencies[21]. The trend of the "privatization of war" is most clearly seen in the course of military operations of the United States and NATO in Iraq and Afghanistan, but it also has its manifestations in the Horn of Africa.

Currently, a large number of foreign PMSCs operate in almost all countries of the sub-region; however, their greatest number is active in Somalia. The difficult political situation in the country and the continuing fighting between local military groupings and clans provide a high demand for the services of PMSCs. Foreign experts are widely engaged with protecting individuals and various objects and with training local security personnel[22].

In the mid-2000s, the Department of Defense expressed interest in expanding U.S. participation in the implementation of the African Union peacekeeping mission in Somalia (AMISOM). As any loss of American troops was considered unacceptable, the U.S. military engaged a variety of PMSCs.

For example, since January 2007 the U.S. company *DynCorp International (DI)* has actively worked in Somalia on contracts with the Pentagon and the U.S. State Department. At the initial stage of preparation for the deployment of AMISOM, *DI* provided military training, equipment and airlifts of Ugandan and Burundian troops to Mogadishu. Subsequently *DI* delivered armored vehicles, radio equipment, mobile generators, tents, uniforms and other technical and military equipment to Somalia

Armed convoys of this U.S. PMSC were involved in escorting and protecting civilian personnel and humanitarian transports of AMISOM during their movement through Somali territory. To date, *DI* has airlifted more than 12,000 peacekeepers of AMISOM and delivered by air, rail and sea transport to and from Somalia more than 15 million pounds of cargo, organized more than 280 flights to Mogadishu and other areas in Somalia. To support its operations in Somalia and other African Horn countries, *DI* has offices or authorized agents in Kampala (Uganda), Mogadishu, Addis Ababa (Ethiopia) and Djibouti[23].

In addition, military instructors of *DI* in cooperation with another PMSC, which was affiliated with the U.S. oil and gas company *Halliburton*, fulfilled a contract with the U.S. Defense Department and the UK to provide training for military and police of the transitional Somali government. They also participated in the military training of Somali special forces and intelligence services. The training of special forces was carried out both on Somali territory and in military training centers in Ethiopia. As a rule, such contracts are funded from the budget of the Pentagon and the U.S. State Department. The funds come from lines budgeted for African peacekeeping missions.

Various Western private military companies, working on contacts with military authorities, are typically used to collect intelligence and information of economic nature. According to some reports, U.S. PMSCs working in Somalia on contracts with Texas oil company *Halliburton* under the guise of AMISOM assessed Somali and offshore oil and gas fields in order to secure them for the U.S. company.

In conclusion, it is necessary to consider one more form of the use of military force in the Horn of Africa, which in fact is most important from the point of view of Western military policy: forward military presence. The main forms of military presence (according to U.S. policy) are: permanent stationing of troops; periodic and temporary deployment of troops; joint exercises; port visits and other visits; preventive deployment of military assets; humanitarian presence; deployment of security teams; state aid; contacts between militaries; assignment of military attaches[24].

One should also take into account such indirect instruments of military policy in third countries as military aid (deployment of military trainers and advisers) and military-technical assistance (including sale and transfer of military equipment and weapons and their storage in other countries)[25].

Geo-strategy, military policy in Africa and AFRICOM

The main motivation for expanding NATO's forward military presence in the Horn of Africa is certainly its extremely favorable geostrategic position.

Firstly, it is the location of a key transportation hub with a center in Djibouti. Major international shipping routes (including for hydrocarbons) from North America to Asia and back, as well as from the Middle East to Africa, lie along the Horn. Given the availability of modern weapons, weapon delivery systems and radar tracking, the territory of the Horn of Africa provides the ability to control not only the Gulf of Aden and the Red Sea, but also access to the Arabian Sea and the Strait of Hormuz. The latter are the main transportation routes for oil from the Persian Gulf[26].

Secondly, the special significance of the Horn of Africa lies in the fact that it borders the oil region of the Greater Middle East as defined by Western strategists from the south. Not coincidentally, in the 1970-1980s the Horn was the scene of intense rivalry between the U.S. and the USSR for supremacy in regional forward military presence. One can say that it was the struggle for basing rights in Somalia, Djibouti and Ethiopia that was the determining factor when Moscow and Washington made the most important foreign policy decisions with regard to these countries during the Cold War.

Without going into too much detail on this vast subject, which requires a separate historical study, one episode should still be highlighted. According to some opinions, the decisive factor determining the reorientation of the Soviet Union from the support of the Somali leader Siad Barre towards the provision of military aid to the Ethiopian regime of Mengistu Haile Mariam was the opportunity to use Ethiopian infrastructure – namely, the port of Assab and the Dahlak Islands. According to the Soviet military leadership , the use of these facilities by the Soviet Navy opened up more opportunities for control of the Red Sea than the former naval base in Berbera, Somalia[27].

After the end of the Cold War, in the ensuing post-bipolar era, the Horn of Africa has by no means lost its geostrategic significance[28]. Moreover, today one can speak about its growing significance, especially against the background of the well-known processes in North Africa and the increasing confrontation in the Middle East, as well as the increasing tension over Iran. In current conditions, the Horn of Africa is once again becoming a region of an increased attention by NATO, which is now increasingly competing with China and India.

Currently in the sub-region there is permanent military presence of the U.S., other NATO countries, Japan and China. Land and sea units of these states are stationed in Djibouti on various contractual and legal bases, which give them long-term rights to deploy military personnel and equipment. This small in territory and population African country is now euphemistically referred to as "the geographical dwarf turning into a geopolitical giant".

Today, the territory of Djibouti houses U.S. Combined Joint Task Force – Horn of Africa (CJTF-HOA)[29] and two military bases and several military facilities of the French military. Djibouti also provides territory for command centers, temporary bases, fuel storage depots and other storages, and military liaison missions of the militaries and navies of Germany, Spain, Portugal, Italy, UK and Japan. The Government of China is currently considering the possibility of establishing a permanent base in Djibouti.

According to some reports, a number of similar military installations have been or are being deployed in Somalia, particularly in the unrecognized breakaway republic of Somaliland in the area of the port of Berbera, in some parts of Ethiopia and oil-rich South Sudan, which is adjacent to the Horn of Africa.

The United States Africa Command (AFRICOM or Africa Command)[30] has become a recently new instrument of military policy on the African continent as a whole and in the Horn of Africa in particular. It is responsible for U.S. military operations in all of Africa except Egypt[31].

Next is a brief analysis of the declared and real goals of AFRICOM and its role in the implementation of U.S. policy in Africa. According to one of the initiators of the idea of creating a separate command for Africa, U.S. President George W. Bush, the new military-political structure is designed to ensure the development of cooperation between the U.S. and Africa in the field of security.

According to U.S. officials, AFRICOM would enhance U.S. efforts to bring peace and security to the people of Africa and promote the common goals of development, health, education, democracy, and economic growth in Africa[32]. According to other statements by U.S. officials, AFRICOM should base its activities on the so-called 3d concept: defense, development, diplomacy.

Thus, Africa Command is positioned as a model of "the military-political structure of a new format and content" launched in the new post-Cold War foreign policy environment. In this regard, its objective is presented by the U.S. propaganda as primarily the coordination of humanitarian, peacekeeping, and diplomatic efforts, while actual military activities are at the bottom of the priority.

However, internal U.S. military presentations provide a different view on the objectives of AFRICOM:

– controlling African regions rich in natural – primarily hydrocarbon – resources, preventing disruptions in African oil production and exports;

– meeting the political and economic challenge of China in Africa;

– controlling "weak" African states and ungoverned regions to counter transnational extremism or influence of unfriendly regimes;

– dealing with instability (including by the means of peace enforcement) in the most volatile regions and selected countries of Africa[33].

Thus, it seems that the retention and, more recently, the expansion of the military presence of the U.S. and its Western allies in the Horn of Africa is in line with the offensive and aggressive policy of NATO. The U.S. and NATO military bases in the sub-region are considered by the American military command as the second echelon and reserve support point for the coalition forces deployed against Iran. The strategic importance of the Horn of Africa to the United States is also increasing due to the worsening political and military situation in North Africa and the need for military protection of the oil production areas in the U.S.-allied countries of the Middle East.

It should be noted that some Western politicians use various challenges and threats to international security (terrorism, piracy) as pretexts for increasing the use of military force in the Horn of Africa and surrounding maritime areas, although they do the same in other regions of the continent.

Increasingly obvious is the fact that the prospects for real and lasting stabilization of the situation in the Horn of Africa, like elsewhere in the world, are not associated with the build-up of foreign military presence. The resolution of problems of sub-regional security, including overcoming the existing intra- and inter-state conflicts, lies primarily in the political, economic and social fields and depends on the development of international economic cooperation.

Since the Cold War and until recent events in Somalia, Côte d' Ivoire, Tunisia, Egypt, Libya and Mali the cases have demonstrated that any kind of foreign – especially military – intervention, under whatever plausible humanitarian disguise it is conducted, produces inversely proportional results, exacerbating existing problems and creating new ones. This is largely due to the fact that the humanitarian motives of outside interference are very often mixed with own political goals and aspirations of external players. On the other hand, foreign mediators do not possess enough knowledge of the real situation on the ground and understanding of political, ethnic and religious processes and clan and tribal relations in ongoing internal conflicts.

It follows from the above that it is possible to argue, with a high degree of certainty, that the lower the level of external influence on the countries of the Horn of Africa is, the more stable are long-term prospects of its development, including in terms of sub-regional security.

---

[1] Historically, demographically, and geographically the Horn of Africa is the sub-region which includes Ethiopia, Eritrea, Somalia and Djibouti. However, geopolitically it also sometimes includes Sudan, which serves as the link between the Horn and the Nile Valley, so the resulting sub-region is often called the Greater Horn (author's note).

[2] One of the main forms of peacekeeping remain peacekeeping operations – one of the main types of the use of military force to restore and maintain peace and to prevent both intra- and inter-state armed violence. The specifics of these operations are that they must be carried out under the mandate and in accordance with UN Security Council resolutions; in certain cases, they are mandated by regional organizations, but typically by the UN Security Council. These operations include the so-called peace enforcement, when peacekeepers conduct combat operations aimed at suppressing aggression and restoring the status quo. A characteristic feature of peacekeeping operations is that military force is used not to capture territory or natural resources, which is a traditional use of armed forces (although this is not completely ruled out), but in order to restore international order, bring peace and security, and undertake the necessary humanitarian actions.

[3] Military Force in International Relations: a Tutorial (Ed. Annenkov V.I et al). M., KNORUS, 2011. P. 306.

[4] *Zaemsky V.F.* UN and Peacekeeping // International relations. M., 2012. P. 242.

[5] A greater number of combat casualties in a single operation over a comparable period of time (1960–1964) has been recorded only in the UN Operation in the Congo (ONUC), in which 245 servicemen were killed, as well as in the course of the mission of the United Nations Protection Force in Yugoslavia (UNPROFOR), in which the casualties totaled 162 in 1992-1995. (see: *Zaemsky V.F.* Op. cit.).

[6] Military Force in International Relations... P. 306.

[7] Ibid, P. 484.

[8] For example, in 2008, by the time of the completion of the UN Mission in Ethiopia and Eritrea (UNMEE), the force of 3369 people consisted mainly of Indian soldiers, while 213 officers from the U.S., Western and Eastern Europe and Russia participated in the mission as military observers. Similarly, the ongoing (since March 2005) UN Mission in Sudan (UNMIS) includes NATO officers largely as military observers. The African Union – United Nations Operation in Darfur (UNAMID) engages Western military representatives as staff officers or military observers of the mission. (Source: author's personal observations obtained during his assignment to the region).

[9] *Cedric de Coning*. Peacekeeping – Peacebuilding: Preparing for the Future. Paper, presented during Conference in Helsinki on 29 May, 2006.

[10] The Wall Street Journal. May 13, 2013, p. 13.

[11] *Krupyanko M.I., Areshidze L.G.* The U.S. and East Asia: the Struggle for a New Order // International relations. M., 2010. P. 7.

[12] ECOWAS is a regional group of West African states. The group has its own collective forces – *ECOMOG*. ECOWAS headquarters are located in Abuja (Nigeria).

[12] http://www.ng.ru/world/2013-02-01/1_usa_mali.html

[13] http://www.ng.ru/world/2013-02-01/1_usa_mali.html

[14] See, for example: *Lansing, Paul and Petersen, Michael*. Ship-owners and the Twenty-First Century Somali prates: The business ethics of ransom payments // Journal of Business Ethics. 2011. Vol. 3. P. 507-516.

[15] *Operation Ocean Shield* (17 August 2009 – present) is an anti-piracy NATO initiative off the coast of the Horn of Africa and in the Gulf of Aden.
Operation Atalanta (8 December 2008 – present) is a current military operation undertaken by the European Union Naval Force to prevent and combat acts of piracy off the coast of Somalia.

[16] http://www.icc-ccs.org/news/865-imb-piracy-report-highlights-violence-in-west-africa

[17] In 2010 the IMB recorded 219 piracy incidents, in 2011 – 237. As of 30 January 2011, Somali pirates were holding 800 crew members on 33 vessels. http://www.icc-ccs.org/home/piracy-reporting-centre

[18] http://www.dni.ru/society/2013/2/19/248480.html; http://www.fontanka.ru/2013/06/18/159/

[19] http://www.advanfort.com/; http://www.imsaltd.com/; http://www.g4s.com/; http://www.mastconfex.com/

[20] This PMSC is better known by its former name – *Blackwater*.

[21] *Nestyorkin B*. German citizens in the service of private military companies // Foreign Military Review. Moscow, July 2006. P. 30.

[22] *Kinsey Christopher Paul, Hansen Stig Jarle and Franklin George*. The impact of private security companies on Somalia's governance networks // Cambridge Review of International Affairs. 2009, Vol. 22, №. 1. P. 147-161.

[23] http://www.dyn-intl.com/what-we-do/somalia-case-study.aspx

[24] Military Force in International Relations... P. 486.

[25] Ibid, P. 46.

[26] On average 10–15 oil supertankers pass through the Strait every day.

[27] See, for example: *Mezentsev S*. Ethiopian-Somali border war of the 1977-78 and reflections on the role and impacts of foreign countries // African Armed Forces Journal. January 2013.

[28] See, for example: The Horn of Africa Intra-State and Inter-State conflicts and security (ed. by R.Bereketea). Nordic African Institute. 2013. P. 87-88.

[29] In 2006, the U.S. signed an agreement with the Government of Djibouti to increase the territory of its base from 90 acres to 500 acres. According to independent military analysts, the U.S. has allocated $6 billion for the development of the infrastructure of the CJTF-HOA base, which at the moment plays the role of the key stronghold of AFRICOM. In particular, the development includes expanding air strip and upgrading port and air field facilities. The official budget for the CJTF-HOA operation is $300 million annually.

According to some reports, in 2011 the strength of the CJTF-HOA military contingent went up from 1,500 to 3,500. Future plans provide for a gradual increase in the number to 7,500.

The visit to Djibouti by US Defense Secretary Leon Panetta in 2011 led to the conclusion of an agreement on the expansion of the base and its use. In particular, the agreement allows the USA to build its new base, turn ownership over to the Djibouti government and then sign a 99 year "service agreement" to use the base. See: *Mountain Thomas C.* Back to Djibouti: Africom and the New White Burden – http://bit.ly/xDQwhn/ (February 14, 2012).

[30] The full name is Unified Combatant Command for Africa.

[31] Prior to the creation of AFRICOM, three Unified Commands had divided responsibility for U.S. military operations in Africa (European Command – EUCOM for West Africa, Central Command – CENTCOM for East Africa, Pacific Command – PACOM for Indian Ocean waters and islands off the east coast of Africa). According to U.S. military experts, such a division had significantly reduced the ability to project force on the continent and the effectiveness of the operational control of U.S. forces in the global war theaters.

[32] The White House Office of the Press Secretary. "President Bush Creates a Department of Defense Unified Combatant Command for Africa". 6 February, 2007.

[33] *Daniel Volman*. Notes based on the Conference on "Transitional National Security: AFRICOM – An Emerging Command". National Defense University, Virginia, 19–20 February, 2008.

Andrey Korotaev
Yulia Zinkina

HOW TO OPTIMIZE FERTILITY
AND PREVENT HUMANITARIAN CATASTROPHES
IN TROPICAL AFRICA[*]

According to the latest UN median[1] forecast published in 2012, the population of such relatively small East African countries as Kenya and Uganda will exceed the population of Russia in the second half of this century; Tanzania will reach Russia's level as early as 2050 and will exceed it by more than double by the end of this century. The population of Nigeria will surpass Russia's population by almost 5 times (see Fig. 1).

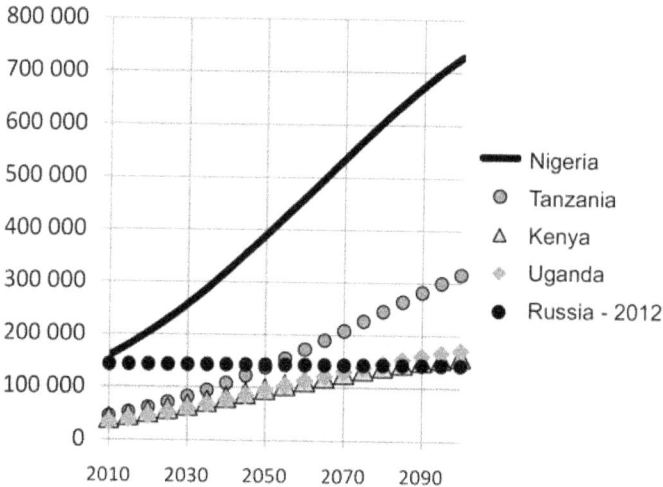

Figure 1. The UN median forecast for the population dynamics (in thousands of people) for selected countries of Tropical Africa in the 21st century[2].

Such explosive growth of the population is clearly able to lead to a large-scale humanitarian disaster in these countries and for the international community in general.

---

[*] First published in *Azia i Afrika segodnya*. Issue 4, 2013.

Figure 2 illustrates the UN demographic forecast for African countries with the highest socio-demographic risks of large-scale humanitarian disasters.

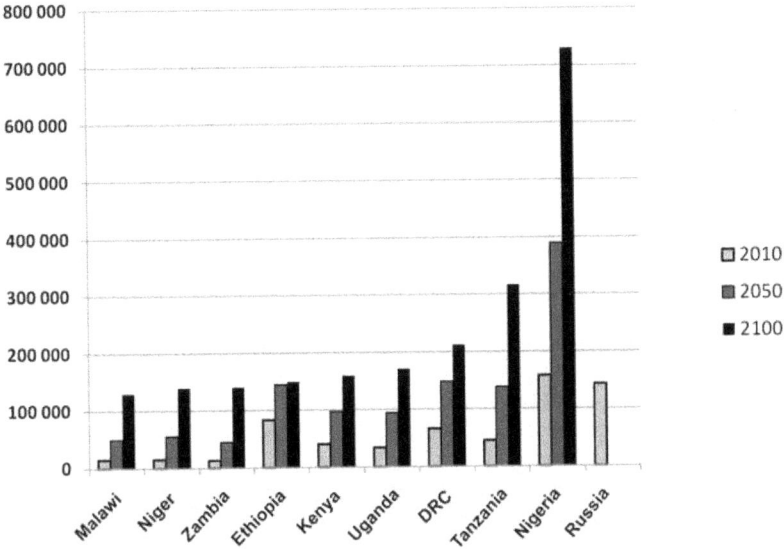

Figure 2. African countries with the highest risks of large-scale humanitarian disasters in the 21st century where population (in thousands) will reach or surpass the current population of Russia[3].

Particularly impressive is Malawi, a very small country in southeastern Africa (area of just over 100.000 km^2, i.e. less than, for example, Vologda region), whose population, according to the UN median forecast, should match Russia's population. On the other hand, it is obvious that the most large-scale socio-demographic collapse – even up to large-scale, bloody civil wars or even a collapse of the state after a long period of conflict and violence, with tens of millions of dead – could happen in Nigeria (unless adequate measures are taken very soon to prevent the explosive growth of the population).

It is important to emphasize that the UN median forecast assumes that fertility in the countries of Sub-Saharan Africa will decline and, moreover, that the rate of decline will accelerate in comparison with the one observed in recent years. However, demographic forecasts indicate that even the projected by the UN acceleration of fertility decline in Sub-Saharan Africa will not be sufficient to prevent large-scale humanitarian disasters.

The situation is further aggravated by the fact that many countries of Sub-Saharan Africa still have not managed to get out of the so-called Malthusian trap[4], which makes the likelihood of a socio-demographic collapse in these countries particularly high[5].

Indeed, in about half of the countries of Sub-Saharan Africa per capita food consumption barely reaches the norms of the World Health Organization (WHO) or is significantly below it. A similar situation in the past has often led to social and political upheavals – even up to protracted and bloody civil wars – in different countries. Increasing per capita food consumption in Africa does not work largely because of the very rapid growth of the population, which literally "eats up" productivity growth, especially in the agricultural sector, where a significant part of the African population is still employed. If the population grows several times over the next decade as it is currently expected, it can turn into a large-scale famine and humanitarian catastrophe.

The problem is still very much underestimated

Nevertheless, despite the urgency of the situation, the problem of the explosive population growth in Sub-Saharan Africa is outside the focus of international development assistance agencies. The matter of fact is that the peak of the alarmist sentiment[6] in the international community with respect to the population explosion in Sub-Saharan Africa took place in the 1970s – early 1990s[7]. It should be noted that at that time the fertility rate in most of the countries of Sub-Saharan Africa began to decline and, moreover, all the more rapidly (see Fig. 3).

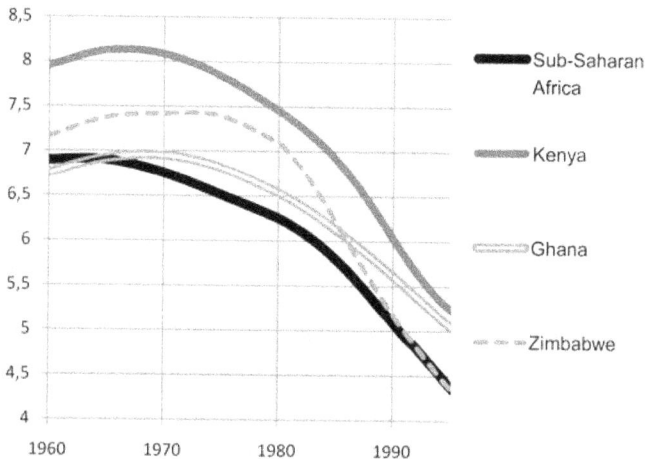

Figure 3. Total fertility rate in Sub-Saharan Africa in 1960–1995.

96

By the early 2000s the information on the reduction of fertility in Sub-Saharan Africa spread among the international community. UN experts predicted stabilization of the population of Sub-Saharan Africa at relatively safe levels (see Fig. 5). Consequently, the international community calmed down[8] as it seemed that the decline in fertility would continue. However, the feeling was premature. In the late 1990s – early 2000s in most countries of Sub-Saharan Africa the decline in fertility slowed down or even stopped, while in some countries fertility even started to grow. Moreover, it leveled off very high, in most cases – at 5.5–6 children per woman (see Fig. 4).

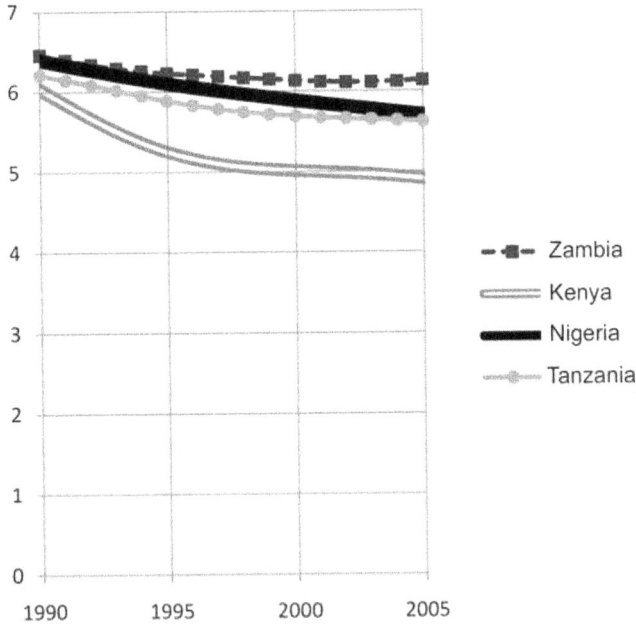

Figure 4. Total fertility rate in select Sub-Saharan countries in 1990–2005.

Considering the leveling off of fertility at a high level, UN experts had to revise their forecasts of ten years ago and increase projected population numbers for many countries of Sub-Saharan Africa by such a dramatic amount that the risk of large-scale social and humanitarian disasters in these countries became very high (Fig. 5).

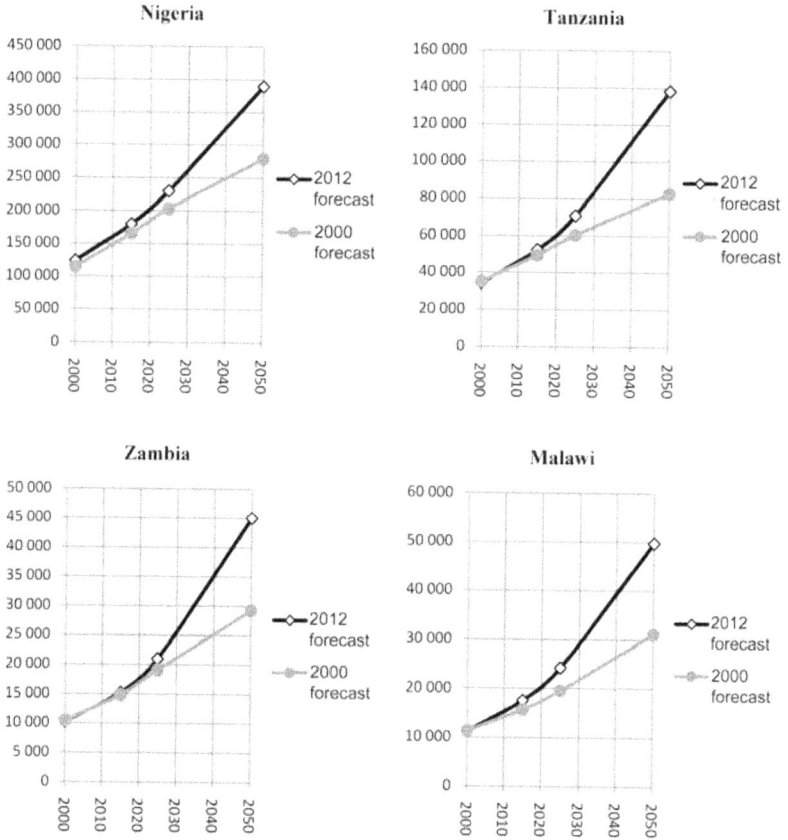

Figure 5. Comparison of two median forecasts of the UN (2000, 2012) for select Sub-Saharan countries (in thousands)[9].

As a result, currently we have to deal with the risk of large-scale humanitarian disasters, which has become much more serious than it seemed just 10 years ago. Meanwhile, the international community is not aware of the resurgence of the terrible threat of large-scale socio-demographic disasters in Sub-Saharan Africa. There is a risk that when the threat is finally realized, it will be too late.

So what can and should be done in order to avert this threat?

First of all, female education...

Among the factors affecting the fertility rate the level of female education is very significant. Well-organized female education reduces fertility and the number of children a woman desires. Better educated women marry later (which is a strong predictor[10] of fertility decline in traditional societies, where contraception is poorly distributed and socio-cultural norms inhibit illegitimate births), have more information and access to family planning, and use contraception more effectively[11]. However, in Sub-Saharan Africa, the effect of raising the level of education on fertility has long been much weaker than in other regions of the world – perhaps due to a weaker spread of female education in the region[12].

Several studies have clearly demonstrated the influence of the improvement of female education in Sub-Saharan Africa on fertility reduction. For example, in the 2000s John Bongaarts, an outstanding American demographer, analyzed data from 30 African countries and concluded that in all these countries the total fertility rate (hereinafter – TFR)[13] was lower among women with secondary and tertiary education than among women with primary education. In 27 countries, the number of children per woman with primary education was lower than per woman with no education[14].

The international community has recognized the need to promote education in Sub-Saharan Africa. The UN Millennium Development Goals include a goal of achieving universal primary education in all countries and for all peoples[15]. However, this objective has been proclaimed without regard to the effect of its implementation on fertility in individual countries and the world as a whole.

Let us now consider how the achievement of 100% primary school enrollment will affect the total fertility rate in the countries of Sub-Saharan Africa. To do this, we will carry out a correlation and regression analysis[16] and analyze the diagram of dispersion[17] that shows the correlation between the proportion of the female population of over 15 years of age who completed at least primary education and the total fertility rate, which is calculated on the basis of censuses conducted at different times in 35 countries of Sub-Saharan Africa (in most countries, there were more than one census) (See Fig. 6).

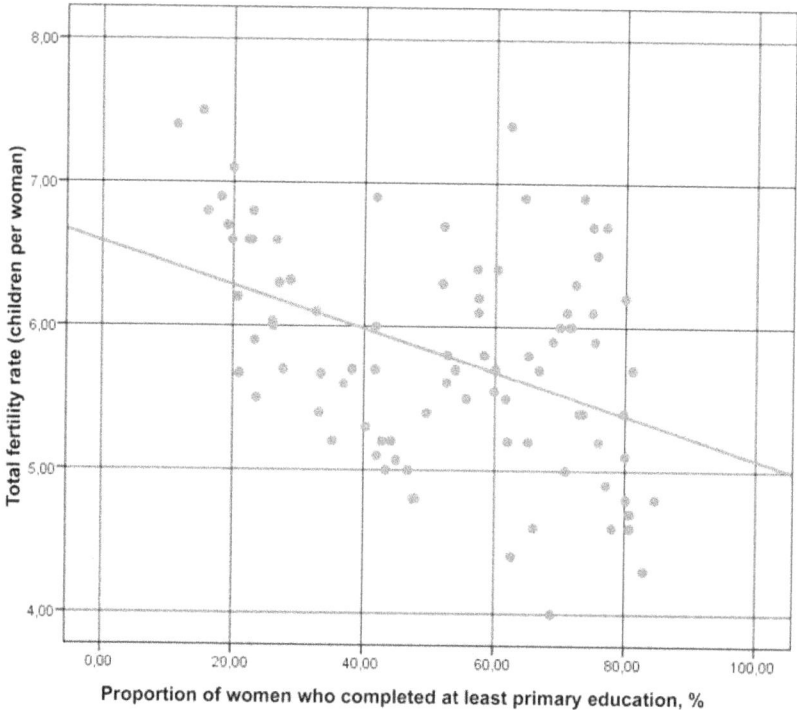

**Figure 6. Correlation between the proportion of the female popula-
tion of over 15 years of age who completed at least primary education
and the total fertility rate in Sub-Saharan countries**

Our analysis has led to an important conclusion: simply eliminating female illiteracy (i.e. ensuring that 100% of the women have at least incomplete primary education) is not sufficient to decrease the fertility rate in Sub-
Saharan Africa to the population replacement level (2.1 children per
woman). The analysis shows that if 100% of the women in Sub-Saharan Africa have at least incomplete primary education, the fertility rate will be little
more than 5 children per woman.

Let us now consider the impact of the expansion of secondary education
on fertility in Sub-Saharan Africa (Fig. 7).

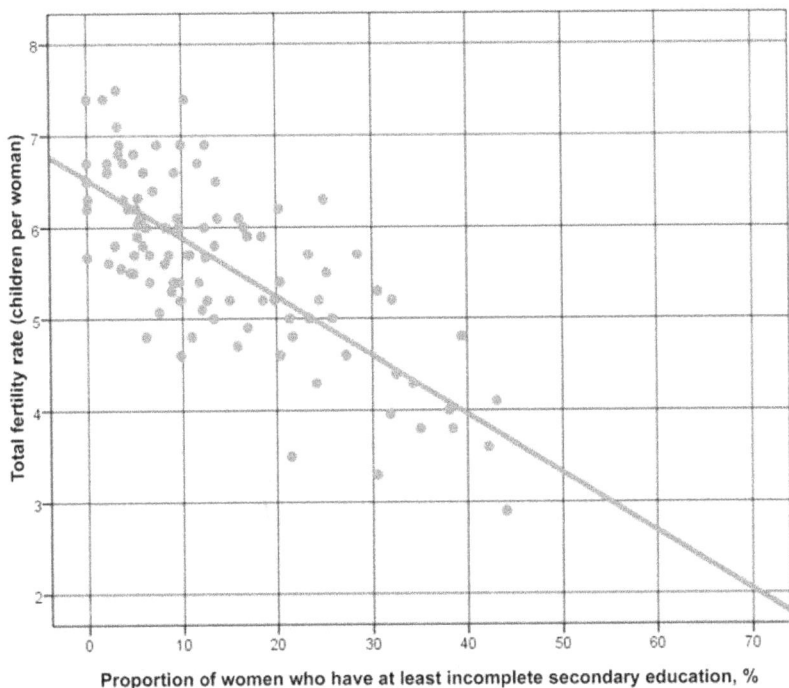

Proportion of women who have at least incomplete secondary education, %

Figure 7. Correlation between the proportion of the female population of over 15 years of age who have at least incomplete secondary education and the total fertility rate in Sub-Saharan countries (diagram of dispersion with a linear regression line[18]).

Our analysis has shown that if 70% of the women of over 15 years of age have at least incomplete secondary (or higher) education, the birth rate in Sub-Saharan Africa should decrease approximately to the population replacement level – to 2 children per woman.

It should be emphasized that it is not as easy as it may seem at first glance to avert the risks of social and demographic disasters in the countries of Sub-Saharan Africa by increasing the proportion of women of over 15 years of age with secondary education to 70%. It is not simply about making sure that 70% of all African girls attend high school (this is also not easy to achieve, but with political will and adequate funding it can be done quickly enough). The fact is that most African women who do not have secondary education have long been out of school age, and it is not realistic to supply secondary education to illiterate African women of over 30 years of age. In our opinion, however, it has long been necessary to expand opportunities for adult Africans to obtain secondary education. Nevertheless, the top priority is to provide secondary education for 100% of the school-age children in general and girls in particular.

In order to prevent the risks of social and demographic disasters in the countries of Sub-Saharan Africa, it is necessary to introduce universal compulsory secondary education in these countries as soon as possible. However, even in this case, a marked increase in the proportion of women of over 15 years of age with secondary education will take place only 8-12 years later, when the students who started learning in the year of the introduction of universal secondary education finish secondary school[19]. This measure will help reduce the population pressure in the Sub-Saharan Africa in two ways – both through fertility reduction and through the acceleration of economic growth (consequently, through the mechanism of the so-called "demographic bonus"[20] and through increased productivity, because educated people almost always work with more dedication and possess higher qualifications).

The introduction of universal compulsory secondary education in Sub-Saharan Africa is certainly a very costly measure, and African countries won't be able to do it on their own. The international community in general and developed nations (including the U.S. and Russia) in particular need to support the region and provide substantial financial assistance[21]. If such support from economically developed countries is not provided in the near future, later these countries will have to provide much more funding for the same purpose, not to mention the problems associated with almost inevitable socio-demographic disasters in Sub-Saharan countries.

...secondly, family planning

In general, it is increasing female enrollment in secondary education that seems to be the key approach to achieving fertility decline in Sub-Saharan Africa. This approach should become the key factor in planning national budgets and distributing international aid. However, increasing the level of female education in a given region, in essence, is a long-term measure, the effects of which will appear gradually, as the girls who have received secondary education enter their active reproductive age. Meanwhile, the UN experts' forecasts indicate the need for the most urgent measures to reduce fertility, and such a time lag (at least 8–10 years) is absolutely unacceptable. Therefore, in parallel with the development of secondary education (which, again, must be an absolute priority for the government), other measures with faster effects need to be introduced to reduce fertility.

Let us consider the experience of countries that have relatively small (less than 10%) proportion of women with incomplete secondary and higher education, which were able to achieve considerable success in reducing fertility. Among them, for example, are Ethiopia and Rwanda.

In Ethiopia, TFR declined from 5.9 children per woman in 2000 to 4.8 children in 2010, i.e. by 1.1 children per woman, in just 10 years. It is important to note that the birth rate declined steadily both in the cities and in the countryside[22]. If it maintains (or slightly accelerates) the current rate of fertility decline, Ethiopia should approach the population replacement level by approximately 2030, reaching a level of about 2.5 children per woman. A similar forecast for this country is made by the UN Population Bureau. It should be noted that due to a significant decline in the birthrate Ethiopia has become the only major country in Sub-Saharan Africa which has a chance to avoid a demographic disaster: the population is expected to double by 2050 but then it will level off.

Health Extension Program, adopted by the Government of Ethiopia in 2003, has played a huge role in achieving such demographic success. The main objective of the program is to provide the rural population with universal access to primary health care[23] and preventive procedures, including the practice of family planning (mostly through raising public awareness with regard to the dangers that having too many children poses to the country and society). Within the framework of the program, so-called "health extension points" (1 point per 5,000 people) have been created in every *kebele*[24]. These points employ 30 thousand employees (health extension workers) recruited from specially trained local girls and women. They visit families in their district and tell new mothers about family planning and newborn care and teach them hygiene skills. They also speak about balanced diets, infectious disease prevention, etc.[25] Largely due to this program, the use of contraception among Ethiopian women (i.e. the proportion of women who use contraception in relation to the total number of women) of 15-49 years of age increased from 3% in 1997 to 29% in 2010; for the cities the figure was 52.5%, while in rural areas – 23.4%[26].

Rwanda's recent demographic successes are even more remarkable. The country managed to reduce fertility from 6.1 children per woman in 2005 to 4.6 in 2010, or by 25% in 5 years, which is a record for Sub-Saharan Africa and is also very significant by world standards. The fertility rate decreased in all groups of the population: among urban women (from 4.9 children per woman in 2005 to 3.4 in 2010) and rural women (from 6.3 to 4.8), among women with no education (from 6.9 to 5.4), with primary education (from 6.1 to 4.8), with secondary and higher education (from 4.3 in 2005 to 3 in 2010)[27].

Rwanda has achieved such a brilliant result by implementing large-scale government programs to promote family planning practices through the infrastructure of *mutuelles* – health insurance system funded by insurance premiums and state budget[28]. Back in 2007, Rwandan President Paul Kagame said that he knew about Rwanda falling behind the global average in terms of the use of contraception[29]. He set a goal to raise the use of contraception among married women from 17.4 % in 2005 to 70% in 2012 (however, as conducting population surveys takes considerable time, Rwanda has not yet published an official report on the achievement of this goal).

Rwanda achieved a truly phenomenal growth in the use of contraception among married (both registered and unregistered marriages) women aged 15–49 – from 17.4% in 2005 to 51.6% in 2010, with rapid growth observed both in urban areas (from 31.6% to 53.1%) and in rural areas (from 15.2% to 51.4%). Impressive progress was also achieved in other areas: for example, from 2000 to 2010 Rwanda managed to halve infant (from 107.4 to 50 per 1,000 population) and child (from 196.2 to 76 per 1000 population) mortality[30].

* * *

In conclusion, it should be reiterated that the rate of fertility decline projected by the UN for Sub-Saharan Africa is clearly insufficient and, therefore, it is necessary to accelerate fertility decline dramatically. The main way to solve this problem should be increasing female enrollment in secondary education and raising it to at least 70% of the female population over 15 years. This can be achieved only if universal compulsory secondary education is immediately introduced throughout the region. In addition, we must simultaneously take other measures to reduce fertility, which can produce faster effects. In particular, it is necessary to implement a large-scale program for distribution of contraception and provide access to services (and information about them) for the population, especially in rural areas. The combination of strategic (universal secondary education) and tactical (large-scale distribution of contraception) measures is, of course, very expensive, but for the majority of African countries it is the only way to avoid an abrupt slowdown in development and many other problems, including major humanitarian disasters and social upheavals.

---

[1] The term "median forecast" means that there are at least another two forecasts – the maximum and the minimum ones. Obviously, the "median forecast" seems to be the most reliable.

[2] See: United Nations. Department of Economic and Social Affairs. 2012. Population Division Database. World Population Prospects – http://esa.un.org/unpd/wpp/unpp/panel_population.htm

[3] Ibidem.

[4] The Malthusian trap is a formal corollary to the Malthusian theory. According to the corollary, countries where population growth outstrips production growth "fall"

into this trap. It follows that their population is doomed to experience unemployment, hunger and poverty if it does not resort to birth control.

[5] *Korotaev A.V., Khaltourina D.A., Bozhevolnov Y.V.* The laws of history. Centennial cycles and millennial trends. Demography. Economy. Wars. 3rd ed. Moscow: LKI/URSS, 2010; *Khaltourina D.A., Korotaev A.V.* Population pressures and political turmoil in contemporary Sub-Saharan Africa // Vostok. 2006. Vol. 2, p. 52-69.

[6] Alarmist sentiment (from French "alarm" – "to arms!") – a mindset characterized by anxiety and seeing the future in very gloomy, pessimistic shades, as well as demanding that urgent measures are taken to stop or delay the impending catastrophe.

[7] See: *Ehrlich P.R.* The Population Bomb. New York, NY: Ballantine, 1968; *Ehrlich P. R., Ehrlich A. H.* The Population Explosion. New York, NY: Simon & Schuster, 1990.

[8] *Cohen J.* Population and planet: the twentieth century and the twenty-first // Harvard Magazine. 1999. Vol. 102, No. 2, p. 38–40; *Cohen J.* The future of population // What the Future Holds: Insights from Social Science, ed. Richard N. Cooper & Richard Layard. MIT Press, Cambridge, MA, 2002, p. 29–75; United Nations. 2012. Population Division Database. World Population Prospects – http://esa.un.org/unpd/wpp/unpp/panel_population.htm

[9] See: United Nations. 2012. Population Division Database. World Population Prospects – http://esa.un.org/unpd/wpp/unpp/panel_population.htm

[10] Predictor – a prognostic parameter and a forecasting tool. Originally it was a purely mathematical term (a part of extrapolation function) but is currently used in other fields of knowledge.

[11] See, for example: *Caldwell J.C.* Mass education as a determinant of the timing of fertility decline // Population and Development Review. 1980. Vol. 6, No. 2, p. 225–255; *Caldwell J.C.* The global fertility transition: the need for a unifying theory // Population and Development Review. 1997. Vol. 23, No. 4, p. 803–812; *Jejeebhoy S.* Women's Education, Autonomy, and Reproductive Behaviour: Experience from Developing Countries. Oxford: Clarendon Press, 1995; *Kirk D., Pillet B.* Fertility levels, trends, and differentials in sub-Saharan Africa in the 1980s and 1990s // Studies in Family Planning. 1998. Vol. 29, No. 1, p. 1–22; *Uchudi J.M.* Spouses' socioeconomic characteristics and fertility differences in sub-Saharan Africa: does spouse's education matter? // Journal of Biosocial Science. 2001. Vol. 33, No. 4, p. 481–502; Fertility behaviour in the context of development: evidence from the World Fertility Survey. United Nations, New York, 1987.

[12] See, for example: *Cleland J.G., Rodriguez G.* The effect of parental education on marital fertility in developing countries // Population Studies. 1988. Vol. 42, No. 3, p. 419–442; *Cochrane S., Farid S.* Fertility in sub-Saharan Africa: Levels and their Explanations. Washington DC: The World Bank, 1986; *Rodriguez G., Aravena R.* Socioeconomic factors and the transition to low fertility in less developed countries: a comparative analysis // Proceedings of the Demographic and Health Surveys World Conference. Columbia, Maryland: IRD/Macro International, 1991.

[13] This indicator shows the average number of children that would be born to a woman of a certain generation over her lifetime if she were to experience the exact

current age-specific fertility rates and to survive from birth through the end of her reproductive life.

[14] *Bongaarts J.* The Causes of Educational Differences in Fertility in Sub-Saharan Africa // Poverty, Gender, and Youth Working Paper. Vol. 20. Population Council, New York, 2010.

[15] See: The Millennium Development Goals Report 2010. United Nations, 2010.

[16] Correlation and regression analysis is a more general concept of another statistical and mathematical term – correlation analysis, which is a method of processing statistical data, which measures the strength of links between two or more variables.

[17] Diagram of dispersion is a two-dimensional graphical representation of the correlation between the two series of measurements, in this case – between fertility and female education. The more points there are on a diagram of dispersion, the higher is the probability that the correlation results (and the results of the research in general) turn out to be reliable.

[18] A line that most accurately reflects the distribution of the experimental points on a diagram of dispersion, and the steepness of which characterizes the correlation between two interval variables.

[19] The period will be 6-8 years in those countries where universal primary education has been introduced in practice.

[20] A high proportion of people of working age in the population age structure. Usually this phenomenon is observed in a country at the completion of a demographic transition – as fertility drops to population replacement level, new generations become much less numerous than the previous generation, which was born at a relatively high birth rate. At the moment when these larger generations come of working age, the country is starting to get a "demographic bonus" – a lot of productive workforce and fewer children and the elderly.

[21] It should be noted that the mathematical modeling of the interaction between the center and the periphery of the world-system, which we carried out in the framework of the RAS Presidium program "System Analysis and Mathematical Modeling of World Dynamics", showed that the amount of aid which the developed countries spend on the development of education in the countries of Sub-Saharan Africa is a factor of stability – i.e. exactly a significant increase in aid can avert socio-demographic catastrophes in these countries.

[22] Ethiopia Demographic and Health Survey 2011. Addis Ababa, Ethiopia and Calverton, Maryland, USA: Central Statistical Agency and ICF International, 2012; Ethiopia Demographic and Health Survey 2005. Addis Ababa, Ethiopia and Calverton, Maryland, USA: Central Statistical Agency and ORC Macro, 2006; Ethiopia Demographic and Health Survey 2000. Addis Ababa, Ethiopia and Calverton, Maryland, USA: Central Statistical Authority and ORC Macro, 2001.

[23] Basic health care in case of sudden injury, acute exacerbation of chronic disease, etc.

[24] A kebele is the smallest administrative unit of Ethiopia

[25] *Federal Ministry of Health [Ethiopia].* Health Extension Program in Ethiopia Profile. Addis Ababa: Health Extension and Education Center, Federal Ministry of Health, 2007.

[26] Ethiopia Demographic and Health Survey 2011. Addis Ababa, Ethiopia and Calverton, Maryland, USA: Central Statistical Agency and ICF International, 2012; Ethiopia Demographic and Health Survey 2005. Addis Ababa, Ethiopia and Calverton, Maryland, USA: Central Statistical Agency and ORC Macro, 2006; Ethiopia Demographic and Health Survey 2000. Addis Ababa, Ethiopia and Calverton, Maryland, USA: Central Statistical Authority and ORC Macro, 2001.

[27] Rwanda Demographic and Health Survey 2010. Calverton, Maryland, USA: NISR, MOH, 2012; Enquête Démographique et de Santé Rwanda 2005. Calverton, Maryland, U.S.A.: INSR et ORC Macro, 2006; Enquête Démographique et de Santé, Rwanda 2000. Kigali, Rwanda et Calverton, Maryland, USA: Ministère de la Santé, Office National de la Population et ORC Macro, 2001.

[28] *Lu C., Chin B., Lewandowski J.L., Basinga P., Hirschhorn L.R., et al.* Towards Universal Health Coverage: An Evaluation of Rwanda *Mutuelles* in its First Eight Years // *PLoS ONE.* 2012. Vol. 7, No. 6, p. e39282; Sharing the burden of sickness: mutual health insurance in Rwanda // Bulletin of World Health Organization. 2008. Vol. 86, No. 11, p. 823–824.

[29] *Kinzer S.* After so many deaths, too many births // New York Times 11.02.2007. URL: http://www.nytimes.com/2007/02/11/weekinreview/11kinzer.html?_r=0

[30] Rwanda Demographic and Health Survey 2010; Enquête Démographique et de Santé Rwanda 2005; Enquête Démographique et de Santé, Rwanda 2000.

Leonid Fituni

"ARAB SPRING": TRANSFORMATION OF POLITICAL PARADIGM IN CONTEXT OF INTERNATIONAL RELATIONS*

In 2011, the spring in North Africa was early and long. It first thundered in January, and then the thunderstorms of social unrest continued for many months and affected vast areas of the Arab world. Over the year revolutionary atmospheric fronts shifted to the south-east and the west, then back to the east – to Asia. In some countries the storms swept away crumbling political regimes. Elsewhere they substantially battered fundamental hierarchical structures. Consequences of the revolutionary weather made themselves felt outside the region, tarnishing the reputation of some politicians and forcing them to look for ways to come clear.

Arab revolts, loud and hasteless

What happened is very well known. The riots and mass protests that started in Tunisia led to the downfall of President Ben Ali and him fleeing the country. The regime of Egyptian President Hosni Mubarak fell on February 11. Two days later riots and demonstrations demanding the resignation of Libyan leader Muammar Gaddafi began in the eastern part of the country. The confrontation between the Libyan authorities and protesters took the form of an armed struggle. On March 18 the UN Security Council adopted a resolution on the establishment of a no-fly zone in Libya. NATO military intervention made a decisive contribution to the fall and death of the Libyan leader in October 2011. In January, large demonstrations began in Yemen, Jordan, Bahrain, and Morocco. However, the events in these countries proceeded in different ways. In Jordan and Morocco, the royal power fairly quickly responded to the situation and swiftly introduced some reforms (as it can be seen now, only cosmetic), which reduced the passions, at least for a while. The events in Bahrain took a bloody turn. The peaceful protests of mainly Shiite population were suppressed with the help of a military intervention of Saudi Arabia. In Yemen, loud protests and regular, sometimes bloody, clashes between the opposing parties still continue. In Syria, since April the government has increasingly been resorting to harsh repressive measures to keep the situation under control.

In almost all Arab countries, Islamic parties and movements and formal and informal associations – both included in the legal political system and banned – remained a strong "silent power" during these events. Initially, they

---

* First published in World Economy and International Relations. Issue 1, 2012.

limited themselves to making public statements in support of the protests, but did not try to lead them or redirect them to the right ideological direction. In full accordance with the Chinese proverb about a wise monkey watching tigers fight from a mountaintop, they had been waiting until the process of democratization cleared the political arena for their active and safe participation. At the same time, they had been making political statements and arranging local protests to remind of themselves. After the victory of the protesters, Islamic parties were among the winners of the carried out or planned elections in Tunisia, Egypt and Libya.

In the light of historical comparative studies

The collocation "Arab Spring", which became the name of the turbulent socio-political (and, to a much lesser extent, economic) processes and changes in North Africa and the Middle East, is certainly intended not to indicate the calendar dates of the events, but to establish an association with the process of awakening and renewal. Structurally, the term is neither new nor original. It is a reminiscent allusion to the similar events in Europe – to the bourgeois-democratic revolutions of 1848 that are known in historiography as the Spring of Nations. This refers not only to formal resemblance. In our opinion, what is happening today in the Arab world may have the same fundamental importance for the formation of a new social balance and for the transition to new types of relations as the 1848 Spring of Nations had for Europe.

As is known, at the time the revolutionary events engulfed almost the entire continent (except the UK, Russia, and the Ottoman Empire) and led to the fall of the monarchy in some countries and to the abolition of absolutism in others. They facilitated a change in the political paradigms dominant in the region. The old "European" and the current "Arab Spring" have a lot of similarities – fundamental and formal, for both the first and the second were the result of a complex combination of reasons, objective and subjective conditions.

At the time of the Spring of Nations, the social upheavals came as a result of deep and multifaceted changes taking place in the European society during the first half of the 19th century. These changes included technological advances, which entailed a certain improvement in the life of the working class; an increase in the number of civil servants and technical specialists; the growing consciousness of many social strata that were previously "politically inert"; the changing place and role of religion in the minds of the masses; slow "dilution" and liberalization of absolutist political systems. New political ideas proclaiming the supremacy of universal values – liberalism, nationalism, and socialism – were gaining in popularity. The essence, nature and methods of political parties were evolving. New ways of transnational dissemination of radical revolutionary views through revolutionary networks were developed and became practically effective.

In order to mobilize the masses for revolutions, new media and technological innovations were used. Popular and affordable press, leaflets and other printed materials (mass illustrated print) became the weapons of propaganda. Two technological breakthroughs in the field of communication and information – telegraph and photography (formerly – daguerreotypes) – at the time were comparable in their significance to today's Internet. Information was transmitted instantly over long distances, overcoming any boundaries. Photographs began to replace drawings in the newspapers, which made the reader a party to the events and raised the level of trustworthiness and accuracy of the disseminated information in one's eyes.

The growth in literacy gave the individual the ability to learn about an event on one's own, collect information, generalize and document the situation, defend one's rights in a more qualified manner, and make demands.

The similarity of the two "springs" can also be seen in the dynamics of economic conditions during the events. The Spring of Nations was preceded by the onset of the deepest global economic crisis (the Great Crisis of 1847–1850), which interrupted a long period of unprecedented economic growth. While the Arab Spring was preceded by a bank collapse in the financial center of the world – the U.S., a similar phenomenon – the Panic of 1847 – took place a year before the European Spring of Nations in the financial capital of the world of that time – the City of London. In both cases, the reason was that banks pumped money in financial bubbles. However, in the 19th century, it was not the bubble of overpriced real estate, as was the case in our time, but the overvalued shares of railway companies. The severity of the situation and the consequences for the international financial system were such that the Bank of England requested a suspension of the Bank Charter Act, which prohibited the issuance of bills not backed 100 percent by gold, until the end of the crisis[1]. Otherwise, the main bank of the country, its emission center, and the government's banker would have been on the verge of a technical default. Very soon the crisis spread to the rest of the Old and New Worlds. The situation was aggravated by a sharp rise in food prices in Europe caused by the disastrous harvests of 1845–46, which greatly increased the degree of discontent among the broad masses of the continent's population.

Thus, we can see that the conditions in which the two revolutionary waves of the 19th and 20th centuries, which became turning points for their regions (and, in fact, for the corresponding cultural and civilizational areas), spilled are typologically very similar if not identical. It is about a destruction of formerly dominant social ties and relations, the technical and communication changes and innovations that contributed to the destruction, as well as the internal and external economic background of the crises. With appropriate adjustments for time, place, and technological advances, one can see similarly significant preconditions, causes and determinants of social unrest both in 19th century Europe and in the contemporary Greater Middle East.

Transitology: three transitions away from a revolution

The aforementioned parallels are by no means provided as curious historical curiosities. Comparative analysis provides a reason to hypothesize that the current Arab Spring (assuming that it really marks the beginning of the region's transformation from a "sanctuary of authoritarianism" to an "experimental field of democracy") is a similar result of a combination of three types of transitions in Arab societies at the turn of the millennia: economic, demographic, and ideological (including informational aspect).

Economic transition is manifested in qualitative transformation of Arab economies in 1990–2010 associated with their forced modernization and adaptation to global economic trends (globalization, integration, liberalization, technologization, and a change in the balance of power in the world economy). Domestic economic situation in the Arab countries became more dependent on the world market than ever before. Economic transition affected, in particular, a general increase in the living standards of the Arab population, its social mobility and material and spiritual needs.

Demographic transition. Most Arab countries are entering the so-called third phase of this transition. There is a real threat that they will fall into a demographic trap. In many of these countries, processes of modernization have led to a significant drop in fertility and slower population growth (Tables 1 and 2)[2]. In Tunisia, Egypt, Algeria, Lebanon, and Saudi Arabia, the fertility rate fell by more than 40% compared to the value before the beginning of transition. As these trends started only 10–15 years ago, and the average life expectancy in the region has reached 70 years, in most countries (but not all!) mortality has hardly increased. Only the proportion of children under 12 years has begun to decline. At the same time, huge numbers of young people aged 15-30 have entered into active life and now quantitatively dominate society. More than 60% of the population of the Arab countries is under 30 years of age. Youth unemployment is extremely high, and their social prospects are limited or uncertain, leading to political discontent and protest moods. Specific configurations of demographic trends have led to social exclusion and radicalization of a part of the youth and a desire to change the existing social paradigm.

Ideological transition in Arab countries follows from the previous two and is manifested in undermining the traditional system of values and broad development of an individual-oriented system, and in the corresponding change in norms of behavior, including demographic and social ones. It is associated with fundamental changes in Arab societies: both with endogenous characteristics of their development (economic conditions, demographic trends, rising literacy and self-consciousness of the masses, for who the framework of social and economic opportunities provided by the existing structure of society is already too narrow) and external influences on the situation inside Arab societies (the penetration of Western culture, stereotypes and value categories, availability of information and means of mobilizing the masses, growing number of those working abroad, dependence of the regimes on external sponsors and on food imports, etc.). There is a significant increase in the degree of freedom in the choice of individual goals and the means to achieve them, not excluding the destruction of traditional values and violent regime changes.

Thus, the dialectic of subjective and objective, and endogenous and exogenous in the events is as follows. Under the influence of global processes and trends, objective prerequisites for the transition to a more modern type of social relations, greater social mobility and wider growth opportunities (career, economic, spiritual) for the citizens have long been accumulating in the region. The need for social modernization was dictated by the outcome of economic development of the past decades and by an improvement in market relations.

Table 1

Widespread improvements in the Human Development Index, 1970–2010

	Life expectancy			Literacy			Gross enrolment			Income		
	Value	% change		Value	% change		Value	% change		Value	% change	
	2010	1970–2010	1990–2010	2010	1970–2010	1990–2010	2010	1970–2010	1990–2010	2010	1970–2010	1990–2010
Developing countries	68	21	8	81	61	21	66	28	24	5873	184	89
Arab States	**70**	**37**	**10**	**74**	**149**	**41**	**64**	**89**	**22**	**8603**	**66**	**44**
East Asia	73	23	9	94	76	18	69	7	31	6504	1183	352
South Asia	65	33	12	66	113	46	59	64	29	3398	162	119
Sub-Saharan Africa	52	19	7	65	183	43	54	109	42	1466	20	28
Latin America	74	24	9	92	27	10	83	59	16	11 092	88	42

Source: The UNDP Human Development Report. N.Y., 2010. P. 2.

Immediately before the Arab Spring the region demonstrated the best sustained economic growth in three decades, and this applied both to the rich oil-producing countries and countries with no oil resources. While there still are very significant cross-country differences, over the last twenty five years

112

the economies of all, without exception, Arab states have considerably advanced along the path of modernization and growth. In all these countries, there was an improvement in real incomes, nutrition, medical care, and access to education. Indeed, somewhere in the world there may have been a more impressive growth, but the Arab region was ahead of East Asia in a number of aspects of human development and ahead of South Asia and Sub-Saharan Africa in all of the aspects (Table 1).

Weak links in the chain of arab autocracies

However, as the history (including Russian) shows, the real and absolute indicators of human development are not always decisive in situations of growing social discontent, flares of "people's wrath", or various "revolutionary" events. In contrast, relative indicators and comparisons (interclass, interethnic, inter-religious, gender, cross-national, etc.) become very powerful tools of mobilizing masses and popular discontent. For the practical use of such tools it is absolutely necessary to have a subjective factor – social forces and their organizations able to implant such comparisons (not necessarily corresponding to the reality) in the minds of members of society and turn them into stereotypes of public perception. In the conditions of the post-industrial globalized information space and virtualization of communication, a subjective factor can be easily transformed into objective reality.

Similar to Russia, where the struggle between the Westerners and the Slavophiles (statists) historically determined the nature and direction of the country's development, in modern Arab societies there are two powerful cultural and civilizational components, which are in dialectical unity and confrontation: one based on the traditional Arab-Islamic values, the other – on the Europe-oriented modernization, which formed in the 19th century and entrenched in the years of colonial rule.

At the time of the Arab Spring the two poles agreed on the need for profound political change and began to seek a regime change singly or jointly. Islamic organizations and liberal democratic movements were equally in opposition to their governments, which usually tried to combine both components in their policies. The fatal miscalculation of the ruling elites in Egypt and Tunisia was that they themselves were de facto integrated in the global society and the global market, becoming part of the international elite, owners of transnational companies, and recipients of the "modernization dividend", and did not take into account that the growing gap in the levels of consumption, access to social benefits and simple creature comforts would not be quietly accepted by other social layers. After all, they also were not isolated from global liberal and democratic trends, *not least thanks to the modernization policies of the authorities themselves.*

All Arab states have been involved in the process of globalization, the fashion and direction of which are defined by highly developed countries with established democratic systems. In this sense, it is no surprise that the revolution breaks "weak links" – Arab autocracies. Egypt and Tunisia are the countries more open to the global trends, more secularized, and with regular and multifaceted ties with the West. At the same time, such countries as Saudi Arabia or Kuwait, which cooperate closely with the United States, exercise their contacts with the West through a more limited number of channels – oil, military, and security ones, but block "unnecessary", from their perspective, ties, and restrict foreign influence in cultural, informational and other fields.

More autocratic Arab states, in which forms of government and the organization of power are much less modern and more distant from the democratic, easily survived the Arab Spring. Thus, when we talk about "weak links" in the chain of Arab autocracies we really mean "not strong (tough) enough autocracies" in Tunisia and Egypt in comparison with, for example, the monarchies of the Arabian Peninsula.

The aforementioned failures of "weak links" are frequently qualified as "democratic revolutions" in the Arab world. How scientifically valid the use of this term is we will only be able to see later, when contemporaries or descendants will have assessed the real impact of these events on the existing socio-political paradigms in Arab societies and apprehended the depth of this impact. In the meantime, we are unwittingly trapped by stereotypes, believing that a revolution entails the introduction of more democratic and progressive principles of governance.

In this sense, the Arab Spring has not had yet such consequences in any country. However, the marker "revolution" has already become associated with the ongoing socio-political discourse, so not to fall out of the boundaries of the latter we are forced to use the rooted terminology.

Nevertheless, it is methodologically incorrect to bracket all externally similar "revolutionary struggles" that unfolded in North Africa and the Middle East. While in Egypt and Tunisia there was a real mass popular uprising (albeit supported from the outside), the course of the events in Libya and Syria was more like an attempt to remove the "deviant" ("wrongly" oriented) Arab regimes under the cover of the Arab Spring.

Between the "youth bulge" and the "pentagram of despair"

The statistics and the actual situation in Tunisia and Egypt – the two countries where popular unrest led to the downfall of existing political regimes – were by no means the worst in the Arab world. Libya's main economic indicators, which characterize living standards and social benefits, were generally better than the average for the region (Table 2). However, the

114

subjective perception by the bulk of the population of the results of economic development and the outcome of the reforms of recent years turned out to be negative. The reason for that is the combination of short-sighted social policy of ruling elites, which appropriated the lion's share of generated income and wealth, on the one hand, and, on the other hand, the incessant anti-government propaganda carried out by Islamic and liberal-democratic political circles.

In any revolution the key is its driving forces, i.e. classes and social groups interested in fundamental changes and trying to introduce them. The protesting masses in Egypt and Tunisia were a motley mix. It included all social strata except possibly for civil servants and law enforcement representatives. In the conditions of the Arab Spring it is quite difficult to identify the narrow social groups concerned. The class approach is not appropriate here.

Table 2

Some indicators of socio-economic development in the Arab countries, 2010–2011

Countries by HDI[1] rank (165 ranked countries)	Population (2011)			Average age of marriage		GDP per capita[2], USD (2010)	Population living on under $2 a day (PPP), %[3]	HDI (2010)	Gini Index, %	Internet users, % (2008)	Satisfaction with Life Index[4]
Algeria (84)	36.3	47	1.4	29	33	4029	26	0.677	35.3	11.9	5.6
Bahrain (39)	1.23	44	2.1	26	30	26000	10	0.801		51.9	
Egypt (101)	84.5	52	1.7	23		2270	39	0.620	32.1	20	5.8
Jordan (82)	6.4	54	1.9	25	29	4216	21	0.681	37.7	26	5.7
Iraq[5]	31.5	61	3.1	23		2090	25				5.5
Yemen (133)	24.1	65	3.0	23	25	1118	58	0.439	31.2	1.6	4.8
Qatar (38)	1.7	34	2.9	26	28	69754		0.803	41.1	34	6.7
Kuwait (47)	2.6	37	2.4	27	29	54260		0.771		34.3	6.6
Lebanon[5]	4.1	43	0.7	27	31	8175	30			22.5	4.7
Libya (53)	6.2	47	0.8	29	32	9714	7	0.755		5.1	
Mauritania (136)	3.3	59	2.2	22	29	921	44	0.433	39.0	1.9	5.0
Morocco (114)	31.7	48	1.0	26	31	2811	25	0.567	40.9	33	5.8

115

Country											
UAE (32)	4.6	31	2.2	24	27	50000	19	0.815		65.2	7.3
Oman[5]	2.7	52	1.9	25	28	16207					
Saudi Arabia (55)	28.7	51	2.1	25	27	14540		0.752		30.8	7.7
Syria (111)	22.2	56	1.7	25	29	2474	30	0.589		16.8	5.9
Sudan (154)	40.2	59	2.4	23	29	1294	40	0.379		10.2	5.0
Tunisia (81)	10.6	42	1.0	27	30	3792	8	0.683	40.8	27.5	5.9

[1] Human Development Index.
[2] At the current exchange rate.
[3] $2 a day is the International Poverty Line according to the World Bank ($1,15 for Sub-Saharan Africa).
[4] Maximum is 10 (Russia – 5.9).
[5] No ranking available.

Calculated based on: http://web.worldbank.org/wbsite/external/topics/extpoverty/ 0,,contentMDK:22569498~pagePK:148956~piPK:216618~theSitePK:336992,00. html; The UNDP Human Development Report. N.Y., 2010. P. 161–163; 176; http://www. internetworldstats.com/stats.htm; http://unstats.un.org/unsd/demo graphic/products/indwm/tab1c.htm;http://unstats.un.org/unsd/demographic/products/ indwm/ tab2b.htm#tech

Formally, the uprisings looked like the struggle for political freedom against the ruling bureaucracies of Tunisia and Egypt. Objectively, for most of the population (especially for the peasants and the urban poor) it is not the most pressing problem. The part of the society potentially to benefit the most from the triumph of revolutionary slogans is the one that was called the "commoners" during the European Spring of Nations, but it is quite a conditional comparison. Besides, it is too early to judge the actual results of the popular uprisings. So far, there has not been a real change of the governing elites.

Both the class and confessional approaches are not suitable for determining the driving forces behind the popular uprisings, with an exception of Bahrain, where the conflict clearly occurred between the Shiite community and the Sunni ruling minority. Frequent clashes between the Christians and the Muslims in Egypt and the confrontation between the Alawites and the rest of the ethnic and religious groups of Syria, which is so strongly propagated by the West, despite their reality do not constitute the essence of the socio-political and economic contradictions in these countries.

The most organized groups in an Arab society are national security, defense and law enforcement agencies, on the one hand, and religious, Islamist

116

associations, on the other. It was believed that secular liberal groups are weak, fragmented and unlikely to become a significant political force in the near future. This, however, did not prevent first the United States and later the European Union from maintaining consistent efforts to support and strengthen these structures – so-called civil society organizations – over decades.

By the end of the 1990s, U.S. foreign policy was increasingly attaching special importance to demographic factors in geopolitical forecasting, strategic planning and implementation of specific foreign policy objectives. With regard to the "failed states" and Muslim regions, a growing attention was paid to the foreign policy approaches[3] based on the theory of the youth bulge[4], according to which developing societies undergoing demographic transition from high to low fertility and mortality rates are especially vulnerable to civil conflict due to the growing number of disaffected youths. The explosive potential, on the one hand, represents a threat to Western interests (primarily in terms of the radicalization of Muslim youth), but, on the other hand, can be used to promote democracy[5]. Since the late 1990s the youth has become the main target group for indoctrination.

In 2009 the National Endowment for Democracy established by the U.S. Congress funded 23 Egyptian, 21 Palestinian, 13 Yemeni, 10 Jordanian, 8 Lebanese, 3 Tunisian, 3 Libyan, 3 Syrian, 3 Algerian and 1 Kuwaiti NGOs, mainly for the purpose of working with the youth audience in different fields of democracy promotion and civil society development. In particular, earmarked grants were aimed at organizing training in mobilizing masses, conducting outreach and propaganda projects, creating online media and websites, circumventing censorship and countering attempts to block information on the Internet. Grant amounts ranged from 19 to 385 thousand dollars per organization[6].

It appears that the choice of the youth as a tool and, at the same time, an object of management of social processes is explained by the following considerations. It is the only easily indentified social group – not by class but by age – with the ability to turn into an effective driving force for the transformation of the political paradigm of Arab societies. In the first decade of the 21st century, sustainable and dynamic economic growth in Arab countries potentially created conditions for the long-awaited breakthrough in the socio-economic standing of older youth groups. However, this did not happen. The age paradigms of income distribution, social benefits, and social influence remained unchanged. Moreover, the age of public recognition gradually increased with the aging of the ruling elite. Due to the immobility of social and political paradigms, the educated middle (20–24 years) and senior (25–30 years) youth groups inevitably found themselves in a deadlock with regard to almost all five key areas of public life: education, work/career, income, op-

portunity to buy own home and build a family. We have called this phenomenon the "pentagram of despair" and schematically depicted relations
and dependencies in the figure.

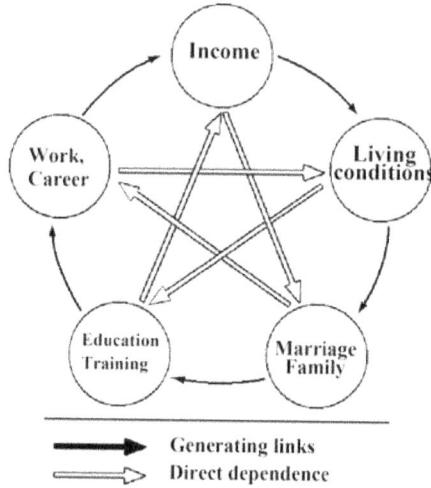

**Figure. "Pentagram of despair" is a vicious circle depicting lack of
social prospects for Arab youth.**

In practice, in the specific conditions of Arab countries the situation is as
follows. Youth unemployment in the region is twice the world average (20-
40% compared with 10–20% world average). Excess incomes of Arab countries from the rent of natural resources (not only oil, but also, for example,
international tourism, i.e. attractive climate, sea, etc.) led to a large increase
in the prices on urban real estate. This limited the opportunities for young
people to purchase their own homes. The lack of money and housing raised
the age of marriage and having first child. However, in the societies where
traditional values are still strong a failure in these areas means far more than,
for example, in the West. As a consequence, in our opinion, a critical mass of
explosive material, which became the driving force of the Arab revolutions,
formed in these countries.

The described "brand of hopelessness" is placed on Arab youth mostly at
the stage of education, which is traditionally focused primarily on preparing
for clerical work in the public sector. This is contrary to the objective needs
of modern Arab economies. Indeed, the past two or three decades have witnessed the vector of development directed in the opposite direction – towards
accelerated growth in the private sector, real industrial production and ser-

vice industry. As a result of such incongruity, graduates are bound to wait for jobs in the public sector for several years. On the other hand, as practice shows, graduates themselves are not very eager to seek less comfortable places of employment.

In *Tunisia*, 70 thousand young people annually receive a quality education of a European (or, rather, French) standard. However, the Tunisian economy cannot absorb even half the mentioned number of graduates. The problem is predetermined by the scale and structure of the economy, on the one hand, and the list of specialties, in which Tunisian graduates are educated, on the other. The selected specialties mostly correspond to humanitarian, economic and law professions.

Authorities tried to solve the problem at least partially by establishing a program to encourage graduates – writers, economists and jurists – to work as teachers in the hinterlands. But there were difficulties here as well. Unlike other Arab countries, Tunisia has very little increase in the number of teaching jobs because of low population growth (even lower than the European average). Young graduates prefer to migrate to the West en masse rather than get a decent but modestly paid work in the Tunisian hinterlands. They dream of finding a job in Europe, preferably in its francophone part, which fits with their contemporary values, ideas and attitudes. They go there in thousands legally or illegally.

Objective negative processes that were specific for Egypt (but not foreign to other Arab countries) were growing against the backdrop of slow but very real social modernization in accordance with the recommendations of its Western neoliberal allies; the processes were registered by the authorities but neglected in the framework of real policies.

The specificity of Egypt is in its relative overpopulation (4% of its territory is home to nearly 95% of its 80 million population, i.e. the actual density is 1540 people per square kilometer, one of the highest in the world). The glaring inequality and human overcrowding make large-scale protests more probable and social conflicts more intense. The authorities, as a rule, tried to solve the problem "manually" – they artificially supported minimum (and even slowly growing) levels of consumption, while actively engaging in the prevention of possible organized protests.

The delicate balance which rested on a complex system of food and agricultural subsidies and measures of direct regulation of agricultural production was gradually upset by economic liberalization. The government abolished the system of compulsory production of certain crops, particularly cereals. In accordance with neoliberal approaches, it changed the concept of food security. If earlier an emphasis was placed on meeting the food needs of the country at the expense of domestic production, now the prevailing opinion is that one must develop industries which

119

have comparative competitive advantages in the world market (e.g. tourism) and import the lacking food with surplus revenues from competitive industries.

The same reasoning was used to eliminate restrictions on agricultural exports. Fellahin gradually switched from supplying the domestic market to growing products for export, for example, early vegetables for the EU, oranges, nuts, etc. As a result, the gap between domestic and global agricultural prices slowly began to decrease, international and domestic food prices began to converge, which was the cherished goal of the reformers. By 2008, the gap was still enormous, but the country was swept with food riots. Some of the riots were suppressed, and the decision to postpone other reforms weakened the rest.

The ruling elite, lulled by successful economic growth (in 2006–2008, GDP grew by more than 6% annually, or by $22 billion), enthusiastically engaged in self-enrichment. While the poorest 20% of the population received only 9% of the country's income, the richest 20% appropriated 41.5%[7]. Increased foreign investment and foreign exchange earnings were used irrationally. Some of the capital was plundered for personal consumption or secretively exported. In 2006 and 2007, capital flight from Egypt associated with the manipulation of contract prices in foreign trade operations, kickbacks, corruption incomes and real estate operations abroad amounted to $13.0 and $13.6 billion respectively. Since the beginning of the crisis and the associated reduction in opportunities for illegal enrichment (due to a reduction in foreign investment, falling trade, and foreign aid) capital flight has declined to $7.4 billion annually[8].

To reduce the impact of the crisis, in 2009 the Egyptian authorities introduced new government subsidies for agricultural exports, and domestic prices resumed their growth. Already in the first half of 2010 inflation amounted to 11% on an annualized basis. At the same time, the prices of basic staples – vegetables – increased by 45% compared to 2009[9].

The worst, however, lied ahead. At the end of August 2010 it was announced that due to an unprecedented drought in Russia Egypt would not receive 540,000 tons of relatively cheap Russian wheat, which were to be delivered under a contract. Russia annually met about a third of the country's demand. However, by the time of the embargo, about 180,000 tons had already been delivered. The Russian embargo did not lead to a famine in the country. Egypt had carryover reserves of 3 million tons (enough to meet the needs for 4–5 months). Upon receipt of the information, the lacking volumes were quickly purchased in France and the United States. However, these purchases cost Egypt an additional $40 per ton[10].

By the fall of 2010, the prices of food and consumer goods increased sharply, while the demand for labor fell. October 25, 2010 an unexpectedly large demonstration of several youth groups and opposition movements was held in front of the Council of Ministers in Cairo. They had not only economic but also political demands. That was two months before the events in Tunisia...

On the democratic principles of internationalism

Indeed, in every country the ripening of a social explosion is a unique process. What is happening is always defined by a set of circumstances, causes and factors, their specific mutual influence and interaction. In the complete absence of internal prerequisites of a social explosion, no external impulse could cause a revolutionary upsurge and mass demonstrations. On the other hand, without a corresponding external background and moral, political, and, last but not least, material support from the outside, the revolutions in Tunisia and Egypt, let alone Libya, would have had no real prospects. The governments of these countries could have suppressed discontent at a greater or lesser cost, as it happened more than once in Arab history (including with the use of weapons and funds provided by friendly Western powers).

However, this time the protests of the opposition forces, which demanded democratization, gained external support. Western democracies provided the protesters with the necessary technical capability to organize and consolidate their forces, whereas in Libya they even participated in the conflict on the side of the opposition. At the same time, the Arab governments were under a constant pressure to avoid taking decisive action that could have lead to the liquidation of the protests and the suppression of the riots.

Why did the West turn its back on its proteges despite the fact that the Arab revolutions, according to Western politicians themselves, caught them by surprise and that it were the most reliable "moderate" Arab regimes, which were in the forefront of the struggle with the Islamists, that fell under attack?

Here we should discuss a very interesting phenomenon in international relations that began with the collapse of the USSR, but fully revealed itself only in the 21st century in the course of the "color revolutions". While the United States has long been preaching the "export of democracy", in Europe the doctrine of "democratic internationalism" – named so due to the well-known analogy – has recently acquired practical outlines. As the experience of recent decades shows, the essence of the doctrine is that countries of "developed democracy" consider it their internationalist duty to help the underdeveloped countries and peoples to step out of the era of totalitarianism and authoritarianism and into the era of democracy. This noble goal is implemented through external expansion – territorial, institutional, regulatory, and, of course, ideological. The danger of this principle is that in the eyes of those who adhere to it, it is a sufficient basis for ignoring or "stretching" norms of international law to fit one's needs and for justifying a direct armed aggression in the name of "democratic expediency". The West seems to have fallen into the same ideological trap that the USSR once did. In some cases, conflicts and changes in the situation directly harm it, at least in the short to medium term (for example, there is an increased risk of acts by terrorists and religious extremists, illegal migration, and conflict areas are getting closer, etc.). However, due to the ideological necessity, it is forced to support the escapades of revolutionary forces that call themselves democratic. *"Democratic internationalism" has become one of the determinants of contemporary foreign policy of the West and consequently a key factor in international relations in the 21st century.*

With regard to the Arab region, the United States and the European Union are implementing a number of official programs for democratization and liberalization of native regimes. It is a system of interconnected measures of political, economic and military-strategic pressure, which is very diverse, has many levels, and all its elements are strategically coordinated. In the United States it is coordinated at the level of the Congress and the State Department, while in the European Union – at the collective level through the so-called European Neighborhood and Partnership Instrument and the European Instrument for Democracy and Human Rights, as well as national programs.

In Egypt the U.S. employed two types of instruments: bilateral agreements and direct grants. USAID alone provided $51 million in 2006–2008 and $20 million in 2009 for the promotion of democracy in Egypt. It was planned to allocate $25 million in 2010–2011, but according to Egyptian press the amount for 2011 alone was twice the figure. In addition, about $3 million was provided in 2009 for the development of civil society and $1 million – in assistance to non-governmental organizations[11]. The programs were carried out in three main areas: rule of law and human rights, good governance, and civil society. Through direct grants the U.S. directly funded Egyptian non-governmental organizations and "other civil society organizations". Meanwhile the American side believed that it was entitled to do so without coordination with the Egyptian government, and Cairo insisted on the opposite.

Assistance to the development of democracy has not ceased with the victory of the revolution. In the summer of 2011 in Egypt there was a scandal in connection with the U.S. refusal to inform the new authorities about the organizations receiving Washington's financial and technical assistance in the run-up to elections scheduled for the autumn of that year. Washington insisted on subsidizing Egyptian civil society organizations directly and "without the permission of the Egyptian government". Cairo rejected this position and demanded that Washington disclosed details regarding the structure of assistance and named its beneficiaries. In particular, there were $42 million allocated for Egyptian organizations in June 2011. The White House refused to make the disclosure, continuing to channel U.S. money to Egyptian civil organizations at own discretion, and the authorities threatened to reject the entire amount of U.S. aid in the amount of $2 billion in the name of protecting Egypt's sovereignty[12].

The main difference between American and European motives to intervene in the region is that it is geographically close to Europe and distant from the U.S. The risk of unexpected developments in the region, which is a key energy supplier to the EU, fuels the desire of the latter to carry out such reforms that would guarantee the region's dependence on the EU for the foreseeable period of time. The EU has compensated for the lack of effective military power with a complex interplay of contractual relations called neighborhood and partnership agreements. These included: the New Integration Strategy of the EU in the Southern Mediterranean (1992), the Barcelona Declaration (1995), the EU's Common Strategy on the Mediterranean Region (2000), a five-year work program adopted at the Barcelona Summit in 2005 (the Barcelona Process), the Union for the Mediterranean (2008), etc.

In this context, regime changes in the southern and eastern Mediterranean would mark the completion of the process of establishing a belt of "young democracies" that would provide security and favorable economic conditions at the southern perimeter of the European Union. If so, in less than ten years we should expect political innovations in the region of the EU's Eastern Partnership as well. Following the successful completion of this process, "Fortress Europe" will be surrounded on the outside by a reliable wall of dependent states, which will recognize the European Union as their "big brother" and diligently reform their political, economic and cultural space in accordance with the stringent requirements of Brussels, which are referred to as "European standards". This in turn guarantees the European Union an opportunity to extract excessive profits in the region for decades to come at the envy of its powerful competitors – the USA and China. After all, the worst case scenario for a united Europe would be the formation of a permanent "crescent of instability" controlled by its competitors and lying along the entire length of the arc stretching from the Atlas Mountains to the Bialowieza Forest.

The preservation of aging "moderate" Arab regimes no longer contributed to resolving the problem of strategic security in the future. Some of them were more loyal to Washington or Beijing than Brussels, and some altogether hostile. A rotation of power was inevitable in the coming years in any case, and it would be better to implement it according to a plan that would simultaneously guarantee some useful institutional changes. However, the West overestimated the willingness of the Arab world to adopt the "export version" of democracy. There has really taken place relative democratization of Arab societies in a number of parameters, but the downside was the strengthening of the position of the Islamists and traditionalists.

Essentially, the Arab spring again raised the question of the possibility and cost of "transplanting" democracy in its Euro-Atlantic incarnation.

For Russia, the changes will mean a definite but not too burdensome complication of conditions for the realization of its own policies and plans (if there are any) in the region. Moscow was unable or unwilling to demonstrate any own interest in the unfolding situation in a determined fashion and once again chose to follow the mainstream trends formed without its active participation. The cost of that may be a substantial (though not critical) reduction in benefits from the relatively insignificant but tangible economic cooperation with the countries of the region. Larger potential losses can be expected if the new model of integration between the EU and the Mediterranean region radically complicates energy cooperation between Russia and the EU.

Thus, for "certain forces" in the world the Arab Spring was an anticipated and welcomed change in the region. From their perspective, the Middle East and North Africa "lagged behind" the rest of the world in terms of democratization, liberalization and transfer of their sovereign powers in the field of economy, culture, and law to supranational democratic structures and entities. The revolutionary shock led the Arab world out of its own version of the "well-off stagnation". Regardless of whether it was the result of a natural internal process or had been artificially stimulated from the outside, the Arab Spring became a catalyst of internal social dynamics of Arab societies but also a factor of destabilization in the region. The probability of the Arab Spring spreading all over the region is low – in fact, if the spring rains pour out in Saudi Arabia, the world oil prices will skyrocket and hurt the already ailing world economy. Is there anyone who needs this?

The history of European democracy indicates that immediately after the Spring of Nations there was a long period of reinvention, "traditional national values" and continent-wide instability, which lasted till the end of the 1930s. The Arab Spring may lead to the establishment of Islamic regimes of a varying degree of enlightenment or conservatism. However, many observers believe that if the Islamic Winter does come, it will come democratically – through elections, referendums, independent mass media and parliamentary law making.

---

[1] See: *Huerta de Soto, Jesús*. Money, Bank Credit, and Economic Cycles. Ludwig von Mises Institute. Auburn (AL), 2009. P. 484.

[2] Hereinafter, unless otherwise indicated, UN is the source of population statistics (UN Demographic and Social Statistics – http://unstats.un.org/unsd/demographic/products/indwm/statistics.htm#Population).

[3] For more information on methodologies of approaches (including mathematical calculations of validity and applicability) see: *I. Abramova, L. Fituni, A. Sapunzov* "Emerging" and "Failed" States in the World Economy and International Politics M., Institute for African Studies. RAS. 2007 (in Russian).

[4] The theory was established by American political scientists J. Goldstone, G. Fuller and German sociologist G. Heinsohn. Its elements formed the basis of the U.S. policy for the practical management of social processes and the promotion of democracy in Arab countries. See: *Goldstone J.* Revolution and Rebellion in the Early Modern World. Berkeley (CA), 1991; *Goldstone J.* Revolutions of the Late Twentieth Century. Berkeley (CA), 1991; *Fuller G.* The Demographic Backdrop to Ethnic Conflict: A Geographic Overview / The Challenge of Ethnic Conflict to National and International Order in the 1990s. Wash., 1995. P. 151–154; *Heinsohn G.* Söhne und Weltmacht : Terror im Aufstieg und Fall der Nationen. Zürich, 2003.

[5] In relation to the practice of U.S. foreign policy, these approaches are disclosed, for example, in articles by Richard Cincotta, an expert at the National Intelligence Council's Long Range Analysis Unit (See: *Cincotta Richard P.* Authoritarianism as a Form of Sustained Low-Intensity Civil Conflict: Does Age Structure Provide Insights into the Democratic Transition? (http://paa2007.princeton.edu/download.acpx?submissionid=70909) and Navtej Dhillon, the Director of the Middle East Youth Initiative at the Brookings Institution (See: *Navtej Dhillon.* The Role of the U.S. in the Middle East (http://www.shababinclusion.org/content/blog/ detail/986/).

[6] According to the latest 2009 annual report of the Endowment. See: http://www.ned.org/publications/ annual-reports/2009-annual-report. The annual report for the previous year is usually published in June, but in June 2011 it did not appear on the official website.

[7] In 2011, the World Bank published data for 2005 (See: World Development Indicators. 2011. The World Bank. Wash., 2011. P. 68). It is most likely that the gap further increased over the next three years of economic boom.

[8] See: http://www.financialtaskforce.org/2011/01/26/now-egypt-there-goes-the-neighborhood

[9] See: http://news.egypt.com/en/2010051110713/news/-business/ egypt-capmas-inflation-hits-11-pct.html

[10] See: http://www.reuters.com/article/2010/08/16/us-grain-russia-drought-idUST RE67F24W20100816

[11] See: Audit of USAID/Egypt's Democracy and Governance Activities. USAID. Audit Report № 6-263-10-001-P. Cairo. October 27. 2009.

[12] See: *Harun, Mohammed.* Khilaf al-Qahira wa Washington 'ala tamwil "al-mujtami'a al-madani" yu'arqilu barnamij al-musa'edat / al-masr al-yaum. 20 yuluyu (tamuz) 2011 (http://www.almasryalyoum.com/node/478990).

Nailia Fakhrutdinova

HAS THE "ARAB SPRING" REALLY HAPPENED? (ANOTHER LOOK AT THE EVENTS IN ARAB COUNTRIES)

Features of the arab political culture and potential for the formation of civil society[*]

The Arabs have a wonderful saying: the bush has bloomed, but the spring has not come. It means that there is something you have long dreamed of and hoped for but it has not happened. The so-called "Arab Spring", which pre-supposed economic growth and the rise in living standards, has failed to bring the expected results. To understand this phenomenon one should consider the characteristics of the political culture of the Arabs.

It is well known that the direct organizer and one of the most active participants of the "revolutions", "days of rage" and marches for change and democracy, as the series of overthrows in Arab countries was called in the world press, was the "Internet youth". However, in all of these countries other forces have benefited from the results of these triumphs. No wonder that the Arabs increasingly often use the term "stolen revolution" in their political lexicon. Many observers predicted the decline of political Islam and noted "an important trend – the decline of its role", that "Arab revolutions" rejected clerical ideas[1]. And indeed, one could not hear religious appeals among the insurrectionists.

However, in Egypt, Libya, and even in the most secular of Arab countries – Tunisia – we can observe a revival of Islamic parties and movements and even their coming to power.

"Fake democracies" – new democracies"?

In an interview with the ITAR-TASS news agency the leader of the "Cedar revolution" General Michel Aoun, who headed a new parliamentary majority in Lebanon in January 2011, said that the events in the Middle East were natural and would not lead to serious instability. According to him, it was a normal maturation process of civil societies. The masses that emerged on the political scene would sweep away "fake democracies", which would be replaced by elected governments. Aoun explained the phenomenon of Islamic movements as a "feature of human nature": under totalitarianism population turns to religion[2].

"Fake democracies" were overthrown, but "new democracies" have not been constructed. The Islamic factor has remained underestimated. The

---

[*] First published in *Azia i Afrika segodnya*. Issue 5, 2013.

Islamists won a crushing victory in Egypt's parliamentary elections. The Freedom and Justice Party (FJP) of the Muslim Brotherhood gained about 45% of all seats. The ultraconservative Salafi al-Nour Party and the liberal Wafd Party took second and third places, respectively[3].

The results of the first free elections in Tunisia were also unexpected. The Islamist Ennahda Party won a landslide victory, receiving more than 40% of the votes. It should be noted that Tunisia is one of the most westernized Arab countries, so a victory of an Islamist party was not expected here. Moreover, Ennahda had been banned. However, its leader Rachid al-Ghannouchi said that in his understanding Islam was not contrary to the democratic principles, and Turkish Prime Minister R. Erdogan during his visit to Tunisia stressed that democracy and Islam were not exclusive.

The turbulent situation in the Arab world forces the leaders of moderate states to take preventive measures. For example, Jordan's King Abdullah II for the first time in the history of the Hashemite dynasty came to the table with the Islamic Action Front (IAF) – the political wing of Jordan's Muslim Brotherhood. Under pressure from the opposition, in February 2011 the king lifted a ban on unsanctioned protests. Secretary General of the IAF Hamza Mansour called the decision of the authorities a "step in the right direction".

What is Islam for the Arabs?

Why do the Arabs again and again return to the Islamic ideology? It seemed that they fought for the democratization of public life, development of civil society, modernization of the economy and change in the leadership of their countries, but they lacked a modern ideology capable of inspiring the masses to achieve these goals.

In order to raise the people to revolt, revolt, just use people's dissatisfaction with their situation and their hatred of the elderly leaders. To lead the country for themselves, need ideas, and their leaders do not have modern.

In order to stir up a rebellion it is sufficient to use people's dissatisfaction with their situation and their hatred of the elderly leaders. To lead a country somewhere, one needs ideas, but their contemporary leaders have none.

The Arabs approach any new idea or trend primarily from the religious perspective. At the same time, as Egyptian scholar Muhammad An-Novaihi aptly noted, they "do not ask if the idea is right or wrong, the trend – useful or harmful, but are interested in whether it fits with their religion or contradicts it"[4]. Precisely this is the uniqueness of the Arab political culture: dominance of the religious worldview in the public consciousness of the population.

It should be emphasized that Islam is not just a religion, but it forms the social structures, influences the judiciary and education.

127

The concept of civil society, which Arabs strive to build, is based on the individual participation of citizen in social development. Religion is a powerful mobilizing force for such participation. The Muslims communicate with God more directly (individually) than the Christians, and their religion is not associated with a particular state or a system of government. This is why Islam has often become the banner of the struggle for a better lot (Algeria, Sudan).

The masses, especially the youth, are looking to religion for a solution to their dire socio-economic situation. At the same time, ruling regimes, opposition parties and movements, NGOs and even trade unions consider religion to be the most effective means of involving citizens in public life because the political slogans sanctified by religion are closer and more understandable to the masses. In this regard it should be noted that the concept of political religion is attributed to David Apter, a former director of the Institute of International Studies at the University of California, who saw it as one of the fundamental characteristics of political mobilization systems[5].

According to Prof. A. Malashenko of MGIMO, unlike Islam, other religions have had fundamentalist manifestations limited both in time and space. In some cases they are constrained by the secular character of the society, in others – they are focused on national or regional problems. "Only Islamism has become a geo-cultural and geo-political phenomenon, which is integrating the Muslim community, influencing not only its inner consciousness, but also its relations with the rest of the world"[6]. Prof. M. Kramer of Harvard University believes that the Islamists are transforming Islam from a traditional mix of faith and politics into an all-out ideological system, a modern "ism".

The image of the religious alternative is present in all Arab countries as a hope and a dream. Even the processes of democratization in these countries are carried out against the backdrop of the Islamization of politics. In this regard M. Sergeev, a well-known specialist in the modern history of the Arab countries of North Africa, formulated the following graphic phase: "every political action becomes religiously colored, and all that is related to religion becomes politicized"[7].

Even many non-religious organizations, initially purely religious and spiritual, later became political. For example, in 1970 in Tunisia there was established the Quranic Preservation Society (*Jamiya Tahfiz Al-Quran*), which enjoyed the support of the adherents of the "new course". According to the statement by its founders, the association had cultural and educational objectives. However, its activity soon acquired distinct political character, and the public started to compare it to the Muslim Brotherhood. In the early 1970s, there emerged a "very simple, almost imperceptible"[8] religious movement, which was masterminded by Rachid al-Ghannouchi (-shi), a teacher, and Abdelfattah Moore, a lawyer. Initially, the movement was limited to lectures in mosques, cultural and educational activities. In the late 1970s, it was renamed the Islamic Tendency Movement (*Al-ittijah al-islami*). Still during the formative period of the Islamic Tendency Movement, another movement called the Progressive Islamic Tendency (PIT – *Al-ittijah al-islami al-taqaddumi*) splintered from it. PIT believes that the problem of citizens is not whether to pray or not to pray, but to pray in the presence of human rights and fundamental freedoms.

In this connection, there is an interesting historical fact. The Muslim Brotherhood, Egypt's well-structured Islamic organization well-known for its political activity, which has branches not only in Arab countries and which is outlawed in many countries, has grown out of Muslim Boy Scouts.

Hassan al -Banna (the founder of the organization) turned to scouting in the early 1930s. He regarded the organization of Muslim Scouts as a union which could take over such functions as physical and combat training, ensuring the security of the meetings of the Muslim Brothers, spreading the influence of the association in Egypt by the means of charitable activities and participation in socially important matters – combating illiteracy, providing medical assistance during epidemics of cholera and malaria. The use of the Scout Movement was one of the first organizational forms that allowed gradually transforming a simple religious association – one of many in Egypt – into a powerful political force.

In the countries where the path of pluralist democracy was taken, Islamic fundamentalists took advantage of greater freedom of expression and elections to strengthen their political influence and compete with the authorities. For instance, Sudanese President Jaafar Nimeiri (1969–1985) flirted with the Islamists, which facilitated the strengthening of the religious phenomenon and establishment of the first Islamic state in Africa. An attempt by Egyptian President Anwar Sadat (1970–1981) to sacralize his policies led to a resurgence of religious extremism in a relatively secular state. For this, in fact, he paid with his life. (A. Sadat was assassinated by Islamic fundamentalist terrorist groups in October 1973 during the annual military parade to mark the anniversary of the Arab-Israeli war of 1973).

Many Arab leaders have tried to restrain this phenomenon by resorting to various means: using the army (Algeria); encouraging splits between organizations, as was the case with the Association of Muslim Youth and the Al-Adl Wal-Ihsan (Justice and Charity) Party (Morocco); attempting to cooperate with the Islamists or, on the contrary, to delegitimize them (Egypt, Sudan, Libya, etc.); introducing the policy of "controlled Islam" (Tunisia, Morocco).

For example, in Tunisia it was relatively quiet until the well-known events. Many Western observers attributed this to the fact that the country had followed a secular path since the independence, which largely determined the level of political culture of its citizens. Tunisia achieved almost universal bilingual literacy: Arabic and French. Educated Tunisians, who read the original Quran, found it difficult to confuse extremist ideas with ones.

Non-political religious organizations are engaged with teaching the basics of true Islam, publishing children books, and doing charity. They are numerous in almost all Arab countries, which fact proves the possibility of the co-existence of religious associations within civil society. This aspect is of paramount importance in terms of the relative failure of the ideas of Pan-Arabism, nationalism, and especially Arab socialism.

Geydar Dzhemal, a prominent Russian specialist in the field of political Islam and Islamic philosophy, believes that historically Islam in the Arab countries can be seen as a civil society in an absolute sense. The community of the Prophet Muhammad in Medina, in his opinion, was not a state, but a "self-organizing, self-governing brotherhood governed only by the authority and will of Allah as transmitted through his messenger"[9]. G. Dzhemal has introduced the term "self-sufficient community", the basis of which even in the contemporary society is a moral imperative. For a Muslim, such imperative, in his opinion, is not to allow yourself to be denied the status of an instrument of divine providence, i.e. not to be deprived of historical responsibility. However, it is precisely the variety of the network structure of non-governmental organizations that provides for the realization of civil society as a collective entity, which ultimately determines the historical and civilizational course. "However," A. Malashenko rightly pointed out, "the voice of the professional theologians is less important today."[10] He was echoed by Mark Sedgwick, professor at the American University in Cairo (AUC): "The most important sources of religious knowledge for Sunni Arabs are the media, the state and, perhaps, also the ulema."[11]

G. Dzhemal was convinced that after Marxism there remained only one universal internationalist approach to global issues: Islamic civilization. He cited the Quranic injunction: "O you who believe, obey Allah, and obey the Messenger, and those in authority from among you" (4:59). "From among you", in his opinion, was the key point.

Modern theologians – advocates of the cooperation of religion with civil society – believe that Islam is a socio-forming religion. In Islam, the social system and its main legal provisions are regulated at the level of the Divine Revelation. In other words, they are not a consequence of the desire of individuals to organize their social life or a result of development and harmonization of social and legal concepts, but an imperative requiring them to create a society based on the principles of Islam and rejecting all

130

other forms. However, when asked about the possibility of Muslim participation in civil society institutions, modern theologians come to very different conclusions – from the inevitability of conflict between classical Islam
(especially in its political form) and civil society to the feasibility of their
peaceful interaction.

Speaking about the role of Islam in the development of civil society in
the Arab world, it would be appropriate to quote the words of former UN
Secretary General Boutros Boutros-Ghali: "For poor countries that do not
have sufficient economic, technological and military power, ideology is their
substitute. Ideology explains their underdevelopment, serves as an instrument for international relations, provides leverage in world politics and a
dream about the future. Without such a dream the life of the poor would be
unbearable"[12].

Islam has become an ideology, a kind of <u>national idea</u> capable of uniting
citizens to solve problems facing their countries. Religion in the Arab countries is the basis of political culture. Of great importance is the emotional attitude of the population to their religion. For the Arabs Islam is not just a religion but a symbol of the former might.

The Turkish model of development – an alternative
to the real Arab "Spring"

Perhaps, that is why the Turkish model of development is currently so attractive for Arabs. The reason is that it promotes a form of government
which, as it seems, combines Islamic values and democracy.

After coming to power in Turkey, in late 2002 the Justice and Development Party (JDP) openly declared its Muslim self-identity in a secular state,
which enabled it to strengthen links with the Arab world . The speech by
Prime Minister Recep Tayyip Erdogan at the summit in Davos in 2009 de-
lighted the Arabs. Erdogan made harsh statements, which condemned Israel
for its military actions against the Palestinians, entered into a dispute with
Shimon Peres and the moderator of the meeting, and then completely left the
international forum, without having an opportunity to respond to the Israeli
president. The move was met with enthusiasm in the Islamic world. In many
countries, including Turkey, there took place mass rallies in support of the
Prime Minister.

Turkish investors have poured into Egypt, Tunisia and other countries;
Turkish culture and educational services are exported. The interest in the
Turkish model can be explained by the demand for modernity, economic development, establishment of political Islam and the desire to demilitarize the
governing structures.

Erdogan's visit to Egypt, Tunisia and Libya in September 2011 was
greeted with much admiration. After all, during his visit to Egypt, for exam-

ple, he promised to increase Turkish investment in the economy of the country by more than 3 times. Such a position is consistent with Turkey's adherence to its policy of neo-Ottomanism.

Features of the Arab political culture besides the predominance of the religious worldview in the public consciousness of the population

A peculiarity of the Arab political culture is worship of their leaders. Leaderism is one of their political priorities. In most cases, a charismatic leader comes at a crucial period in the development of society. In Arab society the charisma has historical traditions[13]. It may appear as the image of a party leader and a cleric (Hassan Al-Turabi in Sudan). Many of the processes occurring in these countries depend on the will and authority of a charismatic leader who has broad and comprehensive support of the masses. In this case, enthusiasm and trust of the population is more important than institutional and legal legitimacy.

Today the Arabs do not have such a person – a leader able to accumulate modern revolutionary spirit and tremendous energy of the masses and direct them to the benefit of the peoples of the Arab countries. Where could he appear from? The Internet community? Arabs need a charismatic leader, real orator, true fighter, diplomat, and, perhaps, revolutionary.

Charismatic leaders such G.A. Nasser (Egypt), Hassan II (Morocco), H. Bourguiba (Tunisia) and others have long been part of the general Arab history. In part it concerns Abdelaziz Bouteflika of Algiers. Possibly that is why it he has avoided the fate of North African presidents.

In this regard, one cannot forget the controversial but certainly great personality of Gaddafi. What has the Libyan opposition achieved? Currently in Libya there is a "war of all against all". Oil and gas deposits are protected by the international forces. No one cares about the population or, especially, the "human rights". Syria is now at the West's gunpoint. Now Bashir Assad has become the "bloody tyrant" who is killing his own people. And although the Syrian president has made considerable concessions – under the new constitution the leading role of the Baath Party has been abolished, a multiparty system has been introduced, the involvement of the opposition in government structures is being discussed – he still does not satisfy the West. One should remember that Gaddafi renounced Libya's nuclear program to please the international community, but it saved neither him nor Jamahiriya.

This creates a situation, which in chess is called zugzwang[14], when a legitimate president can do nothing in case of disorder; whatever he does, all is bad: if he calls hooligans to order, he becomes a tyrant, if he does nothing – a weak ruler.

According to Arab and Western commentators, a kind of a mastermind behind the events in the Middle East was the head of the European Council for Fatwa and Research and the chairman of International Union for Muslim Scholars Sheikh Yusuf al-Qaradawi. He has his own program on the Qatari satellite channel Al Jazeera, which has a huge audience, and speaks on popular Islamic websites. He called on Egyptian police not to shoot at protesters and on Hosni Mubarak to resign.

In his book *Sharia* (2009) Sheikh wrote: "The laws of Islam teach us to confront tyrants, oppression of any people by rulers is reprehensible and forbidden, and jihad against them is necessary... a type of jihad is jihad against evil and corruption among Muslims... Prophet Muhammad praised it and considered it to be the best type of jihad"[15].

However, the same Sheikh forbade Libyan soldiers to fire on opposition, but said nothing to the armed opposition with regard to the soldiers; he also urged the Arab leaders to recognize the Libyan opposition as the legitimate authority, and everyone who had an opportunity – to shoot Gaddafi.

In our view, a national leader, and especially a religious leader, should put the moral imperative at the forefront of his policy rather than call for mass murder. What has become of Libya because of the appeals by al-Qaradawi? Just ruins and blood.

We will not repeat the data on the income of the Libyans in the days of Gaddafi or on the subsidies Jamahiriya paid to its citizens – this is well-known and, unfortunately, in the past. However, the level of development of health services is worthy of mention. One of the anti-Gaddafi TV reports showed a provincial hospital where the "victims of the murderous dictator" were brought. But what a hospital! Five (!) artificial kidney machines. Moscow does not have that. What made Libyans unhappy? Were they really unhappy? Where is the opposition of which so much has been written and shown on TV?

Mustafa Abdul Jamil, the Head of the National Transitional Council, an educated man from the Libyan elite, an opponent of violence, personal humiliation and restriction of freedoms, has always looked as a stranger among his associates. Now that the fighting in Libya has taken the form of a "war of all against all", such a person can hardly change anything.

Today the importance of a strong personality as a motivating factor for the development of civil society in the Arab countries is particularly high. In the presence of a national leader the so-called "democratization from above" and "dosed democracy" become possible." For example, the process of democratization of the Moroccan society during the 1980–90th was directed by King Hassan II and was manageable. Noteworthy are his words: "...democracy, so desirable for everyone, in order to take root and thrive must be introduced in carefully examined doses"[16].

133

But what if he is right? If one wants all at once, a country may be pushed back for years to come. For instance, Zbigniew Brzezinski, former national security adviser of President Carter, believes that "democracy is a complex process that requires a lot of development time", and so far Arab countries are "characterized by social and economic frustration"[17]. At the same time, the experienced politician recommends the West to respect the desire of these countries to maintain national dignity and to overcome the last vestiges of colonialism.

Indeed, the problem of leadership in the Arab world is extremely acute today. Selfless revolutionaries are long gone. The cornerstone of the current activities of the "fighters" with the ruling regimes are vested interests. Did Libyan or Syrian rebels think about their homeland? What about the warlords of Darfur? How many times have they broken off peace talks with the Sudanese government to grab a piece of the pie?

A true leader acts in the interests of his country; it is necessary to adjust the course, learn to express his disagreement, lead a dialogue with the authorities, so that the economy does not come to a halt and no blood is shed. Arab wisdom maintains that 10 years under a bad ruler are ultimately better than one night of anarchy and chaos.

The balance of common and individual

Another feature of the Arab political culture is the fact that individualism, which in the West is the foundation of civil society, is to some extent alien to the Arabs. In the Arab countries there is a deep sense of common destiny of their peoples. Remarkable are the words by Boutros-Ghali, an Egyptian: "When we see Palestinian brothers living under the thumb of the occupation, we all feel like Palestinians whose rights are violated, we feel anger and bitterness of losing a homeland. After all, the Arab world is a single whole. The Arabs still regret the loss of Andalusia"[18].

The Arabs perceive themselves as part of the two major communities: the common Arab culture and history, on the one hand, and the huge Muslim Ummah, on the other. Until 2011 this was true . But what is happening now? The mouthpiece of the Arab world, the satellite channel Al Jazeera, which has always protected the interests of all Arabs, is giving one-sided and clearly biased information, the authenticity of which is often questioned. Furthermore, consider the position of the League of Arab States (LAS). Its members "hand in" to the West one leader after another. With the acquiescence of the Arab League, Sudan has split and continues to break up before our eyes. Morocco is preparing a resolution against Syria at the UN. What happened to the Arabs? Of course, there have always been disagreements. But it had never happened that leaders of sovereign states were obstructed in the international arena. Obviously, such price has to be paid for a chance not to be next in the line of deposed rulers.

Nevertheless, common is to a certain extent closer to an Arab than individual. Besides, "Sharia is based on the idea of obligations imposed on the people rather than on the rights that they may have"[19]. An individual in Islam has subjective rights primarily in such areas of private interest as family, property, etc. In other social spheres he has, as a rule, <u>duties</u> towards God, the Arab world, the Muslim Ummah, etc. In other words, the Arab world has a somewhat different balance between individual freedoms and responsibilities from the one in the West.

However, in today's world the respect of individual rights is becoming a criterion of civilization. Trying to keep up with the times, Arabs also create such documents. In this area, there is a certain international standard, which is based on the 1948 Universal Declaration of Human Rights and the 1966 International Covenant on Economic, Social and Cultural Rights. The Arab analogues include the Arab Charter on Human Rights, the Universal Islamic Declaration of Human Rights, and the Project for an Islamic Constitution. The analysis of these documents in terms of the impact of Islam suggests that their Muslim form is used only as a means to secure the rights and freedoms contained in the Universal Declaration of Human Rights and other UN papers on human rights. It is characteristic that in the Arab world there are many corresponding organization, e.g. the Tunisian Human Rights League, the Moroccan Advisory Council on Human Rights, etc.[20]

"Civil spirit" of the Arabs

Some Western political scientists, while questioning the possibility of the establishment of civil society in Arab countries, point out the insufficient development of "civil spirit" among the Arabs. The recent events have proved otherwise. Many facts, including the abundance of NGOs, associations, societies, etc. established in Arab countries, also prove the invalidity of such opinions. Arabs actively create various associations: human rights agencies, unions of lawyers, teachers, journalists and students, national unions of artists, architects, scientists and even the unemployed.

Virtually every country has associations of graduates of prestigious universities. Some of them, like the alumni associations of Cairo University and Al-Azhar University, have also branches in Tropical Africa. An interesting fact is the existence of the associations of graduates of Russian universities. In Tunisia, for one, such an organization was founded in 1989. At the meeting of graduates of Russian universities, which was held in March 2007 in Sousse, their willingness to promote various, primarily economic, relations with Russia was emphasized.

The revitalization of civil position of the population contributes to the establishment of such socio-economic organizations as the Tunisian National Solidarity Fund, which advocates greater humanity in public relations and helping the poor.[21] In Morocco, there operates the Association for the Fight Against Corruption, which is the national branch of Transparency International (TI) [22]. Similar examples can be given for each country of Arab Africa.

Understanding the need for change has become an omen of modern development in the Arab world. Tunisians have been the first to show how much power rests with the new revolutionary weapons – Twitter and Facebook – in the fight against tyranny. Those who denounce the lies, despotism and immense corruption of the ruling elite have lit the spark that has set off the fire. Now a force is needed that will direct this energy in the right direction: economic progress and civil society development.

The sea of blood which we are witnessing in the Arab world today can hardly be called "Arab spring", a better name would be "Arab madness" and Western state terrorism.

The event that took place shocked not only the Arabs but also Arabists. Indeed, the socio-political and economic situation in these countries required changes, but to a much lesser extent than in many others. All the talk about difficult demographics, slow growth, corruption, etc. – no more than attempts to explain the situation, but they have not really clarified it. Arabs themselves talked about the need for reform. Why was it necessary to push them? Are there any doubts that there was an intervention from the outside?

The Berkman Center for Internet and Society was founded at Harvard University, USA, in 1997. Then Global voices and the Blog Corpus were established. In recent years, the Centre has worked on two projects: "Civil law in the field of information" (support for those involved in online media and protection of freedom of speech in the Internet) and "Internet and democracy". The main object of research and practical action of the latter project was the Middle East. The project received $1.5 mln in grant money. We have seen the consequences of the performance of such "global voices" and "blog corpuses" more than once. But what scares is a statement produced by General Wesley Clark, who commanded the joint NATO force in Europe in 1997-2000. He claimed that during the bombing of Afghanistan the Pentagon was already planning the war in Iraq; moreover, a memorandum of the defense minister listed 6 more countries against which military action was planned: Syria, Lebanon, Libya, Somalia, Sudan, and Iran[23]. Who will be next?

Nevertheless, it is hoped that economic success – if it follows possible economic and political reforms – will create a new political climate in Arab countries. The sense of belonging to the success of the homeland forms more active citizens, a kind of "civil spirit", which the Arabs are accused of lacking. This fact releases the energy of the masses, liberates and encourages citizens to express their will more actively and more freely, to communicate with like-minded people, and then to assert their positions within a party or NGO.

It is obvious that in the Arab world reforms in all dimensions – political, economic, social and cultural – are long overdue. In the course of debates at international and regional forums, many representatives of Arab civil society stressed that the reforms would not produce a lasting result unless social contracts between the ruling elites and the "street" were concluded simultaneously.

According to researchers of the Cairo Institute for Human Rights Studies (CIHRS), under conditions of the freedom deficit, when the free will of the citizens is significantly limited, such social contracts can be a sham if the elites impose their will on the unfortunate man from the street. In fact, many Arab regimes constantly pursued their own interests. State-owned media mislead people and stuffed them full with lies with the same constancy. Under such circumstances, it is not surprising that the Arab regimes that were not able to offer a compelling and worthy vision of the future of their countries have fallen.

Modernization in the Arab world is inevitable. But it should not be an imposed Westernization brought on by force, but economic and social progress, the establishment of modern welfare economics and civil society, enrichment of the Arab/Muslim world with the best achievements of the world civilization while preserving their identity and their use of great spiritual and material wealth.

Today North Africa has many non-governmental organizations, multiparty systems and democratic elections, but it is too early to talk about the existence of a full-fledged civil society.

The development of civil society in the Arab world is a lengthy process. But the formation of such a society or even some progress towards it will be a stabilizing factor – the force that will bring understanding to achieve harmony and tolerance so needed by the Arabs.

---

[1] See, for example: Ignatenko A. *The decline of political Islam* // NG (Appendix to Nezavisimaya Gazeta). M. 16.02.2011.

[2] Compass. M., 2011, Vol. 7. P. 9.

[3] For more about the elections and their results, see: A. Ignatenko. *Disposable democracy for Egypt* // NG religion. 18.01.2012. P. 7; D. Vinitsky. *Revolt in the Arab world: crops and shoots*; "Mohamed Morsi: we struggle for power, but we preach peace". *Asia and Africa Today*. Moscow, 2011: Vol. 12. P. 2-6.

[4] An-Novaihi M. *To a revolution in religious thought*. Beirut, 1970. P. 3.

[5] Apter D.E. *The Politics of Modernization*. Chicago. 1965. P. 3.

[6] Malashenko A. *The Islamic Alternative and the Islamist project*. M., 2006. P. 65-66.

[7] Sergeev M.S . *The history of Morocco. 20th century*. M., 2001. P. 203.

[8] Ignatenko A. *Caliphs without a caliphate*. M., 1988. P. 51.

[9] Dzhemal G. *Counterstrike*. M., 2005.

[10] Malashenko A. Op. cit. P.75.

[11] Sedgwick M. *Is there a church in Islam?* // ISIM Newsletter. 2003. December 13. P. 40.

[12] Boutros Boutros-Ghali. *Egypt's Road to Jerusalem*. M., 1999. P. 83.

[13] *Africa: the features of the political culture*. M., 1999.

[14] Zugzwang (German) ("zug" – move + "zwang" – compulsion) – a situation in chess in which the obligation to make a move in one' turn is a serious, often decisive, disadvantage. (See: Concise dictionary of foreign words. M., 1971. P. 354).

[15] Quoted from Nezavisimaya Gazeta, 16.03.2011. P. 2.

[16] Sergeev M.S . Op. cit. P. 221.

[17] Tages anzeiger. 28.04.2011.

[18] Boutros Boutros-Ghali. Op. cit. P. 37.

[19] Aref Ali Alian. *The status of a person under Islamic law*. M., 1991. P. 7.

[20] Jeune Afrique. 2006. № 2384. 17– 23 Septembre. P. 42.

[21] Ibid. P. 43.

[22] www.Transparency international.ru.

[23] www.Youtube.com/watch?=OC26X1Xoods

SYNOPSIS

ENCYCLOPEDIA "AFRICA"

Vasiliev, Alexei (Editor in chief) & Ismagilova, Roza (Head of research and project co-ordinator). *Encyclopedia "Africa".* **2 vols. Moscow: Entsiklopedija Publisher, 2010. Vol. 1, 950 p., ISBN 978-5-94802-038-9. Vol. 2, 1037 p., ISBN 978-5-94802-040-2.**

The publication of the two-volume encyclopedia "Africa" is important not only for Russian African Studies but also for global studies in this field. It is the world's largest and a unique edition: it contains more than 4,000 entries on all countries and regions of Africa.

The encyclopedia gives much detailed information concerning Africa's numerous development problems, relevant both in scientific and practical terms.

It shows of the continuity of socio-cultural traditions, values and institutions in different historic periods. Apart from containing specific factual material on various branches of knowledge, which is important on its own, articles of the encyclopedia may be of utility for further research of a typology of world civilizations, new approaches to socio-economic and cultural issues, and new concepts.

Africa is an integral part of the global community. Its problems reach beyond the continent, so they must be solved in the framework of international cooperation. The African problems are often brought up at the G8 summits; G8 nations have created structures for cooperation with African countries and provide them with significant economic assistance.

The 2008 global economic crisis had an impact on African countries. Countries closely integrated into the global economy witnessed a decline in GDP. The UN's Millennium Development Goals for Africa remain unmet both in terms of poverty reduction and in terms of improving health, education, culture, etc.

In recent years there has been an increase in Russia's interest in Africa. Russia's cooperation with African countries is developing, and the trade turnover is growing. The demand for various African resources is also rising. Mutual investment has become a new sphere of cooperation.

The political and ethno-political situation in Africa is very complicated. Persisting ethnic tensions and conflicts in many countries of the continent and aggressive nationalism lead to an increase in both theoretical and practical interest in the problems of self-determination, state structure, various forms of federalism, autonomy (including cultural autonomy), and traditional methods of resolving inter-ethnic conflicts. These and many other problems are addressed in the encyclopedia.

The opening part of the encyclopedia is titled **Overview** (355 p.). It gives a full information on the continent. The table of contents of this part demonstrates the diversity and scientific significance of the peer-reviewed topics: **General information. Geographical and physical characteristics** (Coasts. Landform. Geological structure. Mineral resources. Climate. Water resources. Soils. Flora. Animal world. Natural zoning. Nature protection. The worsening of environmental problems).

The history of geographical discoveries and explorations. It includes Ancient history. Middle Ages. Modern history. Contemporary history. **Philosophy. Law** (Law in Africa. Constitutional law of African countries. International law and Africa). **Africa in international relations. Russian-African relations. Population** (Ethnic composition. Ethnic processes. Anthropological composition. Religious situation. Natural migration. Urbanization. Economically active population: professional and class structure. The situation of workers. Refugees in Africa). **Languages** (Afro-Asiatic. Nilo-Saharan. Congo-Kordofanian. Khoisan macrofamily. Linguistics). **Economic overview** (General economic overview. Least developed African countries. State and economy. Foreign capital. Industry. Agriculture. Agrarian system. Industrial agricultural production. Food problem. Forestry. Transportation. Communications. Finance and credit. Currency systems. Financial flows. Strategy of socio-economic development. Intra-African economic cooperation. External economic relations. External debt of African countries. Globalization and Africa countries). **Health** (Living standards, demographics and public health in Africa. Health care systems. International cooperation between African countries and Russia). **Education. African civilizations** (Civilizations of Tropical Africa. Islamic civilization in Africa). **Literature** (North Africa: Francophone literature. Arabic-language literature. Tropical and South Africa: English-language literature. Francophone literature. Lusophone literature). Literature in local languages (Berber-language literature. Amharic literature. Hausa literature. Literature in Africaans. Lingala literature). **Folklore. Architecture, fine and applied arts. Music. Dance. Theatre. Film. Physical education and sport.**

Next come the A-to-Z entries on a wide range of subjects and topics. There are entries on more than 300 ethnic groups, their way of life and traditional cultures. There are also many entries on wider topics such as nationalities question, nationalism, ideologies, theoretical concepts. The longest articles are dedicated to countries. They give a comprehensive analysis of all aspects of life of modern African states.

The encyclopedia gives much detailed information about more than 1500 personalities: travelers, scientists, politicians, writers, poets, artists, athletes, etc. It contains extensive cartographic material and many colored illustrations. The articles in the encyclopedia are supplied with a large bibliography.

The encyclopedia was prepared by scholars of the Institute for African Studies as well as Africanists and Arabists from other academic institutions, Moscow and St. Petersburg universities, and foreign researchers.

We are grateful to the Russian Foundation for Humanities (RFH) for the financial support in publishing *Encyclopedia "Africa"*.

The overview was prepared by Roza Ismagilova.

ECONOMIC STUDIES

Abramova, Irina. *Africa's new role in the global economy of the 21ˢᵗ century.* Moscow: Institute for African Studies, RAS, 2013. 324 p. ISBN 978-5-91298-137-1.

Such factors as the collapse of the unipolar world, the rise of new economic giants – China, India, Brazil, etc., and the growing influence of the "old" economic heavyweights that have not had the tradition and ensuing economic benefits of colonial rule in Africa (Japan and Germany) have dramatically exacerbated the competition for raw materials of the African continent, which is becoming one of the main diversified and non-depleted resource bases of global significance. The monograph demonstrates that African countries are in fact world-class monopolists in a number of resources (especially those resources that are necessary for the most promising directions of scientific and technical progress). In view of the increasing instability in other energy producers, leading Western countries in their strategic doctrines have designated Africa as the most important supplier of energy resources, primarily hydrocarbons and raw uranium. The continent's natural resources could also play a significant role in the implementation of the Russian government's plans for reform and development of the Russian economy and the implementation of its foreign policies.

Africa's resource potential, backed by the strong economic growth of the last decade (GDP growth in most African countries has remained positive even in the current global crisis), has allowed the continent to influence the world markets more vigorously and to obtain more favorable terms in the international division of labor. As the gravity of resource deficit will only increase in the foreseeable future, Africa is likely to strengthen its position in the global economy.

Another aspect of the inevitable growth of the influence of the African continent on the economic fate of the world is associated with rapid population growth and a gradual change in the qualitative composition of its population. In 2009, Africa's population exceeded 1 billion people and continues to grow at the highest rate in the world. By the mid-21ˢᵗ century, if the current trend continues, 20 to 25% of the world population will live in Africa. The combination of demographic pressure and socio-economic backwardness of most African countries leads to an aggravation and proliferation of a number of economic and humanitarian problems beyond the continent. These problems will then have to be addressed by the entire world community.

There are other equally important aspects of the influence of "African human factor" on the world economy. Europe, to a lesser extent North America, and parts of Asia (including South Korea and China) have experienced

142

or are beginning to experience the problem of aging and a relative reduction in the proportion of the working population. In 20-30 years, a significant portion of the global growth in the world labor market will originate from Africa. In these circumstances, labor resources are the second main channel through which Africa will actively influence the formation of linkages and new paradigms of the global economy in the 21st century.

All the above indicates the high relevance of the issues examined in this monograph, which is devoted to a comprehensive analysis of the main channels through which Africa exerts its influence on global development within the framework of the current world economic model. The author concentrates precisely on endogenous (i.e. originating from Africa itself, not imposed on it by external forces) determinants of the continent's participation in the global economy in the 21st century. According to the author, these are two such determinants: raw materials and population growth. Both determinants are endogenous in nature and are part of the "resource potential" of the continent, as these natural and human resources have always been or will originate in Africa.

Bessonov, Stanislav (Ed.). *African countries: problems and ways of economic development.* **Moscow: Institute for African Studies, RAS, 2013. 174 p. Research papers of the Institute for African Studies, Issue 31. ISBN 978-5-91298-121-0.**

The collective work consists of four sections. Section 1 includes three articles on the problems of modernization: the inconsistency of this process against the backdrop of the two strong concurrent influences of African traditionalism and the effects of the global economic crisis (*Stanislav Bessonov*), as well as the difficulty of the implementation of the Millennium Development Goals (*Irina Matsenko*). The articles in Section 2 are devoted to the external financing of investment in infrastructure programs and the role of the African Development Bank in this process (*Vladimir Pavlov*), as well as the improvement of the investment climate in Africa (*Georgiy Roschin*). Section 3 describes the features of the modern development of the continent in the following areas: industry (*Ludmila Kalinichenko*), maritime transport (*Zinaida Novikova*), business education (*Natalia Matveeva*), as well as new approaches to the assessment of the poverty level (*Elena Bragina*). Section 4 discusses the problem of cartelization of the global gas market with the participation of African countries (*Vladimir Koukoushkin*) and the formation of the "war economy" in Africa (*Tatiana Denisova*).

Fituni, Leonid. *Africa. Resource wars of the 21st century..* **Moscow: Institute for African Studies, RAS, 2012. 248 p. ISBN 978-5-91298-107-4.**

The beginning of this century was marked by rising global competition among the leading world powers for resources necessary for the successful development of their economies and strengthening of their positions in the world arena. The collapse of the USSR and the socialist camp upset the equilibrium in the system of international relations. A perception was gradually imposed on the international community that aggressive expansion and the use of force were legitimate instruments of foreign policy of democratic countries. World politics seemed to have steered back on the track that had led its course in the early 20th century. Countries of the world renewed the struggle for resources, and this struggle has resulted in the redistribution of spheres of influence, as well as in attempts by some countries to enter new markets (both import and export) and in resistance of other international actors, already established in these markets, to these moves.

A conflict of interest between traditional and new players, which are representing respectively "old" and "young" centers of world economic power, is visible on the African continent and in the world at large. The monograph shows that in today's polycentric world less developed world regions have once again become the scene of a tense confrontation between the competing centers of power. Just like a hundred years ago, in recent years there has been a tendency for difficult issues such as control over resources and the terms of their exploitation to be increasingly resolved by force – military, "non-lethal", or soft.

Although the title of the book by L. Fituni orients the reader primarily towards the features of the international competition for raw materials on the African continent, the author considers the research subject in a broader, global context. As a consequence, the work contains many generalizations, significant not only for African studies, but also for studies of the world economy at the beginning of the 21st century.

The author begins by addressing the problem of understanding the role of the natural resource factor in the emerging model of world economic development (MWED). The concept of MWED transition was developed by L. Fituni in cooperation with Irina Abramova, another famous Russian Africanist. Their theory tries to explain the cyclical exacerbation of the "resource confrontation" on a global scale over long time periods.

The book contains a detailed description of Africa's existing natural resources and raw materials, including fossil fuels and other resources (water, forests, land, ecological and climatic). The author analyzes demand for these resources, their readiness and prospects for exploitation. Much attention is paid to the policy of African countries on the use of these resources and to changes in economic regimes and legislation related to their exploitation that have taken place over recent decades. In this context, the book examines new trends in the relations with foreign capital, which operates in the resource-related sectors of African economies.

Indeed, Russia's interests remain the focus of the research. A special chapter of the book is dedicated to specific issues of the Russian-African economic cooperation in the field of raw materials. Throughout the book the author conveys the idea that, despite the apparent decrease in the influence of our country in Africa in comparison with Soviet times, Russia, which remains a world power, is doomed to participate to certain extent in resource battles unfolding on the continent even if it will not seek to be involved. The events of the Arab Spring have confirmed this clearly enough.

In conclusion, the author stresses that despite the importance of the aforementioned provisions on the growing importance of the resource component in international development in the coming decades, in many cases other types of resources – human, financial, intellectual, technological, informational, military, etc. – will play no lesser and even greater role than fossil fuels and raw materials. An important change in the existing world economic model has been the rise of large developing countries, which, despite all crises, can no longer return to old paradigms of consumption of domestic and foreign raw materials and other resources for development. For the West, a guaranteed access to these resources is an opportunity to extend its dominance, contain geopolitical competitors, and transfer existing paradigms of global economic relations and interdependencies into the emerging model of world economic development of the 21st century. According to the author, this means that, unfortunately, it is no longer reasonable to expect that resource wars will cease in the foreseeable future, and that Russia will have to find its place, strategy and tactics in this ruthless and fierce fight.

Morozenskaya, Evgenia (Ed.). *Economic infrastructure of African countries.* **Moscow: Institute for African Studies, RAS, 2012. 295 p. ISBN 978-5-91298-112-8.**

The book discusses in detail the main characteristics and development trends of the key branches of production and social infrastructure in Africa. The specificity of this sector of the economy is demonstrated for different sub-regions and individual countries of the continent. Particular attention is paid to the scientific content and sectoral structure of this part of the economy, the growth of its importance for improving the competitiveness of African countries, and the formation of a modern market economy in these countries.

The monograph is devoted to the analysis of the core infrastructure sectors in African countries. It considers possible ways for their future development and the influence of the production and social infrastructure on the economic and social situation in these countries.

The main stages of infrastructure formation as a separate sector of social production are discussed in **Part 1** (*Evgenia Morozenskaya*). Since the 1980s infrastructure sector has been accepted as the most important factor of economic development and growth of national competitiveness and, simultaneously, as an independent integral system.

On the basis of different scientific classifications, sector and function approaches and definitions of the term "infrastructure", the extended interpretation of this term is proposed. Infrastructure is considered as a multi-sector economic structure with complex horizontal and vertical ties, which provides a number of environmental and servicing functions for material and social production.

Infrastructure, as well as other economic notions, may be classified according to different features: production sector, property type, the method of production management, the level of economic independence, etc. The authors used mainly the complex sector approach, which is a feature of the monograph.

Part 2 deals with problems of production infrastructure. Adequate and efficient transport infrastructure (*Section I, Zinaida Novikova*) is basic to economic growth of African countries. Transport in Africa has been given top priority since the first years of independence. But today's transport conditions are far from encouraging. Modern Africa's transport systems are inadequate, inefficient, costly and poorly integrated compared with other regions of the world.

During the early post-colonial period it became evident that there was an absolute need to establish cooperation between African states and this could be promoted and accelerated by transport because it was recognized that transport was a fundamental prerequisite to economic and social development.

The author analyses modern transport infrastructure, its role in economy and possibilities of ensuring economic development in sub-regions of North, West, Central, East and Southern Africa. The long-term objective is to establish a rational integrated transport system which promotes development and contributes to the economic and social integration of sub-regions. The importance of transit transport systems (so called "transport corridors") cannot be over-emphasized, especially for land-locked countries.

Section II (*Ludmila Kalinichenko, Vladimir Koukoushkin, Andrey Pritvorov*) analyses actual problems of energy infrastructure development in North, Tropical and Southern Africa. The authors of the research emphasise poor condition of contemporary energy sector in most African countries – so-called "energy poverty". In spite of possessing great energy resources including oil and gas, hydro, solar, wind and geothermal sources, sub-Saharan countries may be the only region of the world where the number of people without access to electricity will increase in the next two decades. This issue needs attention and urgent solution with the support of international organizations and developed countries.

Section III (*Leonid Fituni*) touches upon critical problems of the security and exploitation of water resources. Different aspects of the creation of full-fledged water infrastructure on national and regional scales are studied. This branch of infrastructure is linked with the production and social spheres, as well as ecology.

Section IV deals with two most important elements of financial infrastructure: bank credit sector (*Vladimir Pavlov, IV.1*) and the main channels of foreign capital inflow in the form of official development aid or private credit resources (*Georgiy Roschin, IV.2*). Bank credit market partly weakens the contradiction existing in African countries between the demand for intersector capital flow, on the one hand, and growing sector disproportions, on the other. Large volumes of credits and loans from international market of private financial capital are becoming the main sources for paying off chronic state budget deficit and for financing investment. Nearly a third of the national pool of loan capital is formed from these sources.

In **Part 3** activities of social infrastructure are analysed. *Section V* (*Boris Runov*) is devoted to science and information, including the priority directions of information and telecommunication infrastructure development (*V.1*) and specific features of national technical and scientific complexes in sub-Saharan Africa (*V.2*).

Sections VI and *VII* (*Irina Matsenko*) deal with the current state of education and health in Africa. The author proceeds from the premise that meeting the needs of society in education and health is a necessary condition for the reproduction of labour force and improvement of its quality and productive potential, and that investment in human capital plays a key role in increasing public labour productivity and accelerating economic development. It is noted that the solution of problems related to education and health in a situation that is critical in terms of human resources is highly relevant for Africa, which is the most underdeveloped and poorest continent in the world. The following issues are covered in detail – access to education (especially enrolment in primary education), its quality, literacy, «brain drain», access to health care, disease burden (HIV/AIDS, malaria and tuberculosis), hunger and lack of drinking water and sanitation, shortage of financial resources and personnel, government policy and external aid. It is concluded that despite the evident progress made during the last decade the current state of education and health does meet neither the real economic needs of African countries in educated and healthy human resources nor their further independent development.

In the **conclusion** (*Evgenia Morozenskaya*), on the basis of the analysis of different aspects of infrastructure sector formation and development in Africa, there are proposed some possible ways of its reforming with a view to increase the competitiveness of African economy.

Runov, Boris (Ed.). *Industrial, financial, labour, scientific and technical potential of Sub-Saharan Africa.* **Moscow: Institute for African Studies, RAS, 2012. 170 p. ISBN 978-5-91298-103-6.**
The collection of scientific papers is dedicated to the key issues of economic modernization in sub-Saharan economies. It analyzes the situation and prospects for the development of industrial capacity in sub-Saharan Africa: the role of the non-ferrous metallurgy as the backbone industry in some countries of the region (*Zinaida Novikova*); problems of the oil and gas sector (*Ludmila Kalinichenko*); the main direction of Kenya's industrial development (primarily, manufacturing) and prospects of agro-industry (*Natalia Matveeva*). The article on the development of labour potential explores its current state (employment, unemployment, poverty), level and quality of education, situation in the health sector (*Irina Matsenko*). Special articles are devoted to the development of scientific and technical complex in the region (*Boris Runov*) and the problems of the formation of capital markets in the region (*Georgiy Roschin*).

Pavlov, Vladimir, & Ganurov, Ilshat. *Currency, foreign trade and investment regulation in Muslim countries.* **2 vols. 544 pp, 648 p. Moscow: Ankil, 2011. ; Vol. I: ISBN 978-5-86476-315-5; Vol. II: ISBN 978-5-86476-313-1; ISBN 978-5-86476-315-5.**
The reference book presents a detailed analysis of the state regulation of currency operations, foreign trade and investment in the 57 member countries of the Organization of the Islamic Conference (OIC). The book discusses general parameters and specific investment codes in force in African and Asian Muslim countries, including the investment codes of the monetary and economic unions of West African and Central African countries. It includes a detailed analysis of the main provisions of the existing trade and currency legislation (as of 2010) in Asian and African countries, including all of the Arab countries of North Africa. The handbook considers the transformation of the existing investment legislation aimed at facilitating significant inter-country movement of investment capital and promotion of bilateral trade, including exports of industrial and capital goods.

The study allowed the authors to draw the following conclusions:

– there is a tendency to unify methods of monetary and exchange rate management and import duty rates and to introduce collective investment codes, as well as to consistently unify investment laws of individual member countries of the Organization of the Islamic Conference (OIC);

– there is taking place a formation of a single currency, common foreign trade and investment area, which will facilitate the functioning of this important economic grouping – the integrated structure of trade, currency and investment markets of the OIC member states.

Abramova, Irina. *The population of Africa in the new economic model of the world..* **Moscow: Institute for African Studies, RAS, 2010. 496 p. ISBN 978-5-91298-078-7.**

The present work is the first attempt in Russian literature to provide a complex analysis of the emerging world economic model and the role of the African population as part (sub-model) of the modern global economic structure. The work is interdisciplinary as it affects both economic and demographic aspects of the development of the world as a whole and of the African continent in particular. The author focuses on those aspects of the theme that have not been developed sufficiently in Russian and foreign literature. This applies in particular to the role of Africa in the formation of a new economic development model, the analysis of the transformation of global population models and the role of the African component in these processes, a calculation of basic demographic parameters of African countries in 21st century, the comprehensive analysis of Africa's labor resources and migration flows from the African continent, and the identification of the patterns of African urbanization.

In preparing this paper, the main emphasis was placed on the study of primary sources, including national statistics of African countries and general population censuses carried out both by specialized agencies of the UN, the ILO, and the OECD, and by African statistical agencies. In the course of work on the monograph, the author also referred to publications by international organizations: the UN, the World Bank, the International Labour Organization (ILO), the World Health Organization (WHO), FAO, UNESCO, etc.

The monograph provides a theoretical summary of field researches in a number of African and European countries in 1999-2010, which included interviews with a number of Russian and foreign experts, as well as materials collected in research centers, government agencies and other organizations in the respective countries.

The first chapter demonstrates the effect of the fundamental processes in the world economy of the early 21st century on the transformation of the global model of social development, analyzes the causes of the crisis of the existing model, and describes the architecture of renewed global economic relations and new rules of the world economic order.

The second chapter is devoted to the main trends of the world's demographic development, as well as to the formation of a new model of population in the framework of the transformation of the global economy.

The third chapter analyzes the changing role of Africa in world demographic processes, offers a calculation of the key demographic parameters of African countries in the last 20 years and until 2050, and shows the influence of socio-demographic changes on economic growth in African countries.

The fourth chapter reflects the main patterns of African urbanization as a specific component of the quantitative and qualitative growth of the world's urban population. Special attention is paid to the socio-economic features of the process of urbanization in Africa on the example of Egypt.

The fifth chapter is dedicated to the analysis of cross-border migration of African people as an integral part of the global labor market. It discusses problems of the economic activity of African migrants, the impact of remittances on the balance of payments in donor and recipient countries, as well as labor legislation, restrictions on illegal migration, and related criminal and shadow economy.

The sixth chapter analyzes the labor market of African countries. The focus of the chapter is given to the dynamics and structure of employment of the African population, the problems of unemployment and underemployment, as well as quantitative and qualitative characterization of human capital in Africa in the context of globalization.

Abramova Irina, & Morozenskaya Evgenia (Eds.). *Market transformation of African economy.* **Moscow: Institute for African Studies, RAS, 2010. 308 p. ISBN 978-5-91298-067-1.**
The book consists of an introduction, conclusion and fourteen chapters grouped into three sections: "Internal and external aspects of African markets formation", "Markets of economic sectors", and "Production factors markets".

The authors of the book analysed the influence of internal and external factors on the formation of a national market, which is regarded as the system of inter-sectoral linkages and provides opportunities for growth of imports and export production.

Economic growth in African countries has been accompanied by market development. In **Section 1** this trend has been confirmed by the analysis of the internal and external aspects. The authors have come to the conclusion that the mutual impact of these aspects leads to the emergence of a new structure of national economy similar in its tendency to international examples.

As noted in *Chapter I (I.1 and I.2, Evgenia Morozenskaya)*, market formation should not be carried out only by market forces in order to prevent the self-destruction of an economy. The solution of the problem of economic effectiveness is connected directly with the acceleration of economic growth but collides with low productivity in African countries that, in its turn, prevents an increase in demand. The aggregate correlation between economic growth and economic development is one of the key problems in the modern studies of the developing countries. This chapter deals with an important feature of African economy: the great acceleration of economic growth, which was observed in these countries in the 2000s, has not been followed by the marked progress neither in economic nor in social development. The necessary transformation of the economy is hampered by the low level of investments.

The complexity of data analysis of market economy in African countries is explained mainly by the lack or unauthenticity of some part (sometimes the whole) of statistical base. The detailed analysis of the methodology of the calculation of macroeconomic indices *(Ch. 1.3, Morten Jerven, LSE, London)* to some extent raises doubts about the steadiness of the tendency of GDP growth rates in African countries to decrease since the 1980s. One should be very careful in making conclusions based on the statistics for the growth rates in African countries. It is better to compare the rates of growth of different sectors of economy rather than generalized indices.

In *Chapter II (Stanislav Bessonov)* it is underlined that for the countries with dominating traditional economy there is no other way out except for the diversification of economy on the basis of market mechanisms. In addition, the primary direction in the formation of new markets is towards achieving a higher level of exports processing and growth in export-oriented industries and types of economic activities that belong to the global economy rather than the national one. Due to the insufficient impact of new markets on the formation and further development of national economic mechanisms, the economic development in Tropical Africa has been unsteady and has had the tendency to slow down.

Chapter III deals with the versatile role of the government, previously a guarantor of legal regulations' application in the developing market economies, in the acceleration of economic growth *(III.1, Evgenia Morozenskaya)*. The attention is mainly paid to indirect methods of regulation, which are prerogatives of the authorities protecting the interests of the society as a whole – credit and monetary policy *(III.2, Vladimir Pavlov)* and fiscal policy *(III.3, Evgenia Morozenskaya)*.

There are different views concerning the question of whether the regional markets can play the role of a preparatory stage for the transition to an all-African market, or their existence conserves the present economic division on the continent. This problem is researched in *Chapter IV (Vladimir Vigand)*. On the one hand, there is obviously a slight influence of the main five out of 14 regional groups operating in Africa on the process of all-African integration. On the other hand, in the opinion of the experts of the African Development Bank and OECD, substantial progress in regional cooperation has been achieved under the aegis of the African Union. This fact allows the author to suggest that mutual economic efforts of African governments in the area of economic policy will create in perspective the basis for strengthening the regional markets and their gradual expansion.

Section 2 discusses the characteristics of sectoral markets in Africa. It analyses the modern technological base of production, the industrial development on the whole and of the oil and gas industry in particular, the evolution of agricultural markets, the perspectives of the development of transport infrastructure and the shortage of water resources on the continent.

Particularly, the section underlines the isolated character of industrial enterprises and limited opportunities for industrialization (*Ch. VI, Liudmila Kalinichenko*), higher technological level of mining industries in comparison with the average low level of technological development (*Ch. V, Boris Runov*), inadequacy of transport infrastructure to the needs of market economy (*Ch. IX, Zinaida Novikova*).

The oil and gas industry occupies a special place among other sectors of industry. It can become an engine of structural economic transformation due to the favourable conjuncture of the world oil market and discoveries of new oil and gas deposits on the continent (*Ch. VII, Vladimir Koukoushkin*).

The problem of the marketability of agricultural products (*Ch. VIII, Valeriy Morozov*) is of vital importance for Africa. In particular, the potential deferred negative impact of the global financial and economic crisis (2008-2009) on Africa is partly explained by the fact that most of Africa's population lives in rural areas in conditions of natural and semi-natural economy. The fortune of these people depends on natural climatic conditions rather than on the situation on global financial markets.

The problem of drinking water availability is studied in *Chapter X (Nina Semenova)*. It is one of the most important Millennium Development Goals proclaimed by the UN for Africa. The author also analyses water resources as perspective commodity and an object of regional cooperation. Special attention is paid to the latter problem in connection with certain progress made in relations of the member-states of the organizations on the development of the largest river and lake basins.

In **Section 3** different aspects of financial markets formation are considered. The issues of correlation between the volume of investments and GDP growth (in general this possibility is admitted in Harrod&Domar economic growth model, which was developed in the 1930s and then applied all over the world, including developing countries after the WW2) are tightly interconnected with the problem of stock exchange formation. In those African countries where it has already appeared with the help of foreign capital it is demonstrating certain positive dynamics (*Ch. XI, Valeriy Morozov*).

The role of foreign direct investments in African economies is getting more and more complicated as it has created industrial enterprises which, on

152

the one hand, expand the industrial base of national economies, and, on the other hand, conserve their isolated character (*Ch. XII, Georgiy Roschin*).

Bank services markets depend on foreign investors and aim at servicing mainly their own credit needs (*Ch. XIII, 1-2, Vladimir Pavlov*). Insurance market is low-developed and also orientates itself predominantly on the foreign clients (*Ch. XIII, 3, Dmitriy Sukhorukov*).

Of great importance is also the labour market. The assessment of employment structure in African countries and labour market policies is completed along the analysis of human factor. The social characteristic of the latter influences strongly the competitiveness of African entrepreneurship (*XIV, 1-3, Irina Matsenko*).

The situation on the Kenyan labour market is presented as a positive example of local capital activity. Besides, there has been created a system of special structures for implementation of the government programs for small enterprises development (*XIV, 4, Natalia Matveeva*).

The authors didn't aim at covering all economic problems of the contemporary Africa. However, they tried to present the readers with a versatile idea of market formation as an economic phenomenon and possible directions of further market transformation on the African continent.

The overview was prepared by I.O. Abramova, L.L. Fituni, and E.V. Morozenskaya.

SOCIOLOGICAL AND POLITICAL STUDIES

Abramova, Irina & Bondarenko, Dmitri (Eds.). *Conflicts in Africa: causes, genesis, and conflict resolution (ethno-political and social aspects).* **Moscow: Institute for African Studies, RAS, 2013. 459 p. ISBN 978-5-91298-122-7.**

The theoretical section of the book thoroughly examines the origins and peculiarities of conflicts and provides a classification of them. According to N.D. Kosuhin, the study of the causes of armed conflicts allows to identify common patterns of their emergence, which is a necessary prerequisite to successful conflict prevention.

L.M. Sadovskaya in her chapter examines conflict resolution within the constitutional framework. According to the author, a state that is not equipped with effective and independent institutions of governance cannot truly serve its people and prevent conflicts in society. Therefore, one of the major political challenges facing African countries is the implementation of the principle of separation of powers, which is an intrinsic part of good governance.

L.L. Fituni in his chapter affirms the need to study modern technologies of social conflict management. He explores new methods of mobilizing protest movements and achieving political change in the Middle East and North Africa.

N.V. Grishina and V.I. Gusarov analyze the destabilizing role of armed conflicts on the continent, focusing on the increase in piracy in the Horn of Africa. The authors believe that the measures taken by the international community are insufficient.

O.B. Gromova examines the destabilizing impact of conflicts on the social environment. The author discusses the difficult plight of the most vulnerable groups of the population (women and children), who constitute the majority of the victims of numerous ethnic conflicts in Africa. Particular attention is paid to the involvement of children in conflicts – the so-called phenomenon of child soldiers (in Sierra Leone, DRC, Liberia, South Sudan).

The second section of the book presents a country-by-country analysis of contemporary crises.

Analyzing the protests in North Africa, A.A. Tkachenko concludes that the region is currently at a "historic bifurcation point": the depth and extent of the problems are so great that one should not expect their quick solution. The author suggests that there may be the second wave of conflicts with unpredictable consequences.

L.V. Geveling focuses on political violence in Nigeria's Fourth Republic. The author argues that even in countries with civil governments one can encounter the phenomenon of the militarization of the sphere of administration and governance. In Africa, entire law enforcement and repression bodies produce and actively employ local forms of "power corruption". According to the author, the corrupt "money-making" system is expropriated just like the most valuable and marketable national natural resources.

G.V. Sidorova touches on the stirring topic of conflict internationalization and conflation of the role of internal and external factors that are destabilizing the situation in the DRC and in the region of Central Africa. As the author put it figuratively, until the country has exhausted the last kilogram of gold or carat of diamonds, the conflict will continue and the population of the DRC will stay below the poverty line.

Assessing the prospects for the escalation of conflicts in the Horn of Africa, S.V. Mezentsev and N.V. Grishina come to a grim conclusion: besides constant tension in international relations, the lack of drinking water, teeming migration, chronic drought, weak government institutions, etc. can plunge the region into anarchy, make it a zone of unresolved military conflicts.

According to L.M. Sadovskaya, the most striking example of the escalation of a usual ethno-religious conflict into a civil war is the case of Côte d'Ivoire. The author examines the reasons that led the country to the civil war of 2002-2004 and analyzes the post-war situation, which nearly resulted in a large-scale civil war in late 2010 – early 2011.

Considering the genesis of the conflict in Sudan, N.C. Fakhrutdinova emphasizes that the achievement of independence by regional ethnic and religious groups does not always lead to peace. Despite the formation of two independent Sudans – the Republic of Sudan (RS) and the Republic of South Sudan (RSS) – regional hostilities continue.

An example of an internal political conflict continuing for more than 30 years is the struggle of Casamance, Senegal's southern province, for independence. L.M. Sadovskaya explores the causes of this protracted conflict and its implications for the economy of the province and Senegal as a whole. The author also looks at the ways to resolve the conflict.

T.S. Denisova devotes her chapter to the regional dimension of the First Liberian Civil War (1989-1997). It can serve as an example of the transformation of an armed conflict into a real regional war. The events in Liberia are a model of the development of a "war economy", where warring parties gain access to global markets of timber, diamonds, drugs, etc.

The third section of the book examines possible ways of resolving conflicts in Africa.

T.L. Deich analyzes UN peacekeeping in Africa and argues that an external interference in a conflict should not be allowed to turn into a direct military intervention. The author points to the need to follow the principles enshrined in the UN Charter. The Charter states that peacekeeping forces should obtain the consent of the country's leadership prior to a deployment.

L.Ya. Prokopenko considers successful activities of the African peacekeeping mechanism known as the African Peace and Security Architecture. However, the author notes a number of constraints to the activities of the regional peacekeeping centers: the dependence on external financing, the lack of mutual trust among the continent's states, and ambitions of African leaders.

Meanwhile, there are instances when African states managed to stop conflicts, as it was the case, for example, in Algeria, Rwanda, and Burundi. Positive conflict resolution experience can serve as examples for those who seek to stop or, better, prevent massacres in their countries. N.Z. Fakhrutdinova indicates the importance of a real dialogue between society and the authorities. The author believes that many states have a chance of finding a solution to their difficulties without a foreign intervention. Much depends on the goodwill of the leader. The chapter touches on the moral imperative of power.

L.M. Sadovskaya devotes her chapter to the analysis of ethnic conflicts in Rwanda and Burundi – two countries similar in their ethnic composition. The author believes that minorities and their place in the power structure will become one of the key triggers of ethnic conflicts. The chapter examines different approaches of the ruling elites of the two countries to resolving ethno-political problems.

The final chapter of the book (T.L. Deich) analyzes Russia's contribution to the peace process in Africa. The author emphasizes that Russia pays close attention to the situation in the "hot spots", and indicates that an increase in the efficiency of decision-making could improve the image of the Russian Federation.

As a final point, the authors come to the conclusion that regional conflicts are among the most dangerous challenges to the mankind in the 21st century. Conflicts sometimes lead to humanitarian catastrophes, which force people to flee their countries. Uncontrolled migration to Europe has already caused problems, the inevitable escalation of which can affect the stability in European countries themselves.

Gussarov, Vladilen. (Ed.). *Africa: the environment and people (intensifying socio-ecological crisis).* **Moscow: Institute for African Studies, RAS, 2013. 254 p. ISBN 978-5-91298-126-5.**

The book provides an overview of the processes of environmental degradation, depletion of water resources, spread of traditional and new diseases on the African continent, and illustrates the role of national health systems and environmental agencies in addressing social and environmental problems.

Section I characterizes modern ecological conditions in African countries: significant deforestation and desertification, soil erosion, loss of biodiversity, as well as environmental pollution due to the relocation of "dirty" industries from developed countries, construction of refineries, etc.

Weighing all the factors influencing the processes of deforestation and desertification, the authors come to the conclusion that the anthropogenic factor is most important.

The desertification of large swaths of land suitable for agriculture has a very negative impact not only on the socio-economic processes on the continent but also on people, as well as poses a serious threat to the preservation of biological diversity, particularly in the seas surrounding the continent.

The authors emphasize the need for urgent specific actions to restore or rescue natural resources of the African continent, referring, in particular, to the large international project "TerrAfrica".

Section II is devoted to the depletion of water resources in many countries of the continent. It discusses in detail the reduction in water availability in African countries, the state of water infrastructure, conflicts over water sources, as well as assesses sanitation and wastewater management in cities with regard to their supplies of clean drinking water and growing volumes of waste.

Special attention is paid to water availability in African cities, where one can clearly see a link between social and environmental problems. The lack of clean drinking water occupies the first place among negative environmental impacts on urban population.

The authors conclude that devastating droughts in East Africa, which cause an acute shortage of water and food, put the region on the brink of war, especially given the large size of population and historically complex ethnic situation.

Section III examines studies on traditional and new diseases on the continent. The theme, which was previously rather neglected in Russian African Studies, is further developed in the chapters "AIDS as one of the most distressing consequences of human relations with the environment" and "Dynamics of traditional diseases", the latter discussing malaria, tuberculosis, schistosomiasis, and venereal, infectious and parasitic disease.

The authors provide a comprehensive analysis of the reasons for the rapid spread of AIDS on the continent, in particular, polygamy, homosexuality, and the levirate type of marriage.

Chronic poverty generates the conditions conducive to the spread of both traditional and new infectious diseases. Most of the population has no access to preventive measures and cannot afford paid medical care. Hundreds of millions of inhabitants of the continent suffer from the effects of tropical diseases, which prevent them from leading productive lives.

Section IV focuses on the role of national health systems and environmental agencies in addressing social and environmental problems. The authors thoroughly analyze the link between ecology and health of Africans, taking into account factors such as malnutrition, poor sanitation, poverty of lower social strata, and the presence of large numbers of refugees and forcibly displaced persons. They also consider vaccination and immunization activities and indicate the reasons for the shortage or complete lack of medicines.

The section pays significant attention to the crisis of healthcare systems in most African countries, the causes of which include, in particular, budget cuts and the lack of medical personnel. The authors also offer solutions to healthcare problems. It is concluded that the acceleration of negative transformation of the environment leads to a decrease in the already low social indicators, including in the sphere of healthcare.

Intra-African and international collaboration are named as possible ways of addressing environmental problems of the continent and protecting its environment.

In recent years the most common forms of intra-African cooperation in the field of environmental protection have been the establishment of special organizations for tackling the most pressing environmental problems in individual regions of the continent and bilateral cooperation in the framework of sub-regional integration groups.

The United Nations Environment Programme and other UN agencies, which are acting both as donors and research and information centers, are central to the implementation of international agreements in the field of nature preservation in Africa.

Thus, the processes of the escalation of a socio-environmental crisis in Africa, as shown by the authors of this monograph, run in parallel and simultaneously in many spheres of human relations with the environment, as well as in the framework of environmental management itself.

Grishina, Nina. *Healthcare in Tropical Africa (social aspects).* **Moscow: Institute for African Studies, RAS, 2010. 120 p. Research papers of the Institute for African Studies, Issue 29. ISBN 978-5-91298-068-8.**
The book assesses the health situation in Africa as alarming, since government spending on healthcare in low-income countries, which include African countries, grows either very slowly or does not grow at all. The situation is complicated by the dependence of healthcare as a sphere of social welfare on the level of political and economic stability in the country. Attention is drawn to the fact that in the poorest countries, which are most vulnerable to diseases, there are no opportunities for the development or reform of national health systems.

The study places a special emphasis on examining the propagation of tropical and infectious diseases, women and children's health, social aspects of the formation of public health, the place of traditional medicine in modern Africa, as well as the provision of international assistance to national health systems.

The author accentuates the fact that the health and quality of life of contemporary and future generations of Africans are influenced by such elements of the ongoing crisis as low standard of living, social and political instability, and various stressors, which affect a large portion of the population of the continent. The author also emphasizes the significant role of distressing environmental factors, increased political and ethnic migration, disruption of habitual way of life (including nutrition), as well as non-typical activities of migrants.

According to the author, a serious obstacle to preserving and restoring public health is the catastrophic shortage of medical institutions at all levels and the lack of essential medicines, as well poorly trained medical staff, especially in remote areas. The study draws attention to the fact that the emigration of certified medical professionals from their own countries and the continent at large does a lot of damage to national health systems.

The overview was prepared by L.M. Sadovskaya, N.Z. Fakhrutdinova, and N.V. Grishina.

Deych, Tatiana & Korendyasov, Evgeniy (Eds.). *BRICS – Africa: partnership and interaction.* Moscow: Institute for African Studies, RAS, 2013. 304 p. ISBN 978-5-91298-124-1.

The BRICS grouping is increasingly taking the role of a new direction of development of political, diplomatic and international relations of Africa. Research into this problem has shown that the African continent is becoming the foundation for the implementation of the BRICS efforts to change the existing world order. The volume of Africa's trade with the BRICS and the inflow of FDI from the BRICS to Africa are growing. Cooperation with the BRICS countries provides Africa with access to new investments, modern technologies, and favorable export markets. The BRICS are not only changing the traditional system of trade and investment relations of African countries, but also are creating new opportunities for the development of African economies. The BRICS and Africa are expanding cooperation on reforming the UN and the Bretton Woods institutions.

The level of bilateral relations between the BRICS and Africa provides for a diverse and extensive cooperation based on long-term mutual interests. The BRICS grouping is becoming an important factor on the African continent – a real alternative to the traditional partners of African countries.

The book is a study of the phenomenon of the BRICS in terms of its importance for the African continent. The study focuses on the analysis of the influence of the partnership between Africa and the BRICS on the processes of economic development of the continent and on the enhancement of its role and weight in global politics, economics, and governance.

Chapter I is devoted to the BRICS group as a new player on the world stage, especially in Africa. Chapter II, which contains works not only by Russian scientists, but also by researchers from other BRICS countries – China, India, Brazil, and South Africa, – is dedicated to the policies of all BRICS member countries on the African continent. Chapter III contains the analysis of the African agenda of the BRICS. It considers the group's activities in solving such African problems as the implementation of the Millennium Development Goals, food security, infrastructure, new technologies, peacemaking and conflict resolution. Lastly, Chapter IV discusses the formation of the image of the BRICS grouping in the world and in Africa.

Kulkova, Olga. *Great Britain's Africa Policy (1997-2012).* Moscow: Russian Council on International Affairs, 2012. 200 p. ISBN 978-5-98597-256-6.

The monograph contains an analysis of British foreign policy in relation to the African continent between 1997 and 2012. Particular attention is given to features and trends in British politics during the premiership of Tony Blair. It also provides an overview of Africa policies of Prime Ministers Gordon Brown and David Cameron. The book covers a wide range of issues: the ideological justification of Great Britain's Africa policy, London's practical actions for the implementation of its African strategy, and problems of British assistance to Africa, both bilateral and in the framework of the G8 and G20. It also examines the role of Great Britain in resolving African conflicts and issues of British cooperation with a number of African countries.

Shubin, Vladimir, & Korendyasov Evgeniy (Eds.). *Africa in contemporary international relations.* **Moscow: Institute for African Studies, RAS, 2011. 224 p. ISBN 978-5-91298-099-2.**
The authors examine the relations of African countries with the leading countries of the world, as well as the role of African countries in international organizations.

Chapter I (E.N. Korendyasov) offers an analysis of the status and prospects of Russian-African cooperation. The author notes that both sides are objectively interested in the development of mutually beneficial relations, but the scale of cooperation is short of the actual opportunities. Chapter II titled "Africa and the reform of the United Nations" (A.Yu. Urnov) looks at the activities of African countries in the United Nations. Chapter III titled "The EU and Africa: parameters of a dependent partnership" (I.L. Lileev) is dedicated to the continent's relations with the European Union. Chapter IV (M.L. Vishnevsky) examines the view of African countries on U.S. foreign policy. The author argues that most of the countries of the continent tend not to follow Washington's lead on the issues that matter most for them, although there may be some exceptions. Chapter V titled "Great Britain's policy on Africa" (O.S. Kulkova) notes that during the leadership of the Labour Party under Tony Blair and his successor Gordon Brown Africa was among the priorities of British foreign policy. Chapter VI (S.A. Gresh) examines the evolution of Germany's Africa policy. Germany is strengthening its presence in Africa as the continent's importance as a source of natural resources continues to grow. Chapter VII (E.N. Korendyasov, G.M. Sidorova) demonstrates the dynamics of the relations between France and Africa at the beginning of the 21st century. Chapters VIII and IX deal with Africa's relations with so-called "emerging powers". T.L. Deych examines in detail both achievements and problems in relations between African countries and China, as well as the prospects for further development of these relations. The author believes that China's rapidly growing involvement in Africa has been one of the most significant events not only for the continent, but also for the world at large. V.A. Usov looks at the continuity and changes in the modern relations of Africa and India. He argues that India "is coming to Africa in the shade of China", so its penetration into the continent is not of particular concern to Africans. Africa needs Indian investment; Africans are impressed by the entrepreneurial skills of Indian businessmen. Chapter X (V.G. Shubin) touches on the problem of the relations between African countries and the Middle East, including the relations between the African Union and the Arab League, the controversial relations between Africa and Israel, and the increasing cooperation of African countries with Turkey. The chapter indicates the position of African countries and the African Union on NATO interventions in Iraq and Libya.

Urnov, Andrey. *Africa and the UN at the close of the first decade of the 21st century. Development, peacekeeping, and the reform of the UN.* **Moscow: Institute for African Studies, RAS, 2011. 230 p.ISBN 978-5-91298-089-3.**

The book examines positions of African countries at the UN on the problems of development and peacekeeping, illustrates the interaction between African countries, the African Union and the UN on the issues that are vital for the continent, and investigates the degree of effectiveness of this interaction. It provides a detailed analysis of the positions of the African Union and African countries on the reform of the UN, primarily – of the Security Council, where, according to the Africans, they do not have full rights and an appropriate status.

The book consists of two parts. The first part gives a brief historical overview and background information on the problem. The second part is devoted to the 63rd session of the UN General Assembly (September 2008 – September 2009) and the following events. The study widely employs transcripts of the meetings of the General Assembly and the UN Security Council, their resolutions and decisions, other UN sources, and documents of the African Union.

Fituni, Leonid (Ed.). *Socio-economic problems of the developing countries in strategy and tactics of international terrorism.* **Moscow: 2011. 190 p. ISBN 978-591298-087-9.**

The purpose of the book is to demonstrate a direct and very strong link between the worsening problems of the developing societies and the growth of international terrorism. At that, the problems are not limited to the usual range of socio-economic difficulties encountered by certain countries on the path of economic growth and political reform, but include broader civilizational, religious and philosophical meanings.

The book deals with the problem of the influence of the threat of international terrorist on the attempts by African countries to overcome the socio-economic consequences of the global crisis, the link between migration, economic influence of ethnic groups, and the growing terrorist threat, and sectoral and regional aspects of the spread of international terrorism and formation of a favorable environment for the growth of terrorism in developing countries.

Today the success of efforts to counter the expansion of international terrorism is directly linked to the resolution of urgent problems of the developing world. It is apparent that the current aggravation of the problem of international terrorism is largely a result of large-scale social and economic changes that occurred in the world in the last quarter of the 20th century. This does not mean that political terrorism, including its international variety, did not exist before. However, it only now has become a systemic force of global importance. Modern terrorism is usually organized and thus can be characterized as a specific form of organized crime. Hence, international terrorism is a particular kind of transnational organized crime.

The rapid spread of new forms of terrorism, including the use of modern science and technology, is facilitated by global integration processes. After the end of the Cold War and the fierce confrontation between the two socio-political systems – capitalism and socialism, there has been a sharp intensification of international humanitarian exchange. However, the reduction in the threat of military confrontation, the expansion of diplomatic, cultural, and economic ties, the interpenetration of political and social processes between countries and continents, rather paradoxically, have played the role of a factor contributing to the internationalization and spread of terrorism.

Deych, Tatiana & Korendyasov, Evgeniy (Eds.). *Africa and the world in the 21st century.* **Moscow: Institute for African Studies, RAS, 2010. 319 p. ISBN 978-5-91298-062-6.**

The book, which consists of four chapters, presents the results of the study of contemporary international relations of African countries in the first decade of the 21st century. Chapter I is devoted to Russian-African economic relations. Chapter II focuses on the activities of traditional players – the U.S., Great Britain and Germany – in Africa. The chapter also considers the response of African countries to Western policies on the example of their attitude to the war in Iraq. One section of the chapter is devoted to the fight against piracy in the Gulf of Aden. In Chapter III the authors analyze the causes of the growing activity of "new actors" – primarily China and India – on the continent, and look at the activity of Asian TNCs in African countries. The section also highlights the problems of trilateral cooperation between India, Brazil and South Africa, as well as the role IBSA plays in the modern world. Finally, Chapter IV focuses on the link between internal African problems and inter-African relations. The authors analyze conflicts and crisis situations on the continent, as well as the challenges facing Africa in the early 21st century. Particular attention is given to regional integration processes and African regional organizations.

Deych, Tatiana & Korendyasov, Evgeniy (Eds.). *Russia – Africa: new trends in relations.* **Moscow: Institute for African Studies, RAS, 2010. 319 p. ISBN 978-5-91298-062-6.**

The collection includes articles containing an analysis of Russia's policy in Africa and Africa's response to the policy. In the section titled "The African Union: establishment, activities, and prospects of cooperation with Russia" the authors (E.N. Korendyasov, V.A. Usov, V.G. Shubin) examine the problems of the establishment and operation of the African Union and the issues of cooperation between Russia and the AU.

In the sections titled "How does Russia's policy in Africa affect the image of our country on the continent" (T.L. Deych, E.N. Korendyasov, V.V. Lopatov) and "What do South Africans think about us" (A.A. Arhangelskaya, I.I. Filatova, G.V. Shubin) the authors offer a study of the factors affecting the image of the Russian Federation on the continent. In the section, "The double-headed eagle on a red background: "Soviet legacy" in Russia's image in the minds of Africans " (D.M. Bondarenko), the author evaluates the significance of the experience of Soviet-African relations for Russia's Africa policy. The authors try to answer the question of what Russia can do to form a positive perception of its policy by African leaders, African elites and ordinary citizens.

Gromyko, Anatoliy A. (Ed.). *World powers in Africa and Russia's interests.* **Moscow: Institute for African Studies, RAS, 2010. ISBN 978-5-91298-076-3.**

The book is a study of Africa's international relations at the beginning of the 21st century and the place of Russian-African relations in them. It analyzes various aspects of Africa policies of leading world powers (the USA, EU member-states, China), and the response of Africans to these policies. The authors have tried to demonstrate the complexity of the situation in which Russia finds itself amidst the increasing competition for African markets and sources of raw materials and to assess the prospects of Russia's cooperation with other players on the continent.

The overview was prepared by T.L. Deych and L.L. Fituni.

SOCIO-CULTURAL STUDIES

Andreeva, Larisa & Savateev, Anatoly (Eds.). *Religious experience of peoples of Tropical Africa: psychological and socio-cultural aspects.* **Moscow: Institute for African Studies, RAS, 2012. 268 p. ISBN 978-5-91298-113-5.**

The monograph is the first Russian study to attempt to examine religious experience as a modified form of consciousness, as well as forms of its institutionalization in the social and cultural life of the peoples of Tropical Africa.

The main purpose of the study is to consider psychological and socio-cultural aspects of religious experience as defining the basic contours of ethnic culture and playing a huge role in the history of a particular ethnic group.

Structurally the monograph is divided into two parts. The first (theoretical) part deals with problems of theory and methodology, namely the content and forms of religious experience (L.A. Andreeva), altered states of consciousness and religious experience (V.M. Khachaturyan), different approaches to magic as a form of religious experience (A.A. Pelipenko, V.M. Khachaturyan), African religious experience and mythological worldview (A.N. Moseyko).

The second part analyzes the phenomenon of religious experience in the empirical context; the objects of the study include specific historical and modern phenomena of ethnic groups in Sub-Saharan Africa. The authors' attention is focused on two aspects of the problem. In one case, a religious experience is mainly considered as a psychological phenomenon in a particular ethnic and cultural context (A.N. Moseyko, L.A. Andreeva). In the second case, the authors focus on the forms of its institutionalization in religious institutions and traditions, foundations of world order, and political and legal institutions and norms.

The study empirically demonstrates that the social significance of religious experience exists due to its transmission, accumulation and reproduction in religious traditions (A.V. Voevodsky, K.M. Tur'inskaya, N.A. Dobronravin, A.N. Moseyko). In relation to religious experience, religious tradition plays the role of a system link between the present and the past; the link makes possible certain selection, stereotyping of religious experience, and transmission and reproduction of these stereotypes. Religious experience finds its practical expression in the formation of a cult, which provides an ordered structure to worshipping a religious object (L.A. Andreeva). Thus, religious tradition is examined as a particular social structure, which reproduces, stores, and translates the content of representations of the sacred, otherworldly, and "completely foreign", which is gained from experience.

An important place is assigned to the role of myth in the formation of religious experience. The myth exists in every society and is one of the basic components of human culture. Myth reproduces material drawn from perceptual experience in the form of a fairy tale, but at the same time expresses a religious meaning that goes beyond the logic of the perceptual world (A.N. Moseyko).

Religious tradition belongs entirely to the everyday reality and is unable to adequately convey the specifics of a religious experience as a border-line experience. This gap between a social reality and the reality of religious experience can lead to the tradition functioning as something entirely separate from the content of experience. However, the primary source of the authority that the tradition enjoys in society is religious experience. An important point is that religious tradition can exist only in conjunction with the transfer of the authority of the sacred to secular institutions (O.I. Kavykin). One of the main forms of the expression of religious experience is sacred texts and corresponding bodies of interpreting comments (A.D. Savateev, N.A. Dobronravin). Of particular interest is the analysis of mystical experience as predominantly individual (albeit there also exist collective manifestations) through the prism of religious traditions (A.D. Savateev).

Hence, the study applies its broad ethnographic and cultural material to demonstrate that religious tradition not only mediates religious experience, but also serves as a kind of social defense mechanism which routinizes religious experience through institutionalization. Such routinization is one of the most fundamental features of religious institutions (L.A. Andreeva, A.D. Savateev).

The actualization of human experience in traditions and institutions is, of course, not the product of religious activity alone, but a common feature of human existence, without which it would not be possible to lead a social life. Once religious experience becomes an institutionalized social fact of everyday life, it, in turn, is supported by the phenomena it produced in the field of law, politics, philosophy, theology, thereby strengthening the socio-cultural system. In fact, the socio-cultural component of religious experience in its various forms supports social cohesion and social control.

Zherlitsyna, Natalia (Ed.). *Social-cultural aspects of the development of African societies: history and modernity.* **Moscow: Institute for African Studies, RAS, 2012. 194 p. ISBN 978-5-91298-115-9.**

The publication presents the works covering socio-cultural aspects of the development of African countries, including its historical context. A particular attention is paid to the research on the colonial period – the time when the foundations were laid for the contradictions between "tradition", African identity and Western civilization. Africa's orientation towards Western values requires some adjustment for ethnic, cultural and historical characteristics of the continent. The drama of cultures merging leaves many questions and leads to ambiguous assessment. The theme can be traced in the articles by G.M. Sidorova, M.N. Chinyakova, and V.V. Gribanova.

The sustainable development of a particular African state or the continent as a whole depends on solving such complex social problems as the protection and improvement of health care, provision of opportunities for education and cultural development, formation of an information society, and strengthening of the role of women in society. Among the successes of Africa's modernization one should mention the development of a new informational and cultural space, which manifests itself in such forms as the Internet, radio, television, and the press as a field of sociolinguistics that leads to a renewal of a language. This thematic unit includes the articles by N.V. Grishina, L.Ya. Prokopenko, T.M. Gavristova and N.A. Ksenofontova.

The works by A.D. Savateev and N.Z. Fakhrutdinova raise the question of the presence of the potential for the transformation and modernization in Islam, which is regarded as the religious and civilizational cornerstone of North and Tropical Africa. This topic is very relevant in light of the events of the 2011 Arab Spring, when the idea of the Arab-Islamic identity was revitalized.

The articles by S.A. Agureev, V.I. Ryabov, A.A. Shugaev and N.A. Zherlitsyna focus on diverse forms of mutual learning and interaction between the African world and Russia in different historical periods.

Evgenyeva, Tatiana (Ed.). *Russia and Africa. Problems of national and state identity.* **Moscow: Institute for African Studies, 2012. 267 p. ISBN 978-5-91298-110-4.**

The collection is dedicated to the problem of the formation of national and state identity, which is currently relevant not only for Russia and African countries, but also for a large part of the EU, the Arab world and elsewhere.

The study of the topic of national and state identity in political transformations, which are taking place in various regions of the world, is motivated by the emergence of serious global challenges, including the threat to the integrity of states and the localization of their political and cultural influence.

In the first section of the collection the authors summarize the results of the research on the formation of national and state identity, which was based on various theoretical and methodological approaches.

The second section examines examples of the successful formation of a national and state identity.

Kazankov, Alexander. *Traditional music of Africa (except Arab and Somali).* **Moscow: Institute for African Studies, RAS, 2011. ISBN 978-5-91298-075-6.**

The book is devoted to the analysis of regional styles of traditional vocal and instrumental music in Sub-Saharan Africa, as well as to the examination of possible paths of the evolution of African music and the formation of a modern areal map of African music.

The author agrees with the hypothesis that music came before language and created neurophysiologic preconditions for the emergence and development of human language: the modern human species originated 140 thousand years ago, while language appeared only 45 thousand years ago. How did the modern human species do without a modern form of language for about 100 thousand years? In the study the author tries to answer this question, which reflects the worst paradox in the modern theory of anthropogenesis (in the part that relates to the origin of the modern human species). To get closer to resolving the paradox, the author puts forward an assumption that there existed the so-called "musilanguage".

The research on regional styles of traditional African music allows the author to make a contribution to the elaboration of the aforementioned problem. Having compared the styles of the vocal music of the Pygmies and the Bushmen (the so-called Pygmy-Bushmen style), A.A. Kazankov comes to the conclusion that these two styles are identical. Since these two ancient human populations (the Bushmen of South Africa and the Pygmies of Central Africa) separated (reproductively and geographically) not less than 70 thousand years ago, the researcher believes that the formation of these styles can be dated (most conservatively) from this time. Thus, the study of regional styles of African music allows (hypothetically) to make an important contribution to the theory of anthropogenesis.

The overview was prepared by I.V. Sledzevskiy and E.B. Demintseva.

Krylova, Natalia & Prozhogina, Svetlana. *The way to yourself (problems of self-preservation in the processes of the fusion of East and West)*. Moscow: Institute for African Studies, RAS, 2013. 346 p. ISBN 978-5-91298-120-3.

Employing various creative approaches and methods of research, the authors devoted the collective monograph to the study of how an individual tries to find a place in a new and unusual social environment.

The monograph consists of an introduction, the two sections ("Russian" and "North African") devoted to the study of the process of cultural self-identification of immigrants in a host country, as well as of illustrative material (oral stories, biographies, life stories and other documents), which is designed to support the authors' argument that any person needs to have cultural integrity.

Cases when a person lacks integrity of cultural identity in a foreign cultural area are used by the authors of the study as the examples of the destruction of a human personality, which leads either to the radicalization of national or ethnic identity in multi-ethnic societies, to the aggressive reproduction of cultural differences, or to the crisis of cultural identity and the depersonalization of a person.

Thus, the authors attempt to describe and analyze the phenomenon of Russian emigration to Africa and North African emigration to Europe in its gender interpretation, as well as its role in the socio-cultural and other contacts between Russia, Africa and Europe.

Ksenofontova, Natalia & Moseiko, Aida & Kazankov, Alexander. *Man and Woman. History. Culture. Mythology.* Moscow: Institute for African Studies, RAS, 2013. 406 p. ISBN 978-5-91298-128-9.

This monograph is a continuation of a series of books entitled "Man and Woman" (2004–2011), in which the authors investigate the dynamic and peculiarities of gender relations in various socio-cultural contexts.

The first part of the book is devoted to the fates of African women from the times of Ancient Egypt to the middle of the 19th century; it reflects their attempts to be on equal footing with the men at forming the course of history.

The second part deals with the Malagasy civilization theme in its full and rich cultural variety, with an emphasis on gender relations and the social status of women. In addition, the part of the book touches on mythological and ideological themes.

The third part of the book is devoted to comparative mythology. An attempt is made at reconstruction of a number of substantial elements of Proto-

Mythology that presumably existed in communities of Homo Sapiens in the Levant around 45–40 thousand years ago.

The fourth part treats a wide range of problems of emergence and forming of the "new woman" image in the 20th – early 21st centuries, reflecting her unique individuality and creative potential in art, literature, philosophy and science.

Kazankov, Alexander & Ksenofontova, Natalia. *Man and Woman. Search for identity.* **Moscow: 2011. 324 p. ISBN 978-5-91298-097-8.**

The authors of the monograph attempt to reconstruct the dynamics and peculiarities of gender relations in different socio-cultural environments. The scope of social examples ranges from traditional African and ancient societies to modern cultural groups of Russia, Europe and the Americas.

The first part of the book, "Gender and Prehistory", is devoted mainly to a comparison of mythology and comparative linguistic issues. In particular, the authors put forward a hypothesis that there is a connection between the origins of music and the proto-language.

The second part, "The war of the sexes, or the search and discovery of an identity", employs rich historical and literary material to analyze behavior, mentality and life models of men and women in different historical epochs.

Rybalkina, Inna. *The Family in Africa.* **Moscow: Institute for African Studies, RAS,**
2011, 237 p. ISBN 978-5-91298-095-4.

The monograph introduces the features of African family and marriage structures, their typology, forms and trends of their centuries-long evolution. It presents the reader with a modern view on the transformation of traditional family forms in the context of rural and urban communities. A particular attention is paid to the influence of the current socio-economic and financial crisis on the family structure, changes in roles of all its members, and their living conditions. This, according to the author, remains very important because the family was and is the key element of social and economic structure of the African society.

Krylova, Natalia & Ksenofontova, Natalia (Eds.). *Africa. Gender dimension.* **Moscow: Institute for African Studies, RAS, 2010. 366 p. ISBN 978-5-91298-071-8.**

The first section of the monograph titled "Achievements", prepared by N.L. Krylova and N.A. Ksenofontova, provides a detailed analysis of the main stages, tendencies and trends characterizing gender studies by Russian Africanists during the late 20th – early 21st centuries.

The second section, "Origins", includes a selection of articles and frag-ments of monographs by those scientists whose works were published in the 1960s–1990s and which laid the foundations of this research direction and gave momentum to the development of a particular topic. The section pays tribute to the important contribution to the development of this research di-rection of Russian African Studies by such famous scientists as L.E. Kubbel, I.E. Sinitsina, and others.

The third section, "Modern problems of African societies in gender dis-course", contains original articles, many of which were written on the basis of field surveys carried out by the authors themselves.

The study covers a wide and rich range of themes that encompass pri-vate and public life of Africans in the second half of the 20th century and early 21st century, the examination of which allows a deeper understand-ing of the nature and features of inter-gender relations. It also illuminates the issue of the nature of power in the system of gender relations (N.A. Ksenofontova) and the importance of male and female initiations as re-productions of gender sacredness (O.S. Kulkova), reveals some of the demographic and socio-political aspects of the functioning of the African family and some of the peculiarities in relations between mothers and children in polygamous families (I.G. Rybalkina, S.E. Rubaylo-Kudlo). In addition, it addresses the politics of African countries in the context of gender relations. In this respect, the study examines the internal political struggle in South Africa (N.V. Grishina), the struggle of Muslim women for their rights (N.Z. Fakhrutdinova), and the emigration situation in Mo-rocco (E.B. Demintseva).

Literature studies, a distinct historical and philological direction in Afri-can gender studies, are represented by such literary scholars as S.V. Prozhog-ina (The specifics of women's literature in the Maghreb and among the Maghrebi immigration in France), N.Yu. Ilyina (Women's portraits in the works of English writers of Tropical Africa), and A.V. Milto (Women and Nuruddin Farah).

A separate section is dedicated to the multi-faceted topic of "Russian women in Africa". In the section N.L. Krylova, E.S. Lvova, V.S. Belyakov, B.M. Gorelik, N.V. Suhov, O.S. Kulkova, I.A. Iskandarova provide a com-prehensive picture of the lives and destinies of different generations of Rus-sian women in Africa (from the first wave of Russian emigration to Africa and till our days).

Krylova, Natalia & Prozhogina, Svetlana. *Gender aspects of conflicts (the collision of epochs and cultures in the opinions of Russians in Africa and North Africans in Europe).* **Moscow: Institute for African Studies, RAS, 2010. 410 p. ISBN 978-5-91298-064-0.**

The monograph is a study of the problems related to the role and place of women (Russian, North African, European), including psychological aspects, in cultural, social, and military conflicts of the colonial, post-colonial and globalization eras as seen in the broader context of sociological and literature studies.

The authors choose a conflict paradigm to highlight the role of women in efforts to overcome conflicts. The use of scientific works and original sources provided the authors with an opportunity to reconcile diverse (literary, cultural, anthropological, ethno-sociological) studies on interracial and inter-ethnic relations in the gender context. The monograph relies on an interdisciplinary approach to illuminate the complex problem of adaptation of a woman to a new culture. North African literature provides a rich material reflecting the social and psychological mechanisms of the existence of a Muslim woman in the context of European culture. Simultaneously, the authors employ original sociological surveys and interviews conducted in Russia, France, and in colonies of Russian women (married to Africans) and their children in African countries to analyze the fate of Russians in mixed families in Russia, Europe and Africa.The authors argue that the problem is relevant both in Western Europe and in Russia because the marginalization (cultural and political) of the individual is becoming one of the key characteristics of a "split civilization", which makes it very difficult to determine the trajectory of the development of major European countries already in the coming decade.

In addition, the book provides a wealth of material to facilitate the formation of an objective view of modern migration processes and to clarify the migration policy of modern Russia.

The overview was prepared by N.L Krylova and N.A. Ksenofontova.

172

NORTH AFRICAN STUDIES

A reservation should be made that North African countries are often considered in the context of the Arab world at large. Thus, many studies of this region include countries of the Middle East.

Korotaev, Andrey & Issaev, Leonid & Shishkina, Alisa (Eds.). *System monitoring of the global and regional risks: Arab world after the Arab Spring.* **Moscow: URSS, 2013. 464 p. ISBN 978-5-9710-0546-9.**

System monitoring of the global and regional risks began as a research project in 2007. Its purpose is to analyze and forecast trends and risks to the development of the world and individual civilizational macro-regions, and to develop recommendations for managing risks and optimizing scenarios of global and regional development.

This monitoring is the fifth bulletin of the project and offers the reader a comprehensive systems analysis of socio-political upheavals in all Arab countries in any way affected by the events of the Arab Spring. This work contains a detailed analysis of the preconditions of popular unrest, considers its key actors and driving forces, describes the course of events and indicates the main effects of the changes in the Middle East and North Africa. The authors of the monitoring make an attempt to provide a full and complete picture of the events that occurred in 2011 throughout the Arabic-speaking area from Mauritania to the Persian Gulf in order to equip the reader with a comprehensive understating of the phenomenon of the Arab Spring .

Most attention is focused on monitoring North African countries, as the destabilizing processes have first and foremost led to the transformation of political regimes in this region.

The study was conducted on the basis of the modern theory of political systems and took into account the specifics of the Arab world, which are linked to the traditional principles and structural features of Islamic states, as well as to the effects of modernization that have occurred in these countries since their independence and are mostly associated with the ideology of Arab nationalism.

The monitoring aims to explore political systems of North Africa and the Middle East in the retrospective, including their formation, development and state at the start of the Arab Spring.

In addition, the authors analyze political turbulence in the Arab world, identify both universal causes of this phenomenon arising from globalization and specific features of the development of Arab countries that left their mark on and continue to influence these events.

Finally, an important objective of the monitoring is to identify the specificity and varieties of political Islamism and to explain the dead-end quality

173

of political reforms on the basis of political Islam, which clearly manifested itself in a number of countries – above all, in Egypt, Tunisia, and Libya (even earlier – in Sudan).

Sledzevskiy, Igor & Savateev, Anatoly (Eds.) *Protest movements in Arab countries: causes, features and prospects.* **Moscow: LIBROKOM, 2012. 128 p. ISBN 978-5-397-03317-0.**

The authors of the book analyze different aspects of the emergence and development of protest movements in North Africa and the Middle East and come to the conclusion that over the decades of rule by authoritarian regimes these regions not only accumulated a lot of socio-economic, demographic and political problems, but also experienced a change of socio-cultural context of Arab society. Researchers often differ in the assessment of protest movements: some define them as "revolutions", others – as "uprisings", "riots", etc. Opinions on the future of Arab countries, the fate of some of which is largely determined by a direct involvement of the West, vary as well.

Albeit paying tribute to the role of Islam as the civilizational core of the Arab-Muslim world, some researchers link the future of the Arab East with secularization and democratization of all spheres of public life. Others believe that Islam will retain its influence and even strengthen it. While the process of change in this part of the world is far from complete, there may well be an escalation of protests or their reversal.

Increasing instability and volatility characterize the socio-political development of the region of North Africa and the Middle East and can cause further escalation of the revolutionary process and change the geo-strategic position of the region. Therefore, the main focus is made on providing a comprehensive, systematic review of causes and features of the protests in Arab countries, factors of stability and instability of the political process in North Africa, and the political dynamics and prospects for development of the region .

The possibility of the spread of "social network revolutions" to the neighboring countries of Tropical Africa is considered. Much attention is paid to the dynamics of social and demographic development of the region as one of the main factors of increasing political instability.

Much value to the work is added by the articles prepared by immediate observers of the events in Egypt's capital Cairo in January 2011. Their testimonies are coupled with scientific analysis and facilitate deeper understanding of the problems that have accumulated in the Arab region.

The book opens with an article that generally lists factors and preconditions of future revolutionary actions and immediate reasons that force people on the streets (A.M Vasiliev, B.V. Dolgov, V.I. Husarov, A.V. Korotaev and Yu.V. Zinkina, N.A. Filin). Next come the articles dedicated to a study of mechanisms and the progress of anti-authoritarian revolts; the articles also attempt to reveal their social composition and the content and nature of protests against the authorities (L.M. Issaev, A.D. Savateev, E.I. Zelenev, R.G. Landa). The next major section of the collection's articles is devoted to the lessons of popular uprisings, the link between the events in the Arab world and the activities of Western NGOs, and the situation in other regions of the Islamic world and Sub-Saharan Africa (V.V. Orlov, A.A. Tkachenko, Abu Al Hassan Mahmoud Bakri, L.L. Fituni, Yu.N. Vinokurov). The final section of the book presents future scenarios for the region, identifies possible patterns of evolution of the Arab world or the world at large, in which, according to most authors, the current dominant trend is uncertainty and instability (R.S. Bobohonov, E.F. Kisriev, A.G. Suleymanyan). The instability is fraught with the threat that wars of a new type will escalate.

These materials lead to an important conclusion: protest movements in the Arab region, unprecedented in their pitch, depth and scope, were generated primarily by internal reasons – spiritual, moral, social, political, and economic. These movements bear the imprint of the peculiarities of historical development of each of the affected countries. The most important peculiarities include the character of interfaith relations, the nature and stability of the political regime , the role of the tribal factor, the role of leaders, the presence or absence of social and political shock absorbers in society.

The main conclusion of the authors: the old forms of governance in the Arab world – authoritarianism and refusing people the right to decide their own fates – are in conflict with the will of the majority of population and the era of free information flows. The situation in the region as a whole can be characterized as "suspense".

Vasiliev, Alexei & Tkachenko, Alexander (Eds.) *Russia in the Middle East and North Africa in the era of globalization.* **Moscow: Institute for African Studies, RAS, 2011. 142 p. ISBN 978-5-91298-083-1.**
The monograph is devoted to a study of Russian-Arab relations and the impact of the changes that occurred in Russia, the Arab East and the world at large from the end of the Cold War and until the events of the 2011 Arab Spring on these relations.

In rethinking the changes, the authors tried to take a fresh look at the state of Russian-Arab relations during the period to develop a holistic view of their future.

In the first decade of the 21st century, after a period of apparent decline, the business partnership between Russia and the countries of the Middle East and North Africa was on the rise in key cooperation areas. Humanitarian contacts grew, and millions of Russians during the period visited Egypt, Israel, UAE, Tunisia and other countries of the region as guests, tourists, or businessmen. Russia's trade with Middle East countries also increased. However, the progress was limited, reflecting the general economic situation in the partner countries and the world economy.

It is not by chance that the emphasis in the book was made on economic cooperation as the most problematic component of Russian-Arab relations. Political and humanitarian cooperation, which over almost the entire history of bilateral relations between Russia and the countries of the region was developing more successfully, in the early 21st century also faced new challenges, unprecedented in their nature and scope. They are, as the 2011 events in North Africa and the Middle East showed, a consequence of the deep crisis of the authoritarian system of government, which proved unable to carry out the necessary reforms.

New challenges of the early 21st century and the existence of divergent trends at global, regional and country levels greatly impede the achievement of a dynamic and sustainable development of the partnership between Russia and countries of the Middle East and North Africa.

However, the authors believe that there exists the necessary foundation for solving this problem. In this regard, the top priorities include finding a solution to deep crises in individual Arab countries, recovering investment climate, and returning to normal life.

Bogucharskiy, Evgeniy & Podgornova, Natalia & Zherlitsyna, Natalia. *Russia and countries of the Maghreb (Algeria, Morocco, Tunisia).* Moscow: Institute for African Studies, 2011. 130 p. ISBN 978-5-91298-083-1.

The monograph covers virtually the entire 300-year-long history of Russia's relations with the countries of the Lesser Maghreb – Algeria, Morocco and Tunisia.

The authors divided the history into three periods:
– Relations of these countries with the Russian Empire;
– Relations with the Soviet Union;
– Cooperation with the Russian Federation.

The study marks the most important and significant events of these periods.

During the first period, the Russian Empire, which was interested in the development of multi-faceted relations, but above all of maritime trade, with Algeria, Morocco and Tunisia, as well as in protecting the interests of its citizens in these countries, opened consular offices. This laid the legal basis for the subsequent development of comprehensive relations and cooperation between Russia and Maghreb states. At that, Russia, which had no intentions to acquire overseas possessions and did not plan to participate in the territorial division of Africa, in the eyes of Africans looked like a power that did not impose its domination and upheld the principle of maintaining the integrity and autonomy of the countries of the region. This policy not only ensured the stability of Russian-Maghreb relations, but also for some time served as a stabilizing factor in the whole region of North-West Africa.

In the 1950s, the Soviet Union actively supported the rights of the peoples of Algeria, Morocco and Tunisia to independence at the United Nations. When these Maghreb countries gained their freedom and independence, the USSR established with them formal ambassador-level diplomatic relations.

During the years of Soviet cooperation with the Maghreb countries, Soviet specialists assisted in constructing dozens of large enterprises and other objects, primarily in the areas of hydropower, electrification, metallurgy, agriculture, etc. Deposits of valuable natural resources were discovered in Algeria, Morocco and Tunisia, and the industrial development of these resources began. Trade turnover was growing. The range of traded goods and services was constantly expanding.

In the early 1990s, this process somewhat stalled due to the collapse of the Soviet Union. However, in the early 2000s, the Russian Federation – the successor of the former USSR – began to reestablish the ties. In fact, it did so quite rapidly and in many new areas.

The immediacy and concurrence of positions of Russia and the countries of the Lesser Maghreb on many important international issues facilitated the development of cooperation. These issues include the cooperation with the EU and NATO, the Middle East Peace Process, events in Iraq, the fight against international terrorism, the new international economic order, a multi-polar world and international security. The fact that for nearly three hundred years Russia's relations with Algeria, Morocco and Tunisia have been based on the principles of equality, mutual respect, and fruitful and mutually beneficial cooperation favors their further successful development.

The overview was prepared by L.M. Issaev, I.V. Sledzevskiy, and A.A.Tkachenko.

TROPICAL AFRICAN STUDIES

In 2010–2013 the Center for Tropical African Studies published seven reference works focusing on countries of the region. Some of the works came out in their first editions. These include **Pozdnyakova, A.P.** *The Democratic Republic of São Tomé and Príncipe.* **Moscow: Institute for African Studies, RAS, 2012. 148 p. ISBN 978-5-91298-111-1**; Shlenskaya, S.M. *Republic of Rwanda.* **Moscow: Institute for African Studies, RAS, 2012. 174 p. ISBN 978-5-91298-106-7**; Vituhina, G.O. & Nizskaya, L.O. & Smirnova, E.G. *The Republic of Senegal.* **Moscow: Institute for African Studies, RAS, 2011. 264 p. ISBN 978-5-02-036457-8.**

The Center also published in second edition **Smirnov, E.G.** *The Republic of Guinea-Bissau.* **Moscow: Institute for African Studies, RAS, 2010. 127 p. ISBN 978-5-02-036439-4**; Pozdnyakova A.P. *Uganda. Moscow: Institute for African Studies, RAS,* **2012. 218 p. ISBN 978-5-91298-116-6**; Shlenskaya S.M. *United Republic of Tanzania.* **Moscow: Institute for African Studies, RAS, 2010. 250 p. ISBN 978-5-91298-077-0** (available in electronic form on the website of the Institute. The book **Denisova, T.S (Ed.).** *Nigeria.* **Moscow: Institute for African Studies,** *RAS, 2013.* **459 p. ISBN 978-5-91298-118-0** was published in the third edition. The authors of new editions fully took into account all the political, socio-economic and other changes in the focus countries.

All reference works have the same structure, traditional for such publications. It includes chapters that introduce the reader to various aspects of the life of the country. The first chapter provides physical and geographical characteristics of the country: it describes its geographical location, geological structure and mineral resources, topography, climate, soil, flora and fauna, national parks and reserves.

The second chapter is "Population", which informs the reader about the size, age, sex, and ethnic composition of the country's inhabitants, as well as acquaints with the largest cities of the country (their location, population, history, landmarks). The sub-section "Religion" characterizes main religious beliefs of the population.

The chapter titled "History" covers all periods of the country's history – from pre-colonial to contemporary. "Foreign Policy", which follows "History", provides a fairly complete picture of the country's place in the international system, its participation in international and regional organizations, relations with neighboring countries, traditional partners and some other countries, including Russia.

The chapter on "State Structure" presents the reader with the basic provisions of the constitution, state symbols, supreme bodies of state power, administrative-territorial division, armed forces, political parties, public organizations, and the judicial system.

The chapter "Economy" considers the economic development of the country in the colonial period and, in more detail, in the years after the independence. Much attention is paid to the government's general economic plans and programs, including those carried out with the assistance of international financial institutions, as well as to specific industries.

The chapter "Culture" contains a variety of information concerning the educational system, scientific institutions, libraries, museums, media, literature, theater and film, music and the art of dance, architecture, folk arts and crafts, fine arts. The reference books are concluded with relatively short chapters on health care and sports.

The authors rely in their research on statistics published in various foreign journals and on national statistics of the referenced countries. They collect a wealth of factual material that allows them to create a coherent picture of the internal situation in each country and its place in the modern world order. They attempt to highlight the peculiarities of each country, which are particularly easily noticed due to the identical book structure. The structure makes it possible to compare the referenced countries between various parameters.

The referenced countries include the second-smallest African country (only Seychelles is smaller) – the Democratic Republic of São Tomé and Príncipe (1001 km^2) – and the most populous – Nigeria (923,800 km^2). The United Republic of Tanzania (URT) leads by the number of geographical attractions. The reference book notes that the country boasts the highest (Kilimanjaro, 5895 m) and the lowest (the bottom of Lake Tanganyika, 358 m below sea level) points in Africa. Lake Tanganyika is the world's second deepest (1470 m) after Lake Baikal, while Lake Victoria is the largest in Africa and the second largest in the world. Admittedly, these lakes and Mount Kilimanjaro are only partially located within the URT. Tanzania also has world famous reserves – the Serengeti, the Ngorongoro, and the Selous, which are included in the UNESCO's list of natural heritage sites (which also includes the Senegalese parks "Djoudj Bird Sanctuary" and "Niokolo-Koba" and Uganda's "Bwindi" and "Rwenzori").

The mineral wealth of African countries has not been yet fully explored, but, according to the reference works, the already discovered minerals are diverse and valuable. For example, Nigeria has oil, gas, tin and rare metals, the sale of which accounts for more than 90% of export earnings. Senegal and the Republic of Guinea-Bissau are rich in phosphorites, Tanzania – in gold and precious stones, Uganda – in various metal ores, Rwanda – in tin ore.

Looking at the peculiarities of the flora and fauna highlighted in the reference works, one can identify common trends in different countries –

namely, a steady decline in the area of primary forests (in São Tomé they occupy 32% of the territory, while in Rwanda – only 10%) and in the number of species of animals and birds, many of which have become completely extinct outside reserves. The works describe rare species of mammals and birds found in the referenced countries. For example, Rwanda and Uganda are the only countries where it is still possible to see the mountain gorillas, Nigeria is the home of the white-faced monkeys, while a rare bird – hornbill (calao) – lives in Senegal.

A variety of demographic information is to be found in the chapters on population. The chapters include demographic data on the smallest country (of the referenced) – the Democratic Republic of São Tomé and Príncipe – 179.5 thousand people, as well as on the largest – Nigeria – 170 million people. In terms of age and sex, the women and the youth predominate in all countries. In recent years, the average population growth in these countries ranged from 1.6% (São Tomé) to 2.7% (Rwanda and Senegal). Across the region, the annual growth of the urban population, which accounts for 11% of the population in Guinea-Bissau and 50% – in Nigeria, is 4-5%. Rwanda, which is relatively small (26,338 km^2), has one of the highest population densities (326/ km^2) on the continent.

Of particular interest are reference materials devoted to the ethnic composition of the population, because tribal contradictions are the root cause of many conflicts and civil wars in Africa. Most countries have a complex ethnic composition (50 ethnic groups in Uganda and Senegal, 120 – in Tanzania, 250 – in Nigeria). However, not always does polyethnicity create problems. In Rwanda, a bitter conflict arose as a result of intensification of the contradictions between two ethnic groups, while in Tanzania, which has a huge number of tribes, ethnic conflicts are generally not observed.

The corresponding chapter in the reference work on Senegal stands out for its level of detail. In turn, the work on Nigeria devotes a significant space to national languages and the state policy on languages, which is of paramount importance because the country has more than 500 languages. A complex linguistic situation, according to the corresponding reference books, can also be found in several other West African countries: in Senegal, where French is the only official language, although there are local languages; in São Tomé and Príncipe and Guinea-Bissau, where the state language is Portuguese. It is interesting to compare this situation with the situation in Eastern Africa (Tanzania, Rwanda), where, as the corresponding reference books indicate, one of the national languages (Swahili, Kinyaruanda) is official along with English.

All the referenced countries are secular in accordance with their constitutions. Christians predominate in Rwanda, São Tomé and Príncipe, and

Uganda; Muslims – in Senegal (about 90% of the population); the number of Christians and Muslims is roughly the same in Nigeria and Tanzania. According to the authors, the exact number of those adhering to traditional beliefs is impossible to calculate as many self-declared Christians and Muslims participate in traditional rituals and cults.

With regard to the chapters on the pre-colonial history, of particular interest are the descriptions of early states in Nigeria, Senegal, and Rwanda. The books make it possible to compare the French (Senegal), English (Nigeria, Tanzania, Uganda), German (Tanzania, Rwanda), Portuguese (the Republic of Guinea-Bissau, São Tomé and Príncipe), and Belgian (Rwanda) systems of colonial control and management and to get acquainted with the history of the resistance of the peoples of these countries to the colonialists and their struggle for independence.

The history of the modern period allows us to compare different paths of development of these countries after their independence, to get an idea about internal power struggles, civil wars (Nigeria), and the origins of the acute political conflict in the Great Lakes region, which in the late 20th century escalated into a terrible genocide in Rwanda, and the consequences of which are felt to this day not only in Rwanda but also in neighboring African countries. Many authors (L.O. Nizskaya, A.P. Pozdnyakova, E.G. Smirnova, S.M. Shlenskaya) weave the portraits of some of the most prominent historical figures or related world leaders into the fabric of the narrative.

The chapters on state structure lead to a conclusion that such different countries have much in common: all of them are republics, their heads (presidents) are elected mainly for a five-year period (in Rwanda, a seven-year term), all have elected parliaments, unicameral (São Tomé and Príncipe, Guinea-Bissau, Uganda, Senegal, Tanzania) or bicameral (Rwanda, Nigeria). The constitutions of these countries enshrine a multiparty system. Their judicial systems have much in common, though there are some nuances. For instance, the Constitution of Rwanda provides for special courts dealing with cases involving crimes against humanity committed during the period from October 1, 1990 to December 31, 1994 – the traditional *gacaca* courts. Essentially, these are councils of elders, which are responsible for the prosecution of various offenses at the local level. Rwandan leadership decided to revive the *gacaca* courts, which had existed in the pre-colonial period, with a view to relieve the ordinary courts and expedite the prosecution of crimes related to the 1994 Rwandan Genocide.

The reference books give a detailed and multidimensional overview of the economies of the considered countries. The overviews encompass characteristics common for all countries, as well as national peculiarities. The common characteristics include: economies inherited from the colonial period, which are focused on the production of export crops (often, just one

181

crop); cooperation with international financial institutions and the implementation of structural adjustment programs, poverty reduction plan, etc.; high external indebtedness, inflation, a negative balance of payments, etc. All these countries are trying to attract foreign investment by creating a favorable investment climate. Some of them do succeed: for example, in 2010 Rwanda was recognized by the World Bank as the best business reformer (in Africa), and in 2011 it entered the top ten African countries with the most attractive climate for foreign investment.

All the referenced countries, as shown in the economic sections of the works, fall in the category of countries with low human development. In 2012, São Tomé and Príncipe occupied 144th place (among 186 countries), Tanzania – 152nd, Nigeria – 153rd, Senegal – 154th, Uganda – 161st, Rwanda – 167th, Guinea-Bissau – 172nd. Per capita GDP (PPP) in these countries is as follows: Nigeria – \$2,600; São Tomé and Príncipe – about \$2,000; Senegal – \$1,900; Tanzania – \$1,400; Uganda – \$1,300; Rwanda – \$1000, Guinea-Bissau – \$905.

Of all these countries, only the Nigerian economy – the largest in Africa after South Africa and Egypt – rests (as the authors argue in the book) on the production of crude oil and gas; in other countries the main industry is agriculture. The share of agriculture in the GDP of Guinea-Bissau is 50%; Rwanda – 34.6%, Nigeria – 31.9%, Tanzania – 28.4 %, Uganda – 22.9%, São Tomé and Príncipe – 13.9%, Senegal – 13.8%. At the same time, agricultural employment in Guinea-Bissau is 62% of the economically active population, in São Tomé and Príncipe – 62.2%, Nigeria – 70%, Senegal – 73%, Uganda – 77%, Rwanda – 79.5%, Tanzania – 80%. As the authors suggest, agriculture in these countries remains focused on the production of export crops, often – mono-crops. In Uganda, the mono-crops is coffee (the country ranks second in Africa and fifth in the world in terms of coffee production), in Nigeria – cocoa and peanuts, in Senegal – peanuts, in São Tomé and Príncipe – cocoa, in Guinea-Bissau – cashew nuts, in Rwanda – coffee and tea, in Tanzania – cloves, coffee, and tea.

As the reference books demonstrate, these countries have underdeveloped industry. In Rwanda, its share of GDP is 10%, in Guinea-Bissau – 13%, in São Tomé and Príncipe – 23.8%, in Tanzania – 24%, in Senegal – 24.8%, in Uganda – 25.1%, in Nigeria – 32.9%. The largest economic sector in these countries is the service sector – its contribution to the GDP ranges from 35.2% in Nigeria to 61.7% in Senegal.

The reference books examine energy and transport systems, foreign economic relations, finance, and tourism as one of the most dynamic and promising sectors of the economy. The chapters on economy are illustrated with tables, which may seem excessively detailed and overloaded with factual material, but which suit well the reference book genre.

The chapter titled "Education" tells the reader that before the independence about 90% of the population of these countries (with the rare exception of São Tomé and Príncipe) was illiterate. Today the adult literacy rate is as follows: in Guinea-Bissau – 44.8%, Senegal – 42.6%, Uganda – 69%, Rwanda – 71%, Tanzania – 72%, São Tomé and Príncipe – 84 9%. All countries have universities, research centers, some (Nigeria, Uganda and Tanzania) – even academies of sciences.

The reference works reflect the rich cultural heritage of these countries, which includes: folklore, kept and passed down from generation to generation by storytellers, music and dance, crafts, historical and architectural monuments. Some of these cultural attractions are included in the UNESCO list: Osun Sacred Grove (Nigeria), the Senegambian Stone Circles (Senegal); ruins of Kilwa Kisiwani and Songo Mnara; Zanzibar's Stone Town (Tanzania); Tombs of Buganda Kings (Uganda).

The books illustrate the formation of national literatures, which have given the world such renowned names as Wole Soyinka, Cyprian Ekwensi, Chinua Achebe (Nigeria), Ousmane Sembene (Senegal), Shaaban Robert (Tanzania); of theater and film (most developed in Nigeria and Senegal); and of modern fine art, including new and original kinds (for example, *Tinga Tinga* in Tanzania).

While there are many common traditions, as well as processes and trends in cultural development, every country has its own bright, original features and characteristics (unique musical instruments, original dances, etc.). Similar crafts (wood carving, weaving, etc.) sometimes produce items that strike with the quality of workmanship and singularity of design (Makonde carvers in Tanzania) or non-traditional materials (*mbugu* barkcloth made of the bark of rubber plants (Uganda) or cow-dung paintings (Rwanda).

The chapters on health familiarize the reader with the system of health care in the referenced countries. They provide information on the number of medical personnel and medical facilities, the most common diseases and ways to combat them. The sections on sports discuss the most popular sports and the participation of athletes from these countries in the Olympic Games and other major competitions.

All of the above references books include a country map, a list of abbreviations, a chronology of major events, and an index of geographical, ethnic and other names. Unfortunately, only one reference book (Rwanda) is illustrated with photographs (courtesy of Dr. D.M. Bondarenko, who made them during a recent visit to the country).

Despite the relatively small size of some reference books ("Guinea-Bissau", "Rwanda", "São Tomé and Príncipe"), all of them are, in fact, encyclopedias, which can serve as a guide for those interested in the country, including students, Africanists, specialists in international relations, business people that want to establish new or develop existing business contacts in these countries, tourists, etc.

The overview was prepared by S.M. Shlenskaya.

SOUTHERN AFRICA STUDIES

Shubin, Vladimir. *Hot "Cold War". Southern Africa (1960-1990).* **Moscow: LRC Publishing House, 2013. 368 p. ISBN 978-5-9551-0655-7.**

The book is the first study of Soviet motives and actions in Southern Africa during the Cold War on the basis of previously unpublished Russian sources. Among them, of most interest are numerous recordings of conversations with politicians and military personnel from Angola, Mozambique, Namibia and South Africa (including A. Neto, J. Nkomo, S. Nujoma, O. Tambo, S. Machel), previously unpublished memoirs of the people directly involved in the formulation and execution of Soviet policy in Southern Africa, materials from their personal archives, and the author's own records and observations. Such a fundamental basis of unique sources made it possible to reconstruct a detailed picture of the formation and evolution of Soviet policy in Southern Africa. The study provides a detailed review of the scope and nature of Soviet assistance, especially military aid, of the work of Soviet military advisers and instructors in Angola and Mozambique and training of the people sent by national liberation movements to the Soviet Union, and of the Soviet decision-making mechanism. With this, Vladimir Shubin does not gloss over "awkward" for our country episodes and trends.

The author describes the positions of leaderships of national liberation movements in Southern Africa, countries of the region, and Cuba on tactical and strategic issues, analyzes their disagreements, and shows how they were resolved.

Drawing on primary sources, the author refutes myths by foreign researchers about the intentions and actions of the USSR in Southern Africa. The research leads the author to a conclusion that most of the conflicts during the Cold War were not caused by the struggle between the "two blocks", but by internal dynamics in one region or another, even if external forces do interfere.

Tokarev, Andrei. *Portuguese studies in the USSR and Russia.* **Moscow: Institute for African Studies, RAS, 2013. 368 p. ISBN 978-5-91298-131-9.**

This book is the first Russian study to encompass the history of studying Portuguese-speaking countries (including five African) in the USSR and Russia. It is the result of a rigorous collection and analysis of virtually all publications ever published in the Soviet Union and Russia on the history, politics, and literature of Portugal, Brazil, and the Portuguese-speaking African countries, as well as on the Portuguese language and its peculiarities in these countries and regions.

The study reflects translated Lusophone literature (in particular, by African authors) and memoirs.

A large section of the book is devoted to examining studies of various aspects of the development of Portuguese-speaking African countries, as well as to the authors of these studies. The monograph provides a list of theses related to the African theme. The book contains extensive historiographical material, which broadens our understanding of the magnitude and direction of studying the Portuguese-speaking African countries in the USSR and Russia.

Arkhangelskaya, Alexandra. *The Foreign policy of the democratic South Africa.* **Moscow: Institute for African Studies, RAS, 2012. 264 p. ISBN 978-5-91298-109-8.**

The monograph analyzes the formation of South African foreign policy after the fall of the apartheid regime and its influence on the situation in South Africa and other regions of Africa and the world at large.

The study examines the development of relations of South Africa with the leading world countries and African countries, as well as South Africa's position in international governmental and non-governmental organizations. Particular attention is paid to the conceptual foundations of South African foreign policy, among which is the adherence to democratic principles in international relations and to the principles of international law.

The monograph illustrates the specific steps of a non-racial South African government aimed at strengthening regional and pan-African unity and expressed in a fruitful participation of the country in the activities of SADCC and the African Union. The growth of international authority of the democratic South Africa is facilitated by its independent foreign policy executed at the United Nations (where South Africa seeks a permanent seat on the Security Council), in the Group of Twenty leading economies, in the BRICS, IBSA and other international associations.

The book reflects the issues such as the status and prospects of Russian-South African relations, South Africa's attractiveness for the world's leading economies as a source of strategic raw materials, the country's migration policy, etc.

The obtained results lead the author to a conclusion that the democratic South Africa is indeed one of the leaders of modern Africa and the entire developing world and stands for the interests of the latter on the world scene.

Skubko, Yury. *South Africa on the road to a knowledge-based economy: science, universities, innovation.* **Moscow: Institute for African Studies, RAS, 2011. 146 p. ISBN 978-5-91298-082-4.**

This study investigates modern problems of the development of scientific and educational potential of South Africa in the post-apartheid period. It contains a detailed historical account of the development of South African science, which has given the world many outstanding scientists, including four Nobel laureates. The monograph examines the development of R&D, especially in the leading public research centers and universities, and the prospects of innovation in cutting-edge areas such as biotechnology and energy; it analyzes serious problems encountered on the road to a knowledge-based economy and in the course of the country's general socio-economic development.

At the same time, the book contains a critical analysis of the current South African policies in the fields of education, science and social policy.

Prokopenko, Lubov. *New political elites in the countries of Southern Africa.* **Moscow: Institute for African Studies, RAS, 2011. 252 p. ISBN 978-5-91298-092-3.**

The monograph examines the problem of the formation of new political elites in the countries of Southern Africa and the extent to which the ruling and opposition elites perform their social functions. Elites are shown as complex social organisms, which incorporate representatives of various social groups and strata, and which are driven by particular ethnic, regional, corporate and other interests. The study portrays a number of leaders and prominent politicians of Southern Africa.

The book provides comparative characteristics of the region's ruling elites and their performance, which indicate both successes and failures, and illustrates the relations between ruling and opposition elites, which are dominated by tensions, which sometimes escalate into open confrontations.

The study examines the processes of establishing the principles of democratic governance (political pluralism, multi-party system, etc.) and impediment factors (high levels of corruption, lack of political culture, ethnic clashes, economic and social problems). It is only fair to add that a clear gap between the stated ideals of democracy and political practice is present not only in African countries.

In the author's opinion, one of the characteristics of political life in the region is the introduction of the institution of succession, which allows particular political elite to remain in power for a long time.

A separate chapter is devoted to the gender situation in Southern Africa. The women are occupying an increasingly prominent place in the region's political elites, seeking to establish the so-called "gender symmetry". The book also considers the role of mass media and ICT in shaping the image of individual politicians, parties, or the authorities in general.

The overview was prepared by A.A. Tokarev and L.Ya. Prokopenko.

Scientific edition

AFRICAN STUDIES IN RUSSIA
Works of the Institute for African Studies
of the Russian Academy of Sciences

Yearbook 2010–2013

Утверждено к печати
Институтом Африки РАН

Зав. РИО ИАфр РАН *Н.А. Ксенофонтова*
Компьютерная верстка *Г.М. Абишевой*

Подписано к печати 2.04.14. Объем 12 п.л.
Тираж 500 экз. Заказ № 95.

Отпечатано в ПМЛ Института Африки РАН
123001, Москва, ул. Спиридоновка, 30/1

www.ingramcontent.com/pod-product-compliance
Lightning Source LLC
Chambersburg PA
CBHW071023280326
41935CB00011B/1471